The Romantic Ballet
in England

Pauline Duvernay in her *cachucha* Costume
Lithograph from a painting by J. F. Lewis
V. & A. Museum

The Romantic Ballet
in England

Its development, fulfilment and decline

IVOR GUEST

Pitman Publishing

First published 1954
Reissued with new introduction 1972

SIR ISAAC PITMAN AND SONS LTD
Pitman House, Parker Street, Kingsway, London WC2B 5PB
PO Box 6038, Portal Street, Nairobi, Kenya
SIR ISAAC PITMAN (AUST) PTY LTD
Pitman House, Bouverie Street, Carlton, Victoria 3053, Australia
PITMAN PUBLISHING COMPANY SA LTD
PO Box 11231, Johannesburg, South Africa
SIR ISAAC PITMAN (CANADA) LTD
517 Wellington Street West, Toronto 2B, Canada
THE COPP CLARK PUBLISHING COMPANY
517 Wellington Street West, Toronto 2B, Canada

ISBN 0 273 36120 1

Printed in Great Britain by
Morrison & Gibb Ltd, London and Edinburgh
G2(G3513:13)

Contents

Contents

Appendices

List of Illustrations

7

Acknowledgments

I AM GREATLY indebted to Mr P. J. S. Richardson, Mr Walter Toscanini, and Mr G. B. L. Wilson for their kindness in supplying me with information.

Among the private collectors to whom I am grateful for allowing me to reproduce prints and paintings in their possession are Mr Edward Kersley, Miss Lillian Moore, Mr W. B. Morris, and Mr Minto Wilson. Other illustrations are reproduced by kind permission of the Trustees of the British Museum, the Victoria and Albert Museum, the City of Birmingham Art Gallery, the Bibliothèque et Musée de l'Opéra, Paris, and the Harvard Theatre Collection. In selecting the illustrations for this book I have purposely drawn only lightly on the great mass of contemporary lithographs, since most of these have been reproduced often before and many are collected in Cyril W. Beaumont and Sacheverell Sitwell's *The Romantic Ballet in Lithographs of the Time* (London, 1938). Less known, admittedly of less artistic worth, but perhaps more descriptive of the ballets they depict, are the engravings that appeared in the illustrated periodicals. Of these I have made extensive use, and in this connection I am particularly grateful to the Editor of the *Illustrated London News* for courteously allowing me to reproduce many such engravings from the early files of that paper.

I must also thank Miss Mary Clarke for her generous and invaluable assistance in the preparation of the manuscript and for her constant encouragement.

IVOR GUEST

Introduction

England has made some notable contributions to the history of ballet, but unlike France and Russia, these have until recently occurred spasmodically and not along a continuing thread of a developing national tradition. Such a tradition has indeed emerged during the present century but, as will be seen, the great flowering of ballet in the 1830s and 1840s with which this book is mainly concerned was not so much an expression of a national gift for the dance as a vogue for an exotic form of entertainment which relied almost exclusively on foreign talent. There were, of course, some excellent English dancers performing with varying measures of success, but they played a relatively minor part, although not an insignificant one, in the story of the Romantic ballet in London. England's main contribution in that period was to have provided the conditions for choreographers and dancers from the Continent to engage in a burst of activity which had no parallel elsewhere, not even in Paris or St. Petersburg. There, where national ballet companies were firmly established with their own schools, the creative tempo was leisurely by comparison with the flow of new works and the interchange of dancers which were features of the London scene.

Yet this rich flowering was to vanish almost without trace. Within a few years of the *Pas de Quatre*, that choreographic miracle in which four of the greatest ballerinas of the time danced together, the vogue for ballet in London passed. In the opera house, where once it had vied with the opera for public favour, ballet became virtually extinct soon after the middle of the nineteenth century, when it took root in music halls such as the Alhambra and the Empire until the Diaghilev Ballet reawakened an enthusiasm for the dance.

In the introduction to the first edition of this book I suggested that it might aptly have been called 'The Lost Tradition of English Ballet.' Being fascinated by the 'ifs' of history, I imagined the Romantic flowering of ballet in the 1840s stimulating a Victorian Ninette de Valois to form a National Ballet, and the masterpieces of Jules Perrot—*Ondine, Catarina, La Esmeralda*, even the *Pas de Quatre*—being taken as the classical base of

9

an English repertory. Perrot, who was never more creative than when he was working in London between 1842 and 1848, might then have become to English ballet what Charles Didelot and Marius Petipa were to Russian ballet, and August Bournonville to Danish ballet. How great is the loss of Perrot's masterpieces can be sensed from the works of Bournonville which are still preserved by the Royal Danish Ballet. Judging from contemporary accounts of Perrot's ballets, it can be assumed that, at his best, he was superior to Bournonville, whose choreography seems to lack that close interrelation between dance and drama which was so prominent a feature of *Giselle* (in Perrot's production in London) and *La Esmeralda*, and the transcendent poetry and variety of invention which distinguished the *Pas de Quatre*.

In the history of the English theatre the Romantic ballet provides the subject for a glorious chapter, but one which had no direct consequences. In the history of the art of ballet, however, these are among the most significant pages, for it was on the London stage that several of the greatest masterpieces of that time were produced. To the English public, with all its enthusiasm, ballet remained essentially an imported art having its main roots in the Paris Opera. The principal dancers who were engaged from the Continent were almost all French or Italian and most of those who were not products of the Opéra school had either crowned their careers with triumphs in Paris or would go on to do so after their London débuts.

It therefore followed that the factors which influenced the development of ballet in Paris were also at work in London. The key to the popularity of ballet during the early nineteenth century was to be found in the discovery by choreographers, teachers and dancers—as well as the scenarists, musicians and designers—that ballet was specially suited to express the ideas of the Romantic movement. This revitalising movement in European art had taken root in the changing world that emerged from a quarter of a century of revolution and war after the final defeat of Napoleon. Such a long turmoil had inevitably left a deep chasm between the present and the pre-war period, and not surprisingly many of the ideas and standards of the old days had lost much of their relevance in the eyes of the younger generation. This was so, in varying degrees, in every branch of human thought, and particularly in the arts.

Fundamentally, the Romantic movement was a movement of revolt against conventions, preserved in the name of Classicism, which had inhibited the expression of artists in former times. Romantic artists did not deny the importance of form, but they rebelled against what they saw as an unhealthy obsession with rules and conventions which were being perpetuated by the Classical establishment.

By seeking new sources of inspiration and attempting to achieve a more intense expressiveness they strove to revitalise their art and give it deeper meaning and a heightened lyricism. The measure of their triumph was seen in the rapidity and the enthusiasm with which their works were accepted by the public. It was as though they had discovered a new language. Soon there was not an art unaffected by this new spirit. Byron and Scott in England, Victor Hugo in France, Heine and Hoffmann in Germany led the way in the field of literature; in music, the new leaders were Schubert, Weber, Berlioz; in painting, Géricault and Delacroix. The theatre, as the mirror of popular taste, was quick to reflect these new ideas: Hugo's romantic dramas were accepted in the stronghold of classical tragedy—the Comédie Française; opera became romantic under the influence of Bellini and Meyerbeer, while its sister art, ballet, was so profoundly transformed by Romanticism that it enjoyed a spell of unprecedented popularity not only in Paris but throughout the civilised world.

Romanticism affected ballet in many ways.* Perhaps its most fundamental effect was the introduction of a more poetic, flowing style under the inspiration of Marie Taglioni. This 'Romantic' style replaced the 'Classical' style with its hard, 'semaphoric' lines which had been predominant before Taglioni's Paris début in 1827. At the same time there was a significant development in the choice of themes. The supernatural, which held a special attraction for Romantic artists, inspired a new type of ballet, in which the principal character was a spirit who became involved with a mortal in a relationship that was incapable of fulfilment in this world. *La Sylphide* was to be the model for a long succession of such ballets, and in it the public was given a new image of the ballerina—a white-clad vision, imponderably defying the laws of gravity and seemingly taking flight as she skimmed across the stage. To achieve this illusion ballerinas developed the technique of *pointe* work, transforming what until then had been little more than a gymnastic feat into a means of artistic expression. In contrast to this was another, more earthly vision—a healthy girl in national costume performing with fiery abandon a dance from some far-off land. Such was Fanny Elssler and her *Cachucha*, but this was only the most famous among many national dances which were adapted to the ballet stage. This predilection for the supernatural and exotic local colour was found also in the work of the designers who, making full use of the scenic effects at their disposal and the recent innovation of gas lighting, filled the theatres with ruined Gothic cloisters, mysterious forest glades, the sunlit landscapes of Italy, Spain and the East, and countless other stage pictures that stirred the souls of the Romantics. Aurally the stage picture was completed by the music, for, although the standard of ballet music in those days was generally low, the composers not only incorporated elements of folk music in their pages but often suggested the setting and the mood of the action—for example, the chilling mystery of some haunted spot or the rippling of water in an underwater scene—by skilful touches of orchestration.

* For a more extensive study of Romantic influences on ballet, the reader is referred to the first chapter of my *Romantic Ballet in Paris* (London and Middletown, Conn., 1966).

To sum up, it is in the general development of ballet as an expression of European culture that the achievements of the Romantic ballet in London should be assessed. Choreographers, teachers and dancers of today are the heirs to a cumulative tradition which has over a long period of time been developed in many centres where ballet has flourished. In this tradition the legacy of the Romantic ballet has been an enduring force. By adding a new dimension of poetic expression through movement, by discovering new possibilities in themes of the supernatural and the exotic, by pointing the way to a closer interrelation between dance and mime, the Romantic masters provided guidelines that have been, and are still, followed by their successors. London's contribution to this tradition is inextricably woven in the ballet heritage, and the magic thread of those great evenings at Her Majesty's Theatre, though long since passed from memory into legend, still casts a spell to enrich the aesthetic pleasure of every lover of the dance.

IVOR GUEST, May 1971

For Lolita de Pedroso

I

Approach to Maturity

'NOVERRE is coming for next winter,' wrote Lady Clarges to her friend Susan Burney, in the autumn of 1781, 'and we are to have operas of two acts and all the rest dancing. They are to dance all Shakespeare's plays and part of the Roman history for the benefit of those grown gentlemen and ladies who have forgot it, or have never read it.' [1]

With Jean-Georges Noverre, whom Garrick called 'the Shakespeare of the dance', ballet reached maturity and for the first time attained a stature of importance among the arts. It was his direct influence which lay behind the great achievements of the Romantic Ballet in the first half of the nineteenth century: his pupils carried on his work and passed on the heritage to their successors, and his great treatise on the dance, *Lettres sur la Danse et sur les Ballets*, was studied most thoroughly by Jules Perrot, the master-choreographer of the Romantic Ballet.[2]

The development of ballet as an art-form before Noverre had been gradual. It had proceeded in many cities, and many ballet-masters and dancers had made their contributions. London, though lacking a state- or court-subsidized Opera, had played a not unimportant part in this development: its theatres were found to be fertile ground for the growth of the *ballet d'action* and the revolt against the strict conventions which reigned at the Paris Opéra.

At the Theatre Royal, Drury Lane, in 1717, the Shrewsbury-born dancing-master, John Weaver, produced *The Loves of Mars and Venus*, which he described as 'a Dramatic Entertainment of Dancing, Attempted in Imitation of the Pantomimes of the Ancient Greeks and Romans', and claimed to be 'the first Trial of this nature that has been made since the reign of Trajan'. Such a claim was not wildly extravagant, and indeed might even be considered to err on the side of modesty, for Weaver's conception was so original that it anticipated by many years the development of the *ballet d'action*.

By a happy coincidence, while Weaver's piece was being given at Drury Lane, there arrived from France to dance at Rich's theatre in Lincoln's Inn Fields two children, Marie Sallé and her brother. The girl was of an impressionable age, and if, as she may well have done, she visited Drury

Lane, she could hardly have failed to be deeply stirred by the expressive performance in the part of Venus of 'the incomparable' Hester Santlow, who was not only a most accomplished dancer but also an actress of outstanding merit. This, added to the experience of appearing in John Rich's pantomimes, would doubtless have had a strong influence in the formation of Marie Sallé's ideas on her art, for she was an original thinker, and perceived more clearly than anyone else in her day the benefit which would accrue to ballet by the introduction of a heightened expressiveness and realism.

Seventeen years later Marie Sallé put her ideas into practice when, at Drury Lane on 14th February 1734, she appeared for the first time in a dance entitled *Pigmalion*, clad not in the cumbersome low-hanging pannier, as was then the custom, but a simple muslin dress which followed the lines of her figure, and with her hair flowing loosely down her back—as, indeed, Hester Santlow had on occasion worn hers. In this short choreographic sketch she expressed, with a sensitivity which at once won the sympathy of the audience, the growing awareness of tenderness as the statue comes gradually to life under the influence of Venus before the enamoured gaze of Pigmalion. With equal success she created the part of the grief-stricken Ariadne in the grand ballet *Bacchus and Ariadne*, and performed *Les Caractères de l'Amour*, 'in which the various passions of love are express'd'. 'The English,' reported the astonished but admiring correspondent of the *Mercure de France*, 'with their cherished memories of the famous Mrs Oldfield, whom they went so far as to bury among the great statesmen in Westminster Abbey, look on her as brought back to life in the person of Mlle Sallé when she plays Ariadne.' [3]

The young David Garrick, then a lad of seventeen, was in the theatre on the night that Marie Sallé took her benefit. The wild enthusiasm of the audience remained in his memory all his life, and he later described to his friend Noverre how people had fought to gain admittance.

By the middle of the eighteenth century ballet was fast developing, as an art, towards a form in which dramatic expression would be first added to, and then fused with, the dance. The credit of inventing the *ballet d'action*, the ballet which develops a plot, can be ascribed to no single person. It was rather the natural culmination of the ideas and the practice of several ballet-masters of the period, perhaps the most talented of whom—and certainly the one with the widest influence—was Jean-Georges Noverre, who first visited London towards the end of 1755 to be ballet-master at Drury Lane. David Garrick was associated in the management of the theatre at that time, and between him and Noverre there grew a mutual admiration of each other's talents and a close friendship which successfully weathered the riots that broke out in the theatre in protest against the engagement of French dancers and led to the untimely withdrawal of Noverre's Chinese ballet from the programme.

This early association with Garrick created a deep impression upon the mind of Noverre, and contributed in no small measure to his thoughts on ballet which he later published in his enduring legacy to posterity, his *Lettres sur la Danse et sur les Ballets*. His pre-eminence as a choreographer and a philosopher of the dance rests not on any priority in realizing the possibilities of the *ballet d'action*—indeed, the realization had come to others, notably Hilverding, before him—but on his formulating in these famous letters principles which remain valid to this day, and on his genius in creating ballets.

When Lady Clarges and fashionable London looked forward to his arrival towards the end of 1781, his ideas had already for some years past been put into practice on the London stage. The focal point of ballet in England had by then shifted from Drury Lane, where Weaver and Sallé had produced their historic works, to the King's Theatre in the Haymarket, London's opera house. Supported by an aristocratic body of subscribers, this theatre could already boast a long tradition as the home of opera in London, and from the middle of the century the dance had assumed there an ever-increasing importance which was to reach its peak in the great flowering of the Romantic Ballet in the eighteen-forties. Hester Santlow and Marie Sallé had both danced on its stage in the theatre's early years, and they were followed by many excellent dancers, including Anna Auretti, Giovanni Gallini, and the Englishman Slingsby. On 13th December 1763, the twenty-one-year-old Dauberval made his début in London there as first dancer, and it was possibly he who arranged the eight new dances which were the feature of the 1764 season: *The Turkish Coffee House, A Tyrolese Wedding, Le Matelot provençal, The Encampment, Le Mariage du village, La Femme maîtresse, Le Tambourin*, and *La Masquerade*. Another name historic in the annals of the dance appeared on the bills during the seasons of 1770 and 1771, that of Vincenzo Galeotti, the choreographer of the oldest ballet now extant (*Les Caprices de Cupidon*, created at Copenhagen in 1786 and still in the repertory of the Royal Danish Ballet).

It was not until 1772 that *ballets d'action* began to form a regular feature of the programmes at the King's Theatre. The first important ballet to be given at the King's Theatre was appropriately a work of Noverre—*Admete and Alceste*, with Anne Heinel, revived by the ballet-master Lépy, who had been with Noverre in Stuttgart. Another of Noverre's pupils, Simonet, was ballet-master during the 1779 season, when London saw the master's panto-mime-ballet, *Annette et Lubin*, little more than four months after its first per-formance at the Paris Opéra; and, two years later, two more of Noverre's ballets were imported to London, *Les Caprices de Galathée* and *Médée et Jason*, both revived, without acknowledgment, by Gaëtan Vestris.

A contemporary described *Les Caprices de Galathée* as 'one of the most superb exhibitions of that kind ever introduced at this theatre',[4] and remarked of Giovanna Baccelli's portrayal of the dying Creusa in *Médée et Jason* that 'it might serve as an useful lesson to our best tragedians'.[5] No longer could the technical virtuoso command supremacy without dramatic talent; ballet was no longer a matter of attractive dances, occupying a minor position in the programme, but a theatrical art in its own right and fast gaining popularity. The rumour which had reached Lady Clarges that Shakespeare's plays were to be arranged as ballets, though it was to be unfulfilled that season, was not beyond the bounds of possibility, and indeed the attempt was to be made before many years had passed.

Noverre had a fine company of dancers in his first season as ballet-master at the King's Theatre. Antoine Bournonville, Pierre Gardel, Slingsby, Louis Nivelon, and Charles Le Picq were numbered among the male dancers, while those of the opposite sex were headed by Giovanna Baccelli and Mlle Théodore, who was to marry Dauberval. With such a company, it was hardly surprising that ballet should have attained an importance it had never had before in London. 'We should say,' declared the *Public Advertiser*, 'the Dance is the principal object of the evening.' [6]

Among Noverre's productions that season were a revival of *Les Petits Riens*, with new music by Bouqueton (replacing the score composed for the original production at the Paris Opéra, which had been largely the work of Mozart); *Rinaldo and Armida* and *Adela of Ponthieu*, both with music by Le Brun; *Medea and Jason* in Noverre's original version with music by Noseri and Gluck; and *Apelles and Campaspe*. These were no loosely connected *divertissements*, but dramas staged by a man with an unfailing sense of theatre, in which the action was forcibly developed through the medium of mime; pieces, too, produced on a grand scale—*Rinaldo and Armida*, for instance, lasted but five minutes short of an hour. The effect produced on the public by Noverre's own works was tremendous. 'M. Noverre', wrote one critic, 'is to be pronounced a genius of no mean rank; *sui generis*, it is true, and of a composite order, made up of qualities such as enter the constitution of the poet, the painter, and the actor.' [7]

Eschewing plots that were complex, Noverre preferred to exploit relatively simple situations. For example, *Adela of Ponthieu* told of the divided loyalties of Adela, who has been promised in marriage to Alfonso, a foreign knight, but loves Raymond of Mayenne, a simple squire. Alfonso discovers the source of Adela's affections, and affronted, accuses the girl's father of breach of faith. Raymond then comes forward and throws down his gauntlet. The challenge is accepted, the two men fight, and Alfonso receives a mortal wound. In order to increase the effect of the duel scene, Noverre had Nivelon and Pierre Gardel take lessons in fencing from the famous Angelo. Such attention to detail gave to Noverre's ballets an impressive realism and earned their choreographer the epithet of 'Nature's own interpreter'.

| *Lord Petersham and Lord Headfort* | *Noblet* | *Lord Worcester* | *Mercandotti* | *Duke of Devonshire, Ball-Hughes, and Lord Fife* | *Lord Westmorland* |

1a. The Green Room of the King's Theatre in the early eighteen-twenties
Drawn and engraved by Robert Cruickshank

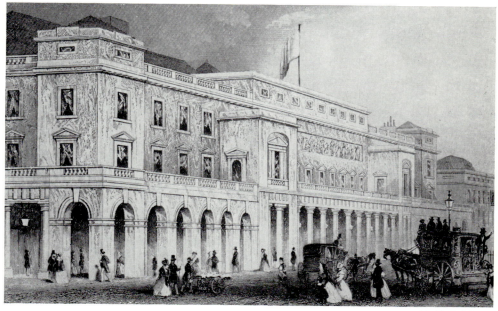

1b. Her Majesty's Theatre at the time of the Romantic Ballet

Coll. of Miss Lillian Moore

11b. Maria Mercandotti in *Cendrillon*

Engraving by R. Cooper from a painting by M. W. Sharp

Coll. of Mr W. B. Morris

11a. Lise Noblet in *La Paysanne supposée*

Engraving by R. Cooper from a painting by F. Waldeck

NOTES TO CHAPTER 1

[1] British Museum: Egerton MSS. 3692.

[2] André Levinson, in *Mastera Baleta* (St Petersburg, 1914), speaks of a copy of Noverre's *Lettres sur la Danse* heavily annotated in the hand of Perrot who had owned it.

[3] *Mercure de France*, April 1734.

[4] *Public Advertiser*, 31st March 1781.

[5] *Public Advertiser*, 3rd April 1781.

[6] *Public Advertiser*, 15th May 1782.

[7] *Public Advertiser*, 12th April 1782.

2

Perfecting the Illusion

FROM NOVERRE's first season in 1782 until the post-Romantic decadence of a century later, the dance maintained an important position in the programmes of the King's, or, as it later became, Her Majesty's, Theatre. Like the opera, which was Italian, it was to be generally a foreign importation, drawing its material principally from France, and a tradition was developed which had a strong affinity with that of the Paris Opéra and was consolidated during the seventeen-eighties by a succession of great French ballet-masters—Le Picq in 1783 and 1785, Dauberval in 1784, and Noverre himself in 1788 and 1789 —who raised the dramatic *ballet d'action* to a position of dignity and at times near-equality with its sister art of opera.

This and the succeeding decade saw a great advance in the development of ballet as a theatrical art. Apart from technical progress, which came with the reform in costume and the introduction of the heelless shoe, this showed itself most particularly in the added emphasis given to the exposition of the plot and to the stage picture itself. The movement was towards perfecting the illusion, an element which was to gain increasing importance as the great period of the Romantic Ballet approached.

A choreographer must first have material in the shape of artistes who can interpret his ideas, and it was not until the arrival in England, towards the end of 1782, of Mme Rossi that the possibilities of mimic drama were revealed to the London public in their full force. 'Her very first step', it was written significantly of her début in a *pas de deux* with Le Picq, 'proclaimed her a perfect mistress in the art of pantomime, at least in that graceful *naïveté* incidental to the character she had to support, namely that of a rural nymph.'[1] Later she was to show her full range in such grand ballets as Le Picq's *Il Ratto delle Sabine* (1782) and *Le Tuteur trompé* (1783), Dauberval's *Le Déserteur* (1784), and even in the unsuccessful *Macbeth* (1785).

As Esila the Sabine in *Il Ratto delle Sabine*, she 'enchanted the audience even to rapture and enthusiasm'.[2] Her love scene with Le Picq, who played the part of Romulus, was described as 'the most masterly piece of acting which pantomime can be susceptible of',[3] the inward struggle between her modesty and her patriotism, and the passion which Romulus has kindled within her, being portrayed in mime with a truthfulness and power which moved even the stoniest-hearted spectators. As a dancer she was in no way inferior. Vigour and grace were most happily combined in her style: in her solo part in the *Chaconne* in this same ballet, she was found 'truly admirable, her elevation in cross-capers uncommon, and her pirouettes or whirlings, and turning round on the tip of her toes, beyond conception'.[3]

Le Déserteur, a choreographic version of the popular opera of the same name, was brought out by Dauberval at the King's Theatre in the summer of 1784 for the benefit of his newly wedded wife, Mme Théodore. Praised as 'one of the most complete tragi-comedies that ever was attempted in panto-mime',[4] it survived in London, in one version or another, until the winter of 1844: the ill-fated Clara Webster was the last to take the principal feminine rôle. Le Picq and Mme Rossi were featured in the original production, and played their parts so successfully that at the end of the first performance Dauberval publicly embraced the former in his gratitude. Crowds filled the King's Theatre whenever the ballet was billed, and often the stage would be so crowded with fashionable spectators who were unable to find a place in the house that the action of the ballet was seriously impeded. These persons were impervious to the hisses of the less refined section of the audience, and one evening, to the latter's satisfaction and amusement, Dauberval himself 'seemed to do some real execution among them when he brandished and discharged a chair'.[5]

'The performance of Le Picq, and yet more of Rossi, yields to no acting extant,' wrote a contemporary critic of this ballet. 'The fainting—the surprise and apparent shock at finding the pardon undelivered—and above all, the shriek, which is the *Siddons stop,* in the finest style, all told prodigi-ously well.'[6] Apparently a scream was not considered amiss in her miming.

Macbeth, probably the work of Le Picq, was performed only once, at Mme Rossi's benefit in 1785. It was a failure, but a very courageous one, and had a few obvious alterations been made, it might well have enjoyed a measure of success. In its original form, however, it contained several unfortunate passages. Spectres appearing to Macbeth and chanting in an Italian accent, 'Macabet! Macabet!' had been greeted by shouts of laughter, and the effect both of the appearance of Banquo's ghost and of the plotting of Duncan's murder had been spoilt by ill timing. Nevertheless a bolder experi-ment in mimed drama had certainly never been made before on the London stage, and that Le Picq and Mme Rossi were not wholly successful in their portrayal of the principal rôles threw no discredit upon them. 'Mme Rossi, as Lady Macbeth, impressed one more with the recollection of Fuseli's painting than of Mrs Siddons's representation,' wrote the *Morning Herald.* 'Her first scene with Macbeth was significant; where she stimulates him to murder, she had also got force. In the banqueting scene, she was deficient in her courtesy to her guests. . . . In the sleeping scene, the comment of language was necessary to give effect to the action.'[7]

Thus far had ballet developed when, on a summer evening in 1789, the first King's Theatre was destroyed by fire. A new Opera House was designed by Novosielski with little delay, but before the building could be completed an impresario named O'Reilly seized the opportunity to present Italian opera and ballet at the Pantheon Theatre in Oxford Street. As a result, when the new King's Theatre was opened in 1791, its manager, Mr Taylor, was permitted to give no more than concerts of music and dancing, although the presence of Gaëtan and Auguste Vestris and Anne-Marguerite Dorival added a lustre which the rival house could not match. Fate, however, soon overtook Mr O'Reilly, whose Pantheon was burnt down in turn in January 1792, and the centre of opera and ballet in London then reverted to the Haymarket, though not until Taylor had agreed to shoulder the responsibility for the debts that O'Reilly had left behind him.

A few days after the second King's Theatre opened for its first full season of opera and ballet on 26th January 1793, with Noverre again as balletmaster, revolutionary France declared war on Great Britain. Not for many years was peace to return, but in London fashionable life, including the annual seasons at the King's Theatre, continued very much as before. Certainly great difficulty was found in obtaining dancers from the Continent, but the management was nevertheless able to present a number of ambitious ballets as the century drew towards its close, the most important being Onorati's *Giustino I* (1794) and *Paul et Virginie* (1795), Didelot's *L'Heureux Naufrage* (1796), and Gallet's *Piçarre* (1797) and *Élisa* (1798).

The choice of grand historical canvases such as the Eastern Roman Empire and Peru during the Spanish Conquest demanded an illusion much greater than had sufficed for the slighter works of a generation before. A new realism was making its way into stage presentation. Before, however, complete illusion could be obtained, the stage had first to be cleared of all persons not participating in the action. The King's Theatre, with its influential body of subscribers to be accommodated, was the last theatre in London to abolish the custom of allowing spectators on the stage. To those watching from the house, this practice was very exasperating. 'The mob of stage loungers', complained *The Times* in 1794, 'render perfection hardly attainable.' [8] Often the gallery shouted abuse at the 'strolling gentlemen', and there were times indeed when there seemed hardly room enough for the dancers—when 'Mme Rose [Didelot], in throwing up her fine muscular arm into a graceful attitude, inadvertently levelled three men of the first quality at a stroke', or when it seemed that only a Hornpipe danced on a pewter plate could be given 'since there is now scarce room enough for Parisot to make her nimble circuit'. [9]

The critic's task was often made very difficult. 'It is impossible', wrote *The Times* in the summer of 1796 of Didelot's *L'Amour vengé*, 'to give any just idea of the new ballet . . . from the crowd of triflers which filled the stage so successfully that neither performers nor machinery could be judged of, nor indeed anything seen but their pretty selves. . . . We can see enough of the boorish lounger and vulgar gentleman in St James's and Bond Street—they should only be exhibited on our stage to excite abhorrence. Our native theatres have exploded the barbarous custom. The King's command should be obtained for the same purpose at the Opera. The aged debauchee will find better game in other haunts, and the young man should not be let loose among those who seem to have put off all shame in their youth.' [10]

Eventually the weight of public opinion began to be felt, and at the beginning of the 1797 season the manager had to issue a notice earnestly entreating gentlemen to withdraw from the stage while the performance was in progress, 'otherwise the request of the Nobility and Gentry, in conformity also to public opinion, of shutting entirely the doors between the audience part of the theatre and the stage, must at last be complied with'. This threat may have cleared the stage for a time, but the loungers soon began to trickle back, and in 1813 a firmer attitude was taken. 'By Command of His Royal Highness the Prince Regent', it was then announced, 'no person whatsoever will hereafter be allowed to stand behind the scenes.'

At long last the stage was left clear, not merely for the performers, but for the creators of illusion, the scene-painter and the machinist, whose magic could be now exploited to transport the audience into the historic past and realms exotic, fantastic, romantic.

NOTES TO CHAPTER 2

[1] *Public Advertiser*, 3rd December 1782.
[2] *Public Advertiser*, 14th December 1782.
[3] *Public Advertiser*, 17th December 1782.
[4] *Morning Herald*, 22nd May 1784.
[5] *Morning Chronicle*, 21st May 1784.
[6] *Morning Chronicle*, 12th January 1785.
[7] *Morning Herald*, 19th March 1785.
[8] *The Times*, 9th December 1794: review of Onorati's *Giustino I*.
[9] *The Times*, 9th May 1796.
[10] *The Times*, 6th June 1796.

3

Two Pre-Romantic Choreographers: D'Egville and Didelot

WHILE THE NAPOLEONIC wars were pursuing their course new influences were making themselves felt in many forms of art, influences that brought a new vitality that men were to call Romanticism. During these crucial years the two foremost choreographers working in London were James Harvey d'Egville and Charles Didelot, whose works bridge the gap between the productions of Noverre, still hampered by stylized scenery and costumes, on the one hand, and the imaginative creations of Aumer, Filippo Taglioni, and Perrot on the other.

James d'Egville was the first English choreographer of note since Weaver. (Plate IXa.) His family was of French extraction, but settled in England before his birth in about 1770. Peter d'Egville, his father—or Dagville or Daigueville: there are several variants—was ballet-master at Drury Lane and Sadler's Wells Theatres during the second half of the eighteenth century, and in 1786 was joint ballet-master at the King's Theatre. Brought up from childhood to follow his father's profession, James, the eldest son, made his first appearance at the King's when a child in 1783, appearing in a ballet by Le Picq, and was a member of the regular company three years later. To obtain a final polish to his style he was sent to France to study under Dauberval, and, being in Paris during the Revolution, became in the ardour of his youth, so it was said, 'a furious democrat'.[1]

On his return to England, he reappeared at the King's under Noverre in 1793 and 1794, and again the following year under Onorati, among the rôles he played being those of Jupiter in Noverre's *Venus and Adonis* and Agamemnon in the same choreographer's *Iphiginia in Aulide*. His aspirations, however, lay in choreography and it was not long before he was given the opportunity to display his talent.

His first production at the King's Theatre was a 'ballet dramatic pantomime', *Le Bon Prince,* produced in 1794, which was warmly praised, although the final *divertissement* was considered a little dull. At this period of life he still had much to learn, particularly the quality of self-control in moments of crisis: there was one evening when the scene-shifters made some unfortunate mistake, and d'Egville, 'who', it was observed, 'perhaps has not made the book of Job his favourite study, lost his temper', with the result that the dancers were so distracted as to lose 'the clue to their exits and entrances'.[2]

In 1799 he became ballet-master at the King's Theatre, and with the exception of three seasons—1803, 1806, and 1807—he retained this post until 1809. During this period he produced many ballets and *divertissements*, and proved himself to be a competent choreographer possessed of taste and invention, though deficient according to one critic in 'knowledge and judgment'.[1]

Among his most successful productions were revivals of four of Dauberval's ballets—*Télémaque* (1799), *La Fille mal gardée* (1799), *Les Jeux d'Églé* (1800), and *Paphos assiégé par les Scythes* (1802). The splendour of the production of *Télémaque* was an indication of the growing importance of ballet at the Opera House: in rapid succession there followed 'a shipwreck, the grotto of Calypso, sylvan views of the island, the aerial departure of Venus in her car, involved in silvery clouds, and last of all, the rocky coast with the ship riding at anchor beneath'—scenes which, 'for richness of colouring and correctness of design are not to be excelled by anything now on the stage'.[3] *Les Jeux d'Églé* was altogether a slighter work, a 'bacchanalian revel with a due mixture of the influence of the tender deity and his wiles', and served to introduce to London Deshayes, who was to become an important figure in the Romantic Ballet, a graceful and agile dancer whose 'manner of escaping from the stage by a spring seemed to be something novel, and was admired'.[4]

In the composition of his original ballets, d'Egville was often inspired by the Classical Anthology. *Hyppomène et Atalante* (1800), *Pigmalion* (1801), *Le Jugement de Midas* (1802), and *L'Enlèvement de Déjanire* (1808) were all founded on stories by Ovid, and *Achille et Déidamie* (1804) derived from the poet Propertius. But classical antiquity was not his only source. He also obtained ideas from Tasso (*Amintas et Sylvie*, 1801), from Cervantes (*Don Quichotte*, 1809), from the history of his own country (*Édouard III*, 1805), and from far-off exotic lands (*Le Mariage méxicain*, 1800; *Irza*, in the Indian style, 1802; *La Fête chinoise*, 1808; and *Mora's Harp*, with a Scottish setting, 1809).

Much of his usefulness to the management of the King's Theatre came, it must be admitted, from the fact that he was proprietor of a dancing school. In times when it was not practicable to recruit a foreign *corps de ballet*, and when principal dancers could be obtained from the Continent only with very great difficulty—generally by way of Lisbon—it was very convenient to have at hand such a ready source of talent, and as time went on more and more of the ballet-master's pupils were drafted into the *corps de ballet*. D'Egville's departure from the theatre in 1809 was not unconnected with the public's revulsion at the sight of untrained dancers, often of very tender years, appearing in public. In justice to d'Egville, however, it should be recorded that he produced some very good, though not outstanding, dancers, such as Miss Cranfield, who played the part of Parisot's reflection in the mirror scene of *La Fille sauvage* (1805), and was good enough to replace a foreign star such as Mme Laborie or Mme Deshayes who might fall suddenly ill, Miss Twamley, for many years a conscientious member of the *corps de ballet*, and the lovely Miss Gayton who, to her teacher's great regret, retired from the stage to marry a clergyman.

A figure of much greater importance, Charles Didelot, the son of a French *premier danseur* at Stockholm, belonged to the same generation as d'Egville. The pupil of Dauberval, Deshayes, Noverre, and Auguste Vestris—a most formidable collection of masters—he quickly won the respect and admiration of the opera-going public of London, both as dancer and as choreographer, and became affectionately known by the nickname of 'O'Diddle'. Both in time and in tendency his career spans the end of the eighteenth century and the beginning of the nineteenth. He came first to London in 1788 on the recommendation of Noverre, and the following year partnered Guimard in the *Menuet de la Cour*, while his last visit to London was in 1814, the year which saw the first fleeting appearance of the child Mercandotti. As a choreographer, his roots, like d'Egville's, were embedded in the traditions of the past, but being much more widely travelled than the Englishman he possessed a greater knowledge of the dances of foreign peoples which he often introduced into his choreography, and he was also a pioneer in the use to which he put the developing technique of stage machinery.

In Didelot's day, ballet was still a young art, and its components of mime and dancing had hardly yet begun to fuse. In his foreword to the printed scenario of *Zéphyr inconstant, puni et fixé* (1812), he drew a sharp distinction between a ballet and a pantomime of action. In a ballet, he observed, 'the graceful, the sportive, the pastoral, the faery, the anacreontic, and the mythological, are the proper sources from which to make dancing paint and display elegance, pleasure, love, and all the evanescent traits of human character'; dancing 'constitutes the leading feature, for the story of dalliance, of mirth, or of *naïveté* is told by dancing'. The field of the pantomime of action, on the other hand, 'embraces every species of grand, historical, and tragic spectacle'; dancing is here but an adjunct, to be brought in incidentally at 'a festival or as an episode'.[5]

Noverre gave Didelot his first opportunity to try his hand at choreography in 1788, when at his benefit the twenty-one-year-old dancer produced a ballet, *La Bonté du seigneur*, and a pantomime of action, *Richard Cœur-de-Lion*. Neither work made very much stir—the first was performed twice, the second only once—but the experience whetted an ambition to create, and when Didelot returned to London as principal dancer in 1796, he produced five successful ballets: two on classical themes, *L'Amour vengé* and *Flore et Zéphire*, and three experiments in *couleur locale*—*The Caravan at Rest*, a *divertissement* in the Indian style, and *Little Peggy's Love* and *L'Heureux Naufrage*, both with Scottish backgrounds, and the latter particularly remarkable for 'the happy adaptation . . . of the Scotch style of dancing'. With these five works, Didelot proved himself 'a man who has a head to contrive, and a power to execute, scenic representations that charm the eye, captivate the fancy, and interest the heart'.[6]

It was during this season of 1796 that Didelot introduced to the London stage the 'flying' of dancers on wires, an effect that was to play an important part in several of the great ballets of the Romantic period. The first attempt was made in *L'Amour vengé* on 2nd June when Cupid and his retinue 'flew about the stage with great ease . . . "sailing on the bosom of the air"', and causing both pleasure and anxiety in the hearts of the spectators,[7] and on 7th July, in *Flore et Zéphire*, the experiment was repeated in a greatly improved form. 'By an airiness of fancy', wrote a critic, '[Didelot] makes all his personages literally fly . . . in a very new and extraordinary manner.'[6]

Having made his reputation as a choreographer, Didelot followed these ballets with other works during the ensuing seasons. In 1797, he produced *Sappho et Phaon* and *Acis et Galathée*, both inspired by Ovid; in 1800, *Laura et Lenza*; and in 1801, *Alonzo the Brave*, a choreographic version of 'Monk' Lewis's story, and a Chinese ballet, *Ken-si and Tao*. After this last season, he took up the triple post of dancer, ballet-master, and teacher at St Petersburg, to which he had been appointed on the recommendation of the Tsar, and which he was to hold for many years, playing a most eminent part in building up a national ballet in Russia.

It was a much maturer artist who returned to be ballet-master at the King's Theatre from 1812 to 1814. Contact with the peoples of Eastern Europe and their dances, and experience of the mechanical resources of the St Petersburg Opera House, had stimulated and developed those two qualities which had always been evident in Didelot's choreography, his interest in *couleur locale* and his reliance on stage effects to produce illusion. He was standing at the threshold of the Romantic Ballet.

His *ballet-féerie*, *Zélis* (1812), was a significant work. It told the story of a young princess whose protecting sylph fulfils her promise to find a match for her; and the introduction of a member of that ethereal race, which was to become so important a feature in the Romantic Ballet, was accompanied by a liberal and splendid display of stage magic. After an opening dance of sylphs the scenery parted to show a Prince out hunting—this was Armand Vestris seated on a live horse, and followed by a retinue on wooden steeds!—and when a sylph was sent to draw him in pursuit of her, the hunter and the hunted were seen 'like forms in a vision, alternately appearing through the haze of distance, and lost in the shades of the forest'. Marvellous things were performed by the stage hands. 'Forests sprang up in the middle of cottage floors; palace walls, with all their pride of battlement and statue, advanced and receded majestically from each other; and whole colonnades of verd-antique and porphyry rose and fell and floated in the air in utter scorn of the laws of gravity.'[8]

A second version of his successful ballet on the subject of Flora and Zephyr, *Zéphyr inconstant, puni et fixé* (1812), with a new score by Venua, again struck the audience with terror at the daring flights of the *corps de ballet*; and other works produced by him during these three seasons in London introduced stylized versions of folk dances he had seen during his travels. In *La Chaumière hongroise* (1813), with its 'most picturesque and characteristic scenery', the dances 'pretended to be really Hungarian',[9] and a Russian *divertissement* staged the same year included national dances from Russia, Tartary, Poland, and Bohemia.

Didelot was the precursor of the Romantic Ballet, for his works indicated the direction that the art was to take to arrive finally at the sublimity of the works of Perrot a generation later. A perceptive critic writing in *The Times* in 1812 was able, as a result of seeing his works, to sense the possibilities of which ballet was capable. The *corps de ballet*'s 'richness and variety of move-ment—their classic grouping—their connection with the scenery—and the mellow and harmonious depth of the lights, as they fall, softened and shaded, through the whole succession of moving forms', he wrote, 'might, under the hands of a master, produce the finest illusions of the stage. Groups from Italian paintings, Poussin's landscapes, studies of Rosa's wilder and more romantic character, with some of the vigorous conceptions of the modern English school, should be perpetually before his eye; while Shakespeare, Ariosto, and the *Arabian Nights,* the graceful adventures of European chivalry, the powerful interest of English drama, and that splendid mixture of human and supernatural grandeur, the magic and the magnificence of that "older Eastern time" which finds admirers in every age, are all waiting for his selection. By pursuing those views of the capabilities of his art, the ballet might raise itself from the degradation of unmeaning dance and vulgar pantomime into the rank of a highly attractive and expressive performance; the eye would not be wearied by the endless gestures of a favourite dancer, nor the better sense disgusted by the story of faded licentiousness; and after the ablest exhibitions of our native stage, a new pleasure might be prepared for us in the mute eloquence of a foreign ballet'.[10]

NOTES TO CHAPTER 3

[1] *Monthly Mirror*, March 1809.

[2] *The Times*, 16th June 1794.

[3] *Morning Post*, 27th March 1799.

[4] *True Briton*, 13th January 1800. *The Times* of the same date wrote: 'His steps and changes are distinguished for neatness and strength and he finishes in the style of Vestris.'

[5] These quotations are not from the original Foreword, but from a short précis of it published in the *Morning Chronicle* of 8th April 1812.

[6] *True Briton*, 9th July 1796.

[7] *True Briton*, 3rd June 1796.

[8] *The Times*, 16th January 1812.

[9] *The Times*, 22nd April 1813.

[10] *The Times*, 29th June 1812.

4

Ballet in the Post-war Years

THE COMING OF peace after the defeat of Napoleon brought a wave of
prosperity to the theatres of London. Foreign visitors and officers coming
home from the wars swelled the theatre-going public, and soon it became
apparent, as one observer remarked, that 'our native gentry, who have
returned from abroad after their several excursions from six days to six
months, have some of them acquired, and more of them learned to affect,
that foreign *penchant* which sends every living thing in Paris and elsewhere to
some theatre or another the moment they have dined'.[1]

It was not long before this prosperity was reflected in the splendour of the
ballet at the King's Theatre, where, on the other hand, the standard of the
corps de ballet was still lamentably low. After the departure of James
d'Égville, a dancing academy had been set up at the theatre in 1810 under
the direction of Louis Boisgirard, 'an amiable and agreeable individual . . .
a Frenchman of good extraction',[2] who had emigrated to England after being
implicated in the escape of Sir Sidney Smith from Paris in 1798. Boisgirard
remained responsible for the training of the *corps de ballet*, holding the post
of assistant ballet-master for many years until his death in 1827 or 1828, and
laid the foundations for the excellent troupe which in later years served
Laporte and Lumley so well. His task was not easy, for ballet was considered
in England at that time very much as a foreign importation, and few artistes
were prepared to devote the time and trouble merely to play in the shadow of
visiting luminaries from abroad. The chances of an English girl attaining
celebrity as a dancer at the Opera House were remote, and it was significant
that the most talented English dancers of the period were often astonishingly
versatile: Clara Webster, as well as dancing, sang, acted, and even on one
occasion played the piano in public, and the burlesque stage throughout the
century counted many excellent dancers among its players.

'The rage for foreign finery', wrote *The Times* of the state of the ballet at
the King's Theatre in 1815, 'has forced upon us a bastard sort of elegance in
the shape of the ballet, wherein we have been and shall ever be excelled by
our Parisian rivals; not so much as to the principal personages of the ballet
(since the present managers of the King's Theatre have done wonders in
that line) as with regard to the whole subordinate tribe of *figurants* and

figurantes who are with us a disgusting rabble, and who can never be expected to cope with the better selected vagabonds of the Rue de Richelieu, until we have a fund equally extensive out of which to furnish them—that is to say, until we have become a nation of Opera dancers, amongst whom the sensual taste is everything, and its union with the intellect, or with the more refined sensibilities, so far from being felt as a source of delight, is hardly known as a subject of speculation.'[3]

Napoleon being for the moment exiled on Elba, it had been possible for the first time for many years to engage a body of principal dancers from Paris for the season of 1815. Armand Vestris, the son of the great Auguste, was engaged as ballet-master, and his father too was to give a number of performances. The company was also to include the graceful Baptiste; the slender, long-featured Mélanie, who according to Ebers had most beautiful hands and feet; and the vigorous Signorina Del Caro, from Vienna, a dancer possessed of 'the limb and muscle of a tiger, and almost the agility'.[4]

Auguste Vestris had not been seen in England since 1791 when he was at the height of his powers. Now he was fifty-five and, as was to be expected, 'somewhat on the wane', although still surprisingly active. There was, however, 'nothing of age in his appearance, except that stronger contraction of physiognomy and a few of those intrusive wrinkles which spare public beauty no more than private', and as he advanced to the front of the stage accompanied by his son, in whose ballet, *Le Calife de Bagdad,* he had just danced, he bowed with all his wonted grace to the welcoming cheers of the audience. Later in the season he created the rôle of Mars in his son's *Mars et l'Amour,* and later still, partnering Mlle Narcisse, danced the *Menuet de la Cour* 'with vast pomp and bodily dignity'.[5]

Never before had London seen such good ballet as during the season of 1815, the year of the final victory over Napoleon after his return to France from Elba. Armand Vestris staged a number of ballets in which, had the audience been gifted with prescience, the shades of Romanticism might have been detected. The lure of foreign parts was evidenced in the light work, *Les Petits Braconniers,* which was set in Scotland, 'a country', commented *The Times,* 'which appears to be to foreigners what Sicily was to the Greek or Africa to the Roman poet—a place for adventures and monsters'.[6] Yet more Romantic in its atmosphere was *Le Prince troubadour,* a choreographic version of La Fontaine's *Joconde,* with spectacular mediaeval settings designed by Ciceri, Zara, and Orm, settings which presented the audience with a wonderful illusion: one scene resembled a landscape by Claude, while another, the most effective of all, showed 'the banks of a river richly luxuriant, lighted up with the beams of a setting sun, seen through the ruins of an old abbey',[7] a truly Romantic picture.

Although a Frenchman, Armand Vestris had apparently no qualms about arranging the dances for the ballet-cantata, *Caesar's Triumph over the Gauls,* which was staged in commemoration of the defeat of Napoleon and for the benefit of dependants of soldiers who had fallen some days before on the field of Waterloo, nor did the public sense anything extraordinary in French members of the company taking part in this patriotic demonstration.

Armand Vestris was again ballet-master in 1816, when several of his former successes were revived and what was undoubtedly his most important work, *Gonzalve de Cordoue,* was produced. Based on a story by Florian this ballet was a study in the mediaeval exotic, the action taking place in Granada during the Moorish dominion.

It was, wrote the critic of *The Times,* 'beyond all comparison by much the most splendid, interesting, and attractive [ballet] that has ever been brought forward at the King's Theatre. The subordinate agents are well selected and judiciously employed. Great use is made of the adverse tribes of the Aben-cerrages and Zegris, and actions allotted to them throughout the performance well suited to the recorded characteristics of each. Bands of troubadours, peasants, etc., fill the stage and animate the spectacle. The scenery—in particular, the interior of the Alhambra palace, the cottage and wood scene, and the fortress of Vilhamara, where the final battle takes place—must be allowed the praise of extraordinary richness and beauty. The dancers all exerted themselves with infinite success. . . . Even the renowned Gonsalvo and his royal bride condescended to add the amusement of dancing to the superior luxuries of love and war; and neither Mlle Mélanie nor M. Vestris seemed to fear any loss of dignity or glory by the exercise'. [8]

The infusion of French talent into the ballet at the King's Theatre had wrought a miracle indeed. By the end of the 1816 season the ballet there had 'reached an extraordinary pitch of elegance and maturity for the meridian of London'.[1] Many lovers of opera were mortified at the realization that the Opera House was attended by many for the sake of the ballet, and consoled themselves as best they could by attributing this vogue to the caprice of fashion. But they overlooked the fact that the fashionable world had first to be attracted, and that this had been done only by an unprecedented standard of production during these two years that Armand Vestris was ballet-master. Even among the highest in the land was the taste for ballet now developing. An enthusiastic royal patron had been found in the person of Princess Charlotte, daughter of the Prince Regent, and in the direct line of succession to the throne. 'We could not avoid remarking', wrote one who was present at a performance in May 1815, 'the extraordinary delight with which the Royal visitor seemed to notice the ballet [*Le Calife de Bagdad*] throughout.' Later that same season she returned to see *Le Prince troubadour,* which 'she had particularly asked for'.[9] The following year she and her husband, Prince Leopold of Saxe-Coburg (later to become the first King of the Belgians), were regular visitors, seeing Baptiste's revival of Duport's *Figaro* three times and *Gonzalve de Cordoue* twice. Her untimely death in childbirth in November 1817 deprived the art of ballet of a staunch and powerful patron.

Having attained such a pitch of excellence, the ballet at the King's Theatre then, from 1817 until 1820, fell into a steady decline. This was through no fault of the dancers, among whom there were many talented artistes, but the result of a succession of mediocre choreographers who were engaged to succeed Armand Vestris as ballet-master: Léon in 1817, Favier in 1818, Guillet in 1819, Hullin in 1820. 'This department of the King's Theatre', wrote *The Times* early in 1818, 'is not in a very flourishing state; except Baptiste and Mlle Mélanie, who is a charming dancer, we have no performers capable of conferring dignity on an art which is only to be tolerated by a refined audience in its happiest and most perfect efforts.' [10]

These were lean years. Generally the new ballets produced were lacking in invention and variety, or obscure or crude in the presentation of plot. In Favier's *Acis et Galathée*, the principal characters expressed their sentiments by pointing to writing on the scenery, and in the same choreographer's *La Fée Urgèle*, placards were used, 'written in mis-spelled French and not legible beyond the fourth row of the pit'.[11] Even a revival of Noverre's *Apelles et Campaspe* failed to please, despite the presence in the cast of Teresa Ginetti, recently returned from St Petersburg, who was particularly remarkable for the rock-like steadiness of her poses. Much, if not all, of Noverre's original choreography had probably been forgotten, and the inept Favier who was responsible for the revival could produce nothing better than an unsatisfying and insipid *divertissement*.

There were two events of interest in the 1819 season. The lesser was the début, as Cupid in *Télémaque*, of a child called Louisa Court: the first step in a career which was to lead her in the fifties to the position of ballet-mistress at Drury Lane under the name of Madame Louise. Causing more stir, however, was the first appearance in London on 1st May of Louis Duport and his wife in the former's ballet, *Adolphe et Mathilde*. As a dancer, Duport created a great sensation by the variety and fluidity of his style, his unusual rapidity, and his vigour, while his choreography received great acclaim, particularly in a *pas de deux* which was 'a most delicious treat', and in the 'most masterly' grouping of the *corps de ballet*.[12]

Duport, however, was a luxury the theatre could ill afford, for its finances were in a most sorry state. Throughout the summer of 1820 the management struggled on, but that it had to stint itself to survive became increasingly evident in the staging of new productions. The crash came not very unexpectedly towards the end of the season: on the evening of 15th August a number of spectators, who had not been warned in time, arrived at the theatre to find it closed as a result of an execution having been levied on the premises. The fortunes of the Opera House had reached their lowest ebb.

NOTES TO CHAPTER 4

[1] *The Times,* 12th August 1816.

[2] John Ebers, *Seven Years of the King's Theatre* (London, 1828).

[3] *The Times,* 24th July 1815. The Paris Opéra was at that time in the Rue de Richelieu.

[4] *The Times,* 18th January 1815.

[5] *The Times,* 18th January, 27th February, and 24th July 1815.

[6] *The Times,* 30th January 1815.

[7] *The Times,* 22nd February 1815.

[8] *The Times,* 8th April 1816.

[9] *Morning Post,* 13th May and 19th July 1815.

[10] *The Times,* 2nd February 1818.

[11] *The Times,* 13th April 1818.

[12] *Morning Post,* 3rd May 1819.

V. & A. Museum

IIIa. Caroline Brocard and Mélanie Duval
in *La Naissance de Vénus*
Caricature in water-colour by A. E. Chalon

IIIb. Louis-François Gosselin in *Le Carnaval
de Venise*
Caricature in water-colour by A. E. Chalon

V. & A. Museum

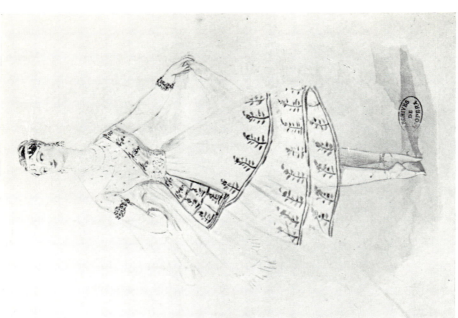

IVb. Marie Taglioni in *La Bayadère*
Water-colour by A. E. Chalon

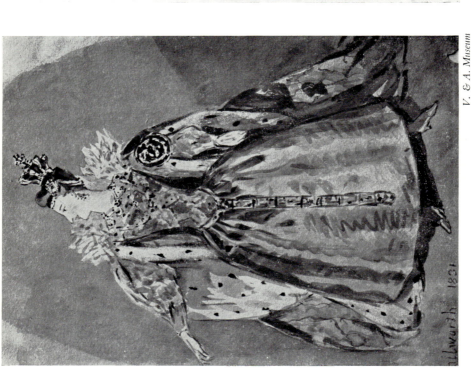

IVa. Zoé Beaupré as Queen Elizabeth in *Kenilworth*
Water-colour by A. E. Chalon

5

The Renaissance of the Ballet under Ebers

IF ONE WISHED to hire a box at the Opera for the night, or obtain a ticket for the pit, during the years following Waterloo, one could not have done better than to call at Ebers's Library at No. 27 Old Bond Street. As a result of acting as a ticket agent for a number of years, the proprietor, John Ebers, gained some knowledge of the working of the Opera House, as well as making the acquaintance and winning the esteem of many of the subscribers; and thus it happened that, when the future of the theatre was in doubt after its premature closing in 1820, it was to him that the leading subscribers turned with proposals to assume the management for the ensuing season. Ebers's association with the King's Theatre was to last until 1827, and was to lead to what must to many have seemed the inevitable fate of all those who meddled in the fortunes of the Opera House—bankruptcy. Though financially disastrous, however, his tenure of office was on the whole artistically successful, and not the least of his achievements was the raising of the prestige of the ballet.

Before his time—even in the days of Armand Vestris—the ballet at the King's Theatre had been very inferior when considered in relation to that of the Paris Opéra. To remedy this, Ebers boldly decided to engage the best French dancers, and his success in doing so was both a measure of his persistence—for the Paris Opéra was naturally not very willing to allow its company to be depleted—and a valuable precedent which undoubtedly eased the task of his successors. Although he early came to an understanding with the Opéra regarding the number of dancers engaged by him at any one time, Ebers still encountered difficulties, but on the whole the arrangement worked very satisfactorily, and he was able to assemble a distinguished company each year, even though at considerable expense in worry and cash: the annual outlay in salaries paid to foreign dancers often approached £10,000.

Hardly a season passed without some brilliant dancer being introduced to the London public. In 1821 came Lise Noblet, Fanny Bias, Julia de Varennes, Albert, and Antoine Coulon, son of the great French teacher; 1822 saw the London débuts of Carolina Ronzi-Vestris and Paul '*l'aérien*', and the return of the lovely Spaniard, Maria Mercandotti, who had been seen as a child some years before; in 1824, Ferdinand was first seen, as also was Pauline Leroux; while the engagements for 1827 included a male dancer from the Scala, Milan, called Carlo Blasis, and Louis-François Gosselin (Plate IIIb), both of whom were to become renowned as teachers.

The sparkling Lise Noblet was a favourite from the very day of her début in March 1821. If her features were not perhaps strictly beautiful, she possessed an infectious vivacity and a perfectly proportioned figure. (Plate IIa.) Ebers and many others held her in the highest esteem, not only as a dancer, but as an actress too. Her dramatic talent was wonderfully brought out in *Nina* (1821), in which the heroine loses her reason at the prospect of being parted from her sweetheart and wedded to another, an affliction which happily proves only temporary. 'This character', wrote Ebers, 'is the most replete with sad and affecting interest that ever fell under my observation in the ballet. . . . Never was the touching sadness of the worst of maladies more truly delineated than in the mute elegance of Noblet's performance. The madness of Nina is not the phrenzied excitement of ungovernable despair, but the melancholy estrangement of a mind retaining, in its ruin, the sweetness and benevolence of its unshaken state. In portraying the workings of this affliction, not a gesture, not a movement of Noblet was idly wasted. Everything was true to nature—everything contributed to the feeling of the piece. Her countenance, expressive as her action was graceful, kept time to every inflection of feeling, and harmonized with all the speaking graces of her deportment.'[1] Her rendering of the rôle of Susanna in *Le Page inconstant* (1824)—a ballet by Dauberval, revived by Aumer, based on *Le Mariage de Figaro*—was 'no less remarkable for its comic power than for the gracefulness with which she executes it'; she and the other players performed the ballet so skilfully that even 'the wittiest dialogue in the world', it was said, 'could scarcely improve the smart and passionate things which these dancers express in dumb show'.[2]

Fanny Bias was a *danseuse de demi-caractère*, excelling in what Ebers described as 'those beautiful little half-steps, which, more than any other, correspond to the epithet "twinkling"'[1]—steps which she performed with astonishing delicacy and no appearance of effort. She was less beautiful (though her feet were 'perfect models') and less graceful than Noblet, who was considered the very model of a perfectly finished and classical dancer, but the 'negligent abandonment and repose in some of her attitudes' gave charm and originality to her style. It was of her that Thomas Moore wrote:

Fanny Bias in Flora—dear creature—you'd swear,
When her delicate feet in the dance twinkle round,
That her steps are of light, that her home is the air,
And she only par complaisance *touches the ground.*[3]

The male dancer was still a figure of importance in ballet during the twenties. 'You dance excellently well,' cried a subscriber while Albert was making his London début in 1821, and his opinion was shared by the rest of the audience. François Decombe, known as Albert, was the son of a cavalry officer in the French Army, and there was perhaps something of the soldier in his bearing and style of dancing. He was, a contemporary wrote, 'unrivalled for the free and yet stately pride of his attitudes, which his uncommon strength of muscle enables him to sustain with a firmness that never trembles from the line of beauty; but there is always an appearance of study about him, which seems never to permit him to enter into the spirit of the dance. His efforts are undoubtedly of the first order; but they are uniformly so conformable to his principles of art, that art alone seems to be his idol'.[4] Another critic observed the facility and elegance with which he executed the most difficult *tours de force*, and remarked that he seemed 'never to exert the full spring of his vigour and elasticity'.[5]

Between the dignified and restrained Albert and Paul, the other great male dancer of his generation, there was a most marked contrast. *The Times* vividly described the former as a 'see-saw' and the latter as a 'jumper'; while Albert 'swims from side to side till he makes our heads turn with vertigo', Paul 'jumps with an agility that might excite envy in a kangaroo'.[6] Paul was seen in London at the very height of his career. Brimming over with an infectious gaiety, he was 'all life and pleasure',[4] exciting delight rather than commanding admiration. 'In agility and grace', wrote *The Times*, 'we have seen nothing more perfect than M. Paul. The elasticity of his spring is admirable, and the play of his limbs, as he seems almost to float in the air, one of the most picturesque objects imaginable. His style is, perhaps, less commanding than that of M. Albert, but in his own manner nothing can excel him.'[7]

Another male virtuoso was Charles Vestris, a nephew of Auguste Vestris, who had made his London début in 1814 and was engaged by Ebers for several seasons together with his wife Carolina Ronzi-Vestris, a sister of the singer Signora Ronzi-de Begnis. *The Times* placed him in a class by himself: he was a 'tee-totum', who 'whirls about with a rapidity which toy-whipping urchins would do well to imitate'.[6]

The sequence of mediocre choreographers who had brought London's ballet so low in public esteem since the days of Armand Vestris was also brought to a close when Ebers assumed control of the theatre. To stage the ballets in which these distinguished dancers were to appear, men of a very different calibre were engaged—Deshayes and Albert (to whom jointly the honour fell of arranging a ballet in honour of George IV's coronation, *Alcide*), Anatole, Aumer, and the veteran James d'Egville.

The most distinguished of these was a pupil of Dauberval, Jean Aumer, whose larger works were marked by a grandeur of theme and conception hitherto unknown in London. Three important ballets were staged by him at the King's Theatre, *Alfred le Grand* (1823), *Le Songe d'Ossian* (1824), and *Cléopâtre* (1825), the first and last having previously been produced elsewhere.

Based on King Alfred's struggle against the Danes, *Alfred le Grand* was a *ballet d'action* in the sense in which the term was then understood. That is to say, the action was expressed in mime, the dances being introduced only incidentally; there was also an elaborately staged battle. 'Every act of this admirable ballet', wrote the *Morning Post*, 'possesses features peculiar to itself; and, what has hitherto been attended to by few of M. Aumer's predecessors, each act is brought to a conclusion with such force and spirit as to allow the impression on the auditory only to escape when the subject is again renewed.' Adding to the effect created by the choreographer's sure sense of theatre were the splendid scenery—particularly the Hall in Count Edelbert's castle, with its Gothic arches and pillars, 'a specimen of fine taste and design'—and dresses 'which almost dazzle the eye with gold and glitter'.[8] The production of *Cléopâtre* was no less lavish, though the choreographer's success was less.

More romantic in spirit than either was *Le Songe d'Ossian*, inspired by the legendary Irish hero. If Aumer took very little advantage of the opportunity to introduce local colour into his dances, he varied his choreography by means of a contrast between the real and the fantastic such as was to distinguish so many of the great ballets of the thirties and forties. The first act was devoted to Ossian's return from the wars, his marriage, and his kidnapping during a hunt, while in the second the mood changed completely: this depicted Ossian's dream in Fingal's cave, with angels appearing dancing in the clouds—'one of the most sublime groupings of female figures', it was remarked, ever to have been seen on the stage.[9] Though it would be extravagant to claim that it influenced the creators of *La Sylphide* and *Giselle*, the composition of *Le Songe d'Ossian* anticipated the structure of these two great ballets.

James d'Egville, who was ballet-master in 1826 and 1827, produced nothing so distinguished. By comparison with Aumer's ballets his works appear old-fashioned. The most successful, *La Naissance de Vénus* (1826), for instance, was a ballet in the anacreontic style that had long been out of vogue. According to Ebers, it had been composed for, but never staged at, the Paris Opéra: to produce his work there was d'Egville's dearest ambition, and one that was not to be fulfilled. A skilfully constructed ballet, it represented the birth of Venus, her initiation into the arts of love, and her choice of Vulcan in preference to her other godly suitors, and was enhanced in performance by the presence as Venus of the beautiful Caroline Brocard. (Plate IIIa.)

Apart from raising the standards of dancing and choreography on the stage of the King's Theatre Ebers also gave an added stimulation to the fashionable cult of the ballet. In imitation of the Paris Opéra, he caused a Green Room to be erected where the dancers could limber up in the moments before their entrances, and reopened the communicating doors separating the house from the stage. (Plate Ia.) The man of fashion was thus ensnared, and the Opera became, as a social observer remarked in the mid twenties, 'the only tolerable place of public amusement in which the varied orders of society are permitted to participate'. He would generally arrive well after the commencement of the opera—for the enjoyment of his dinner was not to be disturbed—but still in good time to watch the *divertissement*, which he might be privileged to do from the wings, if he were an annual subscriber. Afterwards he would perhaps stroll into the Green Room to make an appointment with some preferred dancer for a non-play night before joining 'the distinguished group of operatic *cognoscenti* who form the circle of taste in the centre of the stage on the fall of the curtain'.[10]

The cultivation of 'rather intimate relations with the reigning *favorita*', wrote Tom Duncombe in his memoirs, 'passed for admiration of genius. The "protector" of the beautiful *cantatrice* or *danseuse* was certain of exciting the envy of his less fortunate associates, till the lady left him for a more liberal admirer. This was so expensive a luxury that only an opera-goer with a handsome income could venture to indulge in it; but it was so fashionable that married men, and even elderly men, were proud of the distinction. Highly respectable grandfathers established themselves as patrons of the *prima donna*, while grave and reverend seigniors competed with beardless ensigns for the smiles of the *coryphées*'.[11]

Ballet was essentially a man's art, and the playwright Fitzball, writing in his memoirs of the visit of a number of French *danseuses* to Covent Garden in the eighteen-twenties, indicated another factor of its popularity. 'Silk tights', he wrote, 'were then only tolerated at [the King's] Theatre in the Haymarket. It was then only permitted the aristocracy to be, as old Mrs Bull called it, *un*delicate. Would it be believed by some of our juveniles'—he was writing in the late fifties—'these French ladies were nearly expelled the stage for the very same cause which now sets the theatre in a roar of approbation, and brings down a shower of camellias, azalias, japonicas, and even blushing British roses to their feet. See what an enlightened race we have become, thanks to foreigners whose habits and manners we once so repelled, and who were the first to teach us the "poetry of motion".'[12]

The display of a ballerina's legs was something comparatively recent in ballet. The weight of eighteenth-century female costume had restricted her technique and given the brilliant male dancer—such as the Vestris father and son—the advantage. Towards the end of that century, the liberation of her form from the encumbering layers of skirt and petticoats gave her a greater freedom of movement and enabled her to compete with the male virtuoso. By the twenties, however, complaints were being voiced in London of 'the eternal pirouettes', of ballerinas 'turning round on one leg and putting their limbs into all sorts of the most disagreeable, inelegant, and indecent contortions possible'.[13] For the *danseuse* it was an age of experiment and discovery. With her shoe lightened by the absence of the heel she progressed towards a further technical development, the cultivation of the *pointe*. Its origin was not recorded for it was introduced gradually, almost imperceptibly, but an English lithograph of Fanny Bias in *Flore et Zéphire,* in which she danced at her benefit in 1821, depicts her clearly upon her *pointes.* (Plate Va.) To have shown her thus can have been no fancy on the part of the artist, for the position is of its very nature artificial and has been achieved here no doubt by an upward, hoisting movement of the arms. At first *pointes* must have been used very sparingly by very few dancers, and with no startling effect, for not until 1829 was notice taken of the innovation by the critics in London. But the challenge had been revealed, and in the twenties this challenge—to catch and hold the fleeting impressions of lightness which were to be achieved by this new extension of technique, and to conceal the effort involved by a graceful flow of movement—was accepted. In a very short time it was to seal the triumph of the ballerina and to lead to the Golden Age of the Romantic Ballet.

NOTES TO CHAPTER 5

[1] John Ebers, *Seven Years of the King's Theatre* (London, 1828).
[2] *The Times,* 4th August 1824.
[3] Thomas Moore, *The Fudge Family in Paris* (London, 1818).
[4] *Morning Herald,* 25th April 1822.
[5] *Morning Herald,* 28th March 1821.
[6] *The Times,* 6th January 1823.
[7] *The Times,* 24th April 1822.
[8] *Morning Post,* 12th March 1823; *Morning Herald,* 10th March 1823.
[9] *Morning Herald,* 15th March 1824.
[10] Bernard Blackmantle, *The English Spy* (London, 1825–6).
[11] T. S. Duncombe, *Life and Correspondence* (London, 1868).
[12] Edward Fitzball, *Thirty-five Years of a Dramatic Author's Life* (London, 1859).
[13] *Morning Herald,* 26th March 1827.   The critic of this paper carried on quite a campaign against the pirouette between 1823 and 1830—until, that is to say, the advent of Marie Taglioni.

6

Maria Mercandotti, the Andalusian Venus

In 1808, some three years after his wife had died from the effects of a bite on the nose from her favourite Newfoundland dog, James Duff, a man still in his early thirties, sailed to Spain to offer his services in that country's struggle against Napoleon. By the time he returned to England, having succeeded to the earldom of Fife in the Irish peerage, he held the rank of major-general in the Spanish Army, had been wounded twice in honourable combat and decorated, and in addition had made the acquaintance of a charming widow and her no less delightful daughter. The widow, Señora Mercandotti, came of a respectable family, and her child, Maria, showed a truly astonishing aptitude as a dancer and already possessed 'all the charms of Spanish beauty —the darkly bright and impressive beauty of romance'.[1]

It was said that this young girl first entered the life of Earl Fife when she was appearing as an infant prodigy at the principal theatre in Cadiz. After the performance was over, she was carried round, as was the custom, 'to receive the personal approval and trifling presents of the grandees', and Fife was at once so entranced by her beauty that he adopted her and liberally provided funds for her upbringing. With such affection did he treat her that many erroneously believed that he was her father.[2]

The fourth Earl Fife, as he had then become, returned to England in 1811, and three years later, when the war ended, lost no time in arranging for his young protégée to make her début at the King's Theatre. On the evening of 12th July 1814 it was announced that 'a young lady, native of Spain, recently arrived from that country, now a pupil of M. [Armand] Vestris, will appear for the first time, and dance the favourite national *Cachucha*'.

Maria was then in her thirteenth year, a beautiful little creature, with 'sable hair', a tiny waist, and an exquisite figure. 'We do not recollect', wrote the critic of *The Times* after the first of her few appearances, 'a female dancer with more variety of quick motion. Her agility is such that the eye sometimes can with difficulty trace her movements. In the management of the castanets, her rapidity of execution exceeds all we have seen of those instruments; but this excites surprise quite as much as delight. With many beautiful attitudes, she has some rather fantastic.'[3]

In August she was seen at the Lyceum at a benefit performance, and if several London managers offered her engagements, as they were rumoured to have done, she accepted none of them. According to Ebers, 'she afterwards danced a very few times at Brighton, in the presence of the late Queen Charlotte, and never without unbounded applause'.[1] At the end of September 1814 Lord Fife left England for Paris, and he may have taken Maria with him to place her under one of the great teachers to be found in the French capital.

The following summer, after Napoleon had been decisively defeated at Waterloo, Lord Fife again visited Paris. The French capital was filled with officers and soldiers of the allied armies, and of these the most in evidence were the English. 'The English', wrote Captain Gronow, 'flocked to the Opéra and occupied some of the best boxes,' and several of them, including Lord Fife, were among those privileged to forgather with ambassadors and great state functionaries in the Foyer de la Danse, 'all attired in knee-breeches and opera hats, and with buckles in their shoes, and frills and ruffles of the costliest kind'. [4]

There Lord Fife paid particular court to Lise Noblet, never leaving her for an instant. 'He would carry her shawl, hold her fan, run after her with her scent-bottle in his hand, admire the diamond necklace someone else had given her, or gaze in ecstasy on her pirouettes,' and on his return to England he would amuse the Prince Regent 'with a minute description of the lady's legs and her skill in using them'.[4] When Ebers first engaged Lise Noblet in 1821, Fife placed a carriage at her disposal, lavished presents on her, and invariably entertained her and other dancers at his table at the Pulteney Hotel every Saturday evening. In all, he was said to have spent nearly £80,000 on her.

Influential both at the Paris Opéra and at the King's Theatre in London, where he was appointed a member of the governing Committee in 1821, Fife was well placed to launch his young Spanish protégée, who had now grown into womanhood. With Ebers he paid a visit to Paris in the late summer of 1821. By this time Maria was already studying under Jean-François Coulon, one of the finest of French teachers, and Paris was in expectation of her approaching début at the Opéra, which took place after some delay on 10th December 1821. Lord Fife was of course present, and described the occasion in a letter to the Secretary of the King's Theatre Committee, Mr Allan. 'Maria', he told him, 'made her début under great disadvantages, very much alarmed and wearied to death; but the result was most satisfactory for an artist. I believe it is admitted there has not been so brilliant a début in the memory of anyone. The whole house rose and saluted at the end; of course there are jealousies without number. The whole *corps* are displeased and agitated, and the only thing they can find to say is, that the whole house was packed, when it had only the night before been known certainly that she was to appear.' Other witnesses of the début confirmed the justification for Lord Fife's enthusiasm. 'I think she will be a trump for you,' wrote Lord Lowther. 'Novelty, beauty, and talent attract what you, as a manager, would desire, namely, a full house.' [1]

Some of the French critics were no less impressed—Castil-Blaze declared her to be the prettiest woman he ever saw on the stage, remarking in particular her lovely eyes and her long, lustrous lashes [5]—but Ebers was quick enough to engage her for the 1822 season in London, before the Paris Opéra could lay a legal claim to her services. An indication of the progress she had made since her brief début at the King's as a child can be obtained from the salary—£800—which Ebers contracted to pay her for the season.

Maria reappeared at the King's Theatre on 19th January 1822, in a *divertissement* after the first act of *Le Nozze di Figaro*, and made a favourable impression. 'It is not in the grand style that she can put forward her claims,' remarked the *Morning Post*. 'She has no majesty, no peculiar strength, and but little *aplomb*. But she has grace, lightness, pure attitudes, easy movements, a lovely face, and a shape symmetry itself.' Soon afterwards she played Cupid in *Le Carnaval de Venise*, a rôle to which 'her lovely person was particularly advantageous'. But she was still to be generally appreciated. 'It appears not to be sufficiently known', commented the *Morning Post*, 'what a treasure is possessed in Mercandotti, who moves *comme une petite divinité*.' [6]

The cause of her cool reception was the subject of a letter to the editor of the same paper from a reader who signed himself 'Philomodestus'. 'The taste of the English', he wrote, 'is not yet, thank God, sufficiently vitiated to approve of figures, however lovely, being exposed on the stage in almost a state of nudity, and to this we must attribute it, that in the *Carnaval de Venise*, at the commencement of the season, one of our most elegant dancers met with so little encouragement that she has since been more modestly attired, and is now most deservedly applauded. . . . With respect to the style of their performances, can anything be more ungraceful, more indecent, than that continued whirling round on one leg?' [7]

February saw a revival in one act of *Les Pages du duc de Vendôme*, a ballet with a Spanish setting, for which Anatole had arranged a bolero for Maria and Mlle Roland. Never before, wrote the *Morning Herald*, had 'the matchless graces of Mercandotti, while striking the castanets and moving her arms in unison with her steps', been seen to greater advantage. 'She exercises a singular power over every muscle of her slender frame, which is turned, as it were, to the very form and soul of harmony.' [8]

So popular did she become, after prudently making allowances for English taste, that at the end of March she was entrusted with the title-rôle in Albert's new ballet, *Cendrillon*, the score of which was arranged and in part composed by 'the extraordinary Spaniard, Sor . . . the most perfect guitarist in the world'.[1] The ballet was a great success, and Maria—'this entrancing little creature'—was repeatedly applauded at every performance for the 'grace and native dignity' with which she invested her part and for the tire-less vivacity of her dancing.[9] (Plate IIb.)

Despite the many exacting hours she had spent with Coulon it was still in the dances of her own land that she most excelled. At Lise Noblet's benefit she danced the graceful *guaracha* and 'fascinated every eye. . . . She used, with the most picturesque effect, a scarf which was suspended from her head-dress, and shaped her slender form into every possible variation of beauty'.[10]

Ebers opened his 1823 season on 4th January with *Le Carnaval de Venise*. If it were possible, Maria was even more fascinating than she had been the year before. 'There is', wrote the *Morning Herald*, 'a freshness on her brow, and a brilliancy of expression on her face so beautifully harmonized with the lightness and playfulness of her figure, that admiration almost seeks for opportunities of bestowing applause. Her movements, though perfectly correct, seem not to be merely of the school. She seems not to spring by the rules of science, but to bound in the gaiety of her heart.'[11] In a revival of *Les Pages* she danced the bolero with Lise Noblet, whose movements appeared neglected in contrast to hers.

On 8th March 1823 Aumer staged his grand historical ballet, *Alfred le Grand*, in which Maria was given the part of the King's page. 'Her devotion to her master', described the *Morning Herald*, 'was of that heartfelt and intellectual character which is the attitude of her nation, and she seemed, when her dark eye rested on Alfred, with looks of fidelity and deep attachment, as if the spirit of love had descended from heaven to animate her person and give intelligence to its expression.'[12]

A great future seemed to lie ahead of her, but shortly before the fourth performance of this ballet, Ebers received the following note from her, in consequence of which Mme Ronzi-Vestris prepared to take over the rôle of the page:

Monsieur,

Ma santé étant extrêmement dérangée, j'ai consulté mon médecin, qui m'a conseillé d'aller à la campagne pour passer quelque temps; je m'empresse de vous en prévenir, afin que vous puissiez donner mon rôle à une autre personne.

J'ai l'honneur d'être,

Monsieur,
Maria Mercandotti.[1]

Few were deceived by this letter. For some time past the attentions of a Mr Ball-Hughes had been observed by those who frequented the Green Room, and no sooner had Ebers published Mercandotti's letter than a wit parodied it in these lines:

Sir, being a-miss *et ma santé dérangée*,
Mon médecin declares *qu'il-y-a quelque chose à changer*;
I suppose he means air—*à la campagne je vais*,
So dispose of my rôle *à quelque autre*, I pray,
But Mamma *ne veut pas que je sois paresseuse*,
Bids me go to a ball, and I cannot ref-Hughes.[1]

The successful suitor, Edward Hughes Ball-Hughes, was one of the richest young bachelors in London. Concerning his birth there was some mystery—it was whispered that he was the son of 'a slop seller in Ratcliffe Highway'—but there was certainly nothing nebulous about his fortune, save its habit of trickling from his fingers at the gaming table: 'perhaps the greatest gambler of his day', he was reputed once to have lost £45,000 in a single night at Wattier's Club in Piccadilly. This fortune had been amassed by his forbear, Admiral Sir Edward Hughes, during his command of the fleet on the Indian seas, and when Edward Hughes Ball, as he then was (he took the additional name of Hughes by Royal Licence in 1819), came into it, it yielded him an income of over £40,000 a year. His wealth and education—Eton and Trinity College, Cambridge—gained him admittance to the most exclusive sets in London society and earned him the nickname of 'Golden Ball'. He was a most eligible young man, remarkably handsome, with excellent manners—in short, 'a thoroughly amiable, agreeable fellow, and universally popular'. Mothers considered him as a great match for their daughters, but nevertheless he was refused three times before he fell captive to the charms of Maria Mercandotti.[13]

The power of Maria's attraction may be gauged from the description of her in the book, *The English Spy*, as she was depicted in the engraving of the Green Room at the King's Theatre by Robert Cruikshank. 'Before the mirror,' it runs, 'in all the grace of youthful loveliness and perfect symmetry of form, the divine little fairy sprite, the all-conquering Andalusian Venus, Mercandotti, was exhibiting her soft, plump, love-inspiring person in a pirouette.' [2]

Golden Ball's offer of a handsome settlement was indignantly refused by the dancer, and when at last he realized that he could win her in no other way, he offered her his hand and his fortune. The proposal accepted, Maria and her mother and Ball-Hughes stole quietly out of town and with all speed made for Edinburgh, where Lord Fife, who had given his blessing to the match, was waiting. The ceremony was to have been held there at once, but certain difficulties arose and the party continued their journey to Duff House, the Earl's seat at Banff. There the banns were published three times in one day, and the marriage was duly celebrated on Saturday, 22nd March. Golden Ball and his young bride spent a few days at Dalgety Castle before travelling to the south. They planned a honeymoon on the Continent, but the weather was so stormy when they arrived at Dover that they delayed their departure and spent some days at Broadstairs, where Maria was observed taking the air on a Jerusalem pony.

Their romantic elopement was the talk of the town for some weeks, and sent many wits to their writing-desks to compose a couplet or some verses, often containing the obvious play upon the bridegroom's name. A fair sample of these couplets was one attributed to Harrison Ainsworth:

> *The fair damsel is gone; and no wonder at all,*
> *That, bred to the dance, she is gone to a Ball.*[4]

A longer effusion, whose author is no longer known, dwelt on the qualities of the bride:

> *If she refus'd what most had done,*
> *   Oh bless thy happy lot,*
> *And be content that thou hast won*
> *   Her beauty without spot;*
>
> *If to thy gold she would not yield,*
> *   More than thy gold was worth,*
> *Think thou hast cull'd in virtue's field,*
> *   The loveliest flow'r on earth.*
>
> *If in the movement of the dance*
> *   A moral thou canst see,*
> *'Tis when its grace the charms enhance*
> *   Of thy Terpsichore!*
>
> *An ornament without offence,*
> *   The heart-bewitching face*
> *To Virtue gives, and Innocence,*
> *   The brightest charm to Grace.*[14]

The excitement caused by this escapade soon died away, and the newly wed couple settled down to married life in a house in Greenwich Park. There Ball-Hughes assembled all his old friends about him, entertaining them until two or three o'clock in the morning, and often later. Maria, being a Spaniard and a one-time dancer, was apparently accustomed to late hours, and had lost none of her freshness when the diarist Creevey saw her at Ascot in 1826. She was surrounded by all the dandies in the Duke of York's stand, and was in Creevey's opinion the beauty of the meeting.[15] Eventually, however, there were differences, which led to a separation and a divorce.[16] According to Castil-Blaze,[5] Maria later became Mme Dufresne, and that is the last that history has to record of her.

As for Ball-Hughes, his addiction to gambling caused his fortune to dwindle to a mere pittance compared with what it had once been, but his luck did not run out. Soon after his marriage he had purchased Oatlands, a large estate near Weybridge, formerly the property of the Duke of York, an investment which many at the time considered folly, but he later sold it at a handsome profit for residential development. In his last years he fathered families by two other women, and died at Saint-Germain-en-Laye in March 1863.

NOTES TO CHAPTER 6

[1] John Ebers, *Seven Years of the King's Theatre* (London, 1828).

[2] Bernard Blackmantle, *The English Spy* (London, 1825–6).

[3] *The Times*, 18th July 1814.

[4] R. H. Gronow, *Celebrities of London and Paris* (London, 1865).

[5] F. H. J. Castil-Blaze, *L'Académie Impériale de Musique* (Paris, 1855).

[6] *Morning Post*, 21st and 28th January and 11th February 1822.

[7] *Morning Post*, 16th April 1822.

[8] *Morning Herald*, 18th February 1822.

[9] *Morning Post*, 27th March 1822.

[10] *Morning Herald*, 14th June 1822.

[11] *Morning Herald*, 6th January 1823.

[12] *Morning Herald*, 10th March 1823.

[13] R. H. Gronow, op. cit.; F. Boase, *Modern English Biography* (London, 1892); *Dictionary of National Biography*.

[14] *Morning Post*, 4th April 1823.

[15] Thomas Creevey, *The Creevey Papers* (London, 1903).

[16] Lord William Pitt Lennox, *Drafts on my Memory* (London, 1866).

7

The Dawn of the Golden Age

THE POLICY of featuring ballet on a grand scale, which Ebers had introduced, was continued by his successor, Laporte, who, with the exception of one season, 1832, controlled the Opera House from 1828 until his death in 1841. Under his aegis, the Golden Age of the Romantic Ballet dawned. Its splendour could hardly have been foreseen. Within the span of eleven summers the fabulous pleiad of ballerinas—Taglioni, Elssler, Carlotta Grisi, and Cerrito, any one of whom a single generation would have been fortunate to possess—burst upon London, their greatness being further stressed by the advance being made in the ballerina's technique, most particularly in the use of the *pointe,* and the corresponding eclipse of the male dancer. At the same time an excellent choreographer was found in Deshayes, whose important ballets were built upon elaborate scenarios and enhanced by the collaboration of a talented designer in William Grieve. These factors, imposing themselves on trends which had been developing for some time—the use of *couleur locale,* the ever increasing attention given to the creation of illusion, the introduction of creatures of fantasy, the influence of Romantic literature— led to one of the most glorious phases in the history of ballet, a phase in which the King's Theatre played a distinguished part.

The impact of Taglioni, Elssler, Grisi, and Cerrito was indeed so shattering that the public paid little attention to the male dancers at their side. Often those whom Laporte engaged were barely tolerated, although many possessed excellent qualities. The young August Bournonville, for instance, who visited London in 1828, was well received but made no real impression on the audience, who were more interested in his partner, Louisa Court, an English girl who had been in Paris studying under Maze. Charles Mabille, Coustou, Guerra, and Bretin, who were all talented dancers, likewise received scant attention as they devoted themselves to displaying the graces and talents of the ballerinas they partnered.

The only male dancer who bid to share popularity with the ballerina in the thirties was Jules Perrot, who first visited London in 1830. This was his first appearance in an important opera house—he did not make his début at the Paris Opéra until after his first London season—but though he was only twenty he already possessed a great fund of stage experience, acquired at the

46

Gaîté and the Porte-Saint-Martin in Paris, where he had played both orthodox dancing rôles and parts which demanded acrobatic effort. This had given him an unusual technique, and, had it not been for a chronic weakness in his foot which troubled him from about 1835 and dogged him throughout the remainder of his dancing career, he might, as a dancer, have shared the palms of the Romantic Ballet with Taglioni, as in a later age did Nijinsky with Karsavina.

Jules Perrot made his London début in a revival of *Le Carnaval de Venise* on 6th February 1830, and quickly attracted attention. 'Perrot shines conspicuously,' wrote the *Morning Post* some days afterwards, 'and is evidently destined to be the star of the season. The wonderful ease and agility with which he performs surpasses anything that has hitherto been witnessed on these boards.'[1] His stay in London was short, for he had to return to Paris in April to prepare for his début at the Opéra under the guidance of Auguste Vestris, but he returned again in 1833 and thereafter every season until 1836; in the succeeding decade he was again to become an annual visitor, but then primarily in the rôle of choreographer. As a dancer Perrot possessed both vigour and elegance, and was capable of the most rapid movement without any sacrifice of grace. His most remarkable quality was his buoyancy: 'his power of springing with facility from both or either of his legs singly being as great as if the limbs had all the qualities of Indian-rubber'.[2]

That this great male dancer should efface himself in presenting to the London public his young protégée, Carlotta Grisi, in 1836, was most significant of the eclipse of the male dancer in this period. (Plate VI.) He had come across her at the San Carlo in Naples, where he had been engaged for the Carnival season, and had at once been deeply smitten both by her promise as a dancer and by her fresh, youthful charms. When they arrived in London she was probably already his mistress, for they both lodged in the same building—51 Quadrant, Regent Street.

At the time of her London début, on 12th April 1836, Carlotta was not quite seventeen, yet—as Taglioni had done before her, and as Cerrito was to do four years later—she immediately carried the town by storm. 'She came, curtsied, and conquered,' reported the *Morning Herald*. For a dancer she was somewhat tall; her legs and feet were well shaped, and her head, 'of a Medician smallness', sat 'lightly and airily on a lithe neck and gently sloping shoulders'. Though her execution, at her first appearance, was a little marred by nervousness—the *Morning Post* observed 'an occasional unsteadiness' and 'some of the steps being too wide, and performed by dint of great exertion'—the qualities of her style were fully and immediately appreciated: her freshness, her freedom of movement, her 'great force and bounding agility', her sure musical sense. In particular, 'her revolving motion in bounding across the stage', recorded *The Times*, 'was wonderful for its flexibility and exciting for its novelty'.[3]

47

But the greatest charm of her dancing, even when she was performing the most intricate movements, lay in its seeming artlessness. 'She appeared', wrote the *Morning Herald*, 'to live and move in the poetry of motion, for its sake alone. Her vivacity is the very elixir of youth, her grace the inspiration of nature. Smiles almost breaking into laughter are ever on her cheek, and she evidently cares less for the admiration of her beholders than for the pleasure she derives from efforts that are but recreation. She is as a wild fawn before our eyes, or an Esmeralda, or as one of those spirits of some bright particular star which the Roman painters represented as dancing down the skies and rejoicing in their course.' [4]

Not for nothing, either, was this young dancer the cousin of Giulia Grisi, the great *prima donna*. At Perrot's benefit, and again at hers, she sang the *cavatina*, 'Regnava nel silenzio,' from *Lucia di Lammermoor*, with Bochsa accompanying her on the harp, and the genial and rotund Lablache, the great bass, by her side on the stage to give her encouragement. But though her voice—'a *soprano sfagato* of considerable compass and of average power' —was pleasant it was obvious where her vocation lay when later she and Perrot burst into the 'original' Neapolitan tarantella.

With so much that was novel being introduced there was little wonder that ballet became so fashionable during the eighteen-thirties. Wonderful ballerinas made their débuts in thrilling succession—Taglioni in 1830, Elssler in 1833, Carlotta Grisi in 1836, Cerrito in 1840, all except Taglioni appearing in London before they were seen in Paris—and technical discoveries were continually being made as the possibilities of the *pointe* were explored. Although all four of the great Romantic ballerinas included it in their vocabulary—Fanny Elssler in particular cultivated it to a remarkable degree—not they but Élisa Vaque-Moulin and Amalia Brugnoli were the pioneers of this new genre on the London stage.

Élisa Vaque-Moulin made the audience at the King's Theatre conscious of the *pointes* for the first time when she visited London in 1829. With her this novel extension of technique was probably more in the nature of a physical feat than an enhancement of her style as a dancer, but the impression she made was none the less very great. 'In some respects she is the most extraordinary dancer we have ever seen,' wrote the *Morning Post*. 'She possesses certainly great muscular powers, and leaves nothing to be wished for on the score of agility, vigour, and grace; her manner of standing and walking upon her toes is truly astonishing.' [5]

Brugnoli, who came to London three years later in 1832, had been cultivating her *pointes* for at least ten years. Lady Blessington had thought her style 'peculiar' when she had seen her dance in Italy as long ago as 1823. 'She advances rapidly across the stage', she noted, 'on the extreme point of her toes, without for a moment losing her *aplomb*, cuts into the air, and alights again on the point of her feet, as if she were no heavier than gossamer.' [6] Marie Taglioni also gave Brugnoli credit for introducing this

Coll. of Miss Lillian Moore

vb. Amalia Brugnoli and Paolo Samengo

Coll. of Mr Peter Revitt

va. Fanny Bias in *Flore et Zéphire*
Lithograph by F. Waldeck

VI. Carlotta Grisi and Jules Perrot in *Le Rossignol*
Drawn and etched by T. Jones

'*genre nouveau*', but considered it laboured and lacking in grace.[7] This, however, was a memory from the winter of 1823–4, when they were both dancing in Vienna. When London saw Brugnoli in 1832 she had had nearly ten years in which to develop the feat, and contemporary notices indicate that she had succeeded to a remarkable degree.

Partnered by her husband, Paolo Samengo, Brugnoli performed an astonishing *pas de deux* which mounted towards a thrilling climax. (Plate Vb.) 'The prolonged pirouette and mercurial balance with which they commence agree with the sententious prelude of an overture,' described the *Morning Herald*. Then, as the music gradually quickens in tempo and increases in volume, 'the dancers, redoubling their marvellous exertion, quivering, cutting, interlacing, and glancing, conclude an elaborate coda with one tremendous whirl of pirouette, during which every limb performs peculiar evolutions of its own—the leg shaking or trilling—the arms poising and twining, and the body coiling itself with as many convolutions as would puzzle a Mussulman Fakir, or excite the envy of the dancing serpents of La Vaillant.

'Mme Brugnoli's toe is quite unequalled by anything within our recollection, except Paganini's bow or single string. She performs evolutions on it such as no other dancer could accomplish with their ten, with unerring precision and nonchalance. Her pirouette is inconceivable; her *abandon*, when from her pinnacle of foot she is wafted like a zephyr to her companion's arms, is, as the French said of one of their Ministers, unspeakable; and her *staccato* on the tips of her two toes——!'[8]

Such a discovery was not to be ignored by other dancers. Even Taglioni found something to learn. 'She,' wrote the *Morning Herald* in 1833, 'like the general *corps de ballet*, has, since we last saw her, studied to emulate the wonders of Brugnoli's toe.'[9] Pauline Montessu was observed at Covent Garden the same year performing a 'gracefully slow tip-toe circumvolution'.[10] Angelica Saint-Romain, in 1836, succeeded in astonishing the public by 'the most unnatural trick of performing *capriccios* on the tips of her toes'. Several of her movements appeared quite novel: 'she raises herself', wrote the *Morning Post*, 'on the point of both toes, so as to form an acute angle, and then slides forward on the stage with a gentle undulating motion of the body'.[11]

Although a most revolutionary innovation, the *pointe* was not the only development which distinguished the Romantic Ballet. Indeed, more important still were the contributions to style made by Taglioni, Elssler, Grisi, and Cerrito: the modest grace and delicacy of the first, the fire and expressive mime of the second, the winning graces and poetry of the third, and the speed of execution and fascination of the fourth, brought immeasurable riches to the art of ballet. Technique with them, though never neglected, was concealed and took second place; they were creative artists in the full sense of the term, making a greater contribution to their art than did any

D

choreographer of their day except Perrot, by setting up new standards and serving as models to their lesser companions. They brought new values to rejuvenate an art in which technical 'correctness' had assumed undue preponderance; they breathed the life of Romanticism into the cold marble of Classicism. 'Formerly,' explained the *Morning Post* in 1843, 'dancers' evolutions were as precise as those of soldiers—in their feats they bounded and leapt in the perpendicular line. . . . Now dancers have discovered that the line of beauty in dancing is like that of Hogarth in painting—and that the more it is waving, undulatory, and inclined, the more it is graceful and captivating. They have gone one step further and laid down this axiom: that dancing excels exactly in proportion as it resembles flying. That is the source of all the present triumphs.' [12]

Though overshadowed by the brilliance of the ballerinas, the choreographers of this period included several talented artists. Foremost among these was Deshayes, who had appeared at the King's Theatre in the early years of the century as a dancer, and now added to his achievements the creation of a number of important ballets—*Masaniello* (1829), *Kenilworth* (1831), *Faust* (1833), *Beniowsky* (1836), and *Le Brigand de Terracina* (1837) —and, in his last season in London, 1842, assisted in the production of *Giselle* and *Alma*. 'A more amiable or more courteous personage never existed in the realms of the fantastic toe,' it was written of him shortly after his death at the end of 1846, 'nor was he devoid of inventive talent. . . . Last season he came to visit London again, and being invited to a dinner with Taglioni, Cerrito, and many of the first of the light-footed fraternity, all the memories of his glories were revived, and he had so many toasts on the subject to drink in champagne that he grew glorious himself afterwards, floated in clouds of dreamy reminiscences, like the heroes of Ossian, and instead of going to bed strolled into the fields, and nearly broke his neck in a pit. However, he recovered with broken shins, and lived to die amongst his household gods in Paris, loved and esteemed by all who knew him.' [13]

In the design of his important ballets Deshayes followed in the footsteps of Aumer by selecting a strong story, expressing it in mime, which occupied the greater portion of the ballet, and embellishing it with dances introduced incidentally as occasion offered. He devoted great care to the staging and the exposition of the plot, and in the composition of dances displayed a fertile imagination: his invention ranged wide, from dances of the Spanish type and rustic dances, which he arranged in *Masaniello*, to the mythological masque in the Elizabethan style and the Pyrrhic dance of *Kenilworth*. An objection was raised when *Faust* was produced that his dances bore no relation to the plot, but this criticism he seems to have heeded, for three years later, when he staged *Beniowsky*, he was congratulated by the same critic for the 'excellent dancing, not in the mere commonplace manner of ballets as they are usually got up at present, but characteristic and in harmony with the subject',[14] and Duvernay's *pas seul* before the looking-glass in *Le Brigand de Terracina* anticipated the work of Jules Perrot.

Deshayes was the first choreographer to benefit from the revolution that took place in the scenic department of the King's Theatre under Laporte. 'The old conventional scenes,' wrote *The Times* in 1839, 'which were almost worn down to a display of their naked canvas, and which represented by turns ancient Rome or Greece, modern Italy or Constantinople, have passed away, and given place to scenes which for beauty will not yield to the works of any theatrical artist, while the characters, instead of wearing the first suit of clothes that the gods or the dressmaker (warranted, if required, to convert a suit of armour into a Highland kilt) might provide, have been clad in dresses both appropriate and, if necessary, magnificent.'[15] The names of William Grieve, stage designer at the King's Theatre from 1829 until his death in 1844, and of Charles Marshall who succeeded him in 1845—both artists in their own right—deserve honourable mention in the annals of the Romantic Ballet in London.

One of the most successful of Deshayes's grand ballets was *Kenilworth* (1831), which had the added distinction of introducing to ballet two of the most powerful monarchs of the century: Queen Victoria, who, as the eleven-year-old Princess Victoria, saw it on 19th April, and Napoleon III, then Prince Louis Napoleon, who was in the Duchess of Bedford's box with his mother on 31st May. The ballet adhered to the well-known romance of Sir Walter Scott with unusual fidelity, and though many incidents of the novel had of course to be omitted, what there was left retained both the essential features and the balance of the original story.

The first act opened in the Black Bear Inn, where Tressilian learns of Amy Robsart's presence at Cumnor Place and the intrigues of Varney to arrange a marriage between his master, the Earl of Leicester, and Queen Elizabeth. The scene then changed to Cumnor Place, where the fight between Tressilian and Varney and Leicester's farewell to Amy, whom he has secretly married, are depicted; and finally there was a scene of rustic revelry outside the inn. The incidents in the second act included the Queen's arrival at Greenwich, Raleigh's gesture with the cloak, the reconciliation between Leicester and Sussex, the presentation of Tressilian's petition accusing Varney of having abducted Amy, and Varney's declaring her to be his own wife. For the third act, the scene changed to Kenilworth Castle. After the Queen's arrival a masque is performed before her. When it is over, she retires to a grotto, where Leicester, urged by Varney, joins her. Their tender exchanges are there observed and interrupted by Amy, but Varney, declaring that she is out of her mind, drags her from the grotto. Amy's confidante discloses the truth, and Leicester, acknowledging that Amy is his wife, craves the Queen's pardon. The last scene showed Amy repulsing Varney's advances and escaping from him up a staircase. Across a passage she sees her husband and his friends and runs towards them, but at that moment Varney touches a spring, the floor opens, and she falls to her death to the horror and confusion of all.

The production of the ballet was 'very grand and elaborate'. Grieve surpassed himself in designing the sets: the scene of the Thames at Greenwich, with the arrival of the Queen and the Royal cortège in State barges, and that of Kenilworth Castle ablaze with light for the revels were particularly brilliant. No less magnificent were the costumes, to the preparation of which considerable historical research had been devoted. The whole strength of the company took part in the ballet, which abounded not only in splendid processions and pageantry, but also in passages of expressive mime. Caroline Brocard 'beautifully embodied all the most "poetical imaginings" of the lovely and unfortunate heroine'; Lefebvre enacted the rôle of Leicester; Zoé Beaupré made her first appearance at the King's Theatre in that of Queen Elizabeth (Plate IVa), for which, however, she was more fitted by 'the lightness of her than by the dignity of her form'; and Simon made a sinister Varney.

In his arrangement of the action Deshayes introduced a group inspired by a popular engraving of the time showing Amy Robsart sitting at Leicester's feet, and produced a striking effect in each of the Queen's entrances, particularly that of the third act when she appeared on the stage riding a white palfrey. The final catastrophe was 'terribly real'. The dances came in the third scene of the first act and in the last act, and featured Paul and his sister, Pauline Montessu; they included several *pas* in the classical style, and, in contrast, the masque, which was 'admirably grotesque' and 'produced much merriment'.

At the end there was a general call for Deshayes, and the curtain rose to show him, surrounded by the dancers, 'the principals of whom, with the utmost *bonhomie*, thrust him forward, patting him on the back and applauding him, after the manner of Coulon and Pauline Leroux on the first night of *Masaniello*'.[16]

Masaniello, a ballet version of Auber's opera, *La Muette de Portici*, had been the sensation of the 1829 season, not only because of Leroux's sensitive portrayal of the character of Fenella, but also because of the spectacular production which culminated in 'a sublime representation of an awfully grand eruption of Mount Vesuvius'. 'Grandeur of spectacle' no less distinguished *Faust*, in which Pauline Leroux gave another outstanding performance as Marguerite. *Beniowsky*, which was based on a drama by Kotzebue, afforded both choreographer and designer the opportunity of depicting the imperial splendour of the Court of Catherine the Great, and for its success relied heavily on the mimetic abilities of the cast: Antoine Coulon distinguished himself, and Mme Copère—who danced at the Opera House from

1826 to 1847, and was for a time in charge of the Wardrobe department—gave 'a very fair specimen of royal dignity' as Catherine the Great.

In these ballets by Deshayes, as in the works of his predecessors and contemporaries, a principal feature was often a realistically arranged battle or duel. Perhaps Deshayes's most effective scene of this kind was the finale of *Le Brigand de Terracina*, a ballet inspired by Auber's opera about the bandit chief, Fra Diavolo. A troop of soldiers comes upon the bandits in their mountain lair, and after a bitter struggle vanquishes them. Fra Diavolo—the rôle was played by Antoine Coulon, who was, in the words of the *Morning Post*, 'in these parts unequalled on any stage'—rushes in, desperate. He is assailed from all sides. 'He commences to ascend the fearful heights, and the pursuit becomes most animated. His figure flits across the stage as he gradually mounts, throwing away his jacket, hat, etc., to facilitate his escape. As he gets to the summit of an overhanging rock a shot touches him, and he falls from an apparently lofty elevation into a frightful abyss. He is, however, brought upon the stage, and then expires, the characters forming a *tableau vivant* of the brigand's death. There was an amazing reality about the whole of this scene.' [17]

Other choreographers whose work was seen in London in the thirties were Filippo Taglioni, who devoted his creative talent principally to displaying the art of his wonderful daughter; Albert, who produced *L'Anneau magique* in 1832 and *Le Corsaire*, inspired by Byron's poem, in 1837; Léon, whose *Guillaume Tell* was first given in 1830; and Antonio Guerra, who produced *Robert le Diable* (1839), *Le Lac des fées* (1840), and *La Fille de l'exilé* (1841).

These ballets, even when arranged by an Italian choreographer, were French in spirit, in that the action was confided to dancers and expressed in a restrained form of mime, while the dances were introduced not only as a separate *divertissement*, which was generally designed stylistically to fit into the framework of the ballet, but also, at times, to express some facet of the plot such as the hero and heroine's love for one another. This was in marked contrast to the Italian school, where the action was confided to mimes who took no part in the dancing, which was thus separated from the dramatic aspect of the ballet and relegated to a degree of secondary importance, and where the miming had developed into a form very much more forceful and more gesticulatory than with the French.

London was given the opportunity of judging between these two schools in 1833, when Laporte engaged Antonio Cortesi to stage his ballet *Ines de Castro* with a distinguished body of Italian mimes. The ballet began with the arrival in Portugal of the Spanish infanta Bianca to wed Don Pedro, the heir to the throne, and the discovery that the latter is secretly married to Ines de

Castro. Ines is condemned to death but pardoned by the King, Don Pedro's father. The Spanish party, however, led by one Driego, take the law into their own hands, carry Ines off and imprison her in a castle. Don Pedro follows, but Ines dies of her privations at the very moment of her release, and her bereaved husband takes his revenge by slaying Driego over her body.

'The ballet was a silent tragedy,' observed the *Morning Herald*, 'and the obvious distinction between the French and the Italian performance was that the latter aimed at giving a much more natural expression to their feelings than the former, who habitually indulge in artificial grimace, which neither costs them much effort or their observers much emotion. But although the Italians are in this respect superior, yet they are by no means free from art; on the contrary, they have many palpable mannerisms. They stamp about tremendously both *obbligato* and in chorus, and in the same style they use violent gesticulation, rather too angular to be graceful, so that, in scenes of great excitement, there is a constant advance and retreat towards each other of the *dramatis personae*, shaking their elbows and kicking their heels at each other—all, however, in time—in exact good time. Still, they do produce occasionally a very powerful effect of dumb show, much stronger than their rivals have ever aimed at or succeeded in.

'Mme Pallerini, who appeared in the part of Ines de Castro, is a woman of acknowledged greatness in elevated pantomime. Her person is, however, too short and unshapely to be prepossessing. She has few of the winning graces of our leading French *prime donne*, but surpassed them, and indeed is finest when most excited, although in such instances she gives occasionally an unpleasing although perhaps faithful representation of nature. Thus, when the followers of Driego endeavoured to drag her away to prison, she struggled for life and liberty most lustily, and almost succeeded in capsizing four stalwart Knights of St Jago, while her death was in truth an appalling picture of a gasping and convulsive giving up of the ghost. In both instances it was disagreeable to look at her, while she has all the merit of energy and nature. Mme Cortesi (the Bianca) is tall, well looking, and an active and graceful gesticulator. Signor Ronzani reminds us slightly of young Kean, but is a stouter man. He is an interesting actor, from the seeming ardour of his emotions and his vigorous animation in expressing them. He is, however, a master of the stampeggio. At the last scene on Saturday night, he also seized his adversary Driego so strenuously, and tugged him so heartily by the hair, that we entertained very serious apprehensions for either wig or scalp. This is not English-like, and it only excites our ridicule. Signor Cortesi, who performed the part of the old King, is more quiet, but clever; he was, however, as were all the party, over-zealous in hugging and kissing the two children who figure in their piece, and of whom Signora Lumelli promises well, for she works her limbs with the assiduity of a telegraph. On the whole we felt rather surprised than gratified by this specimen of Italian style of pantomime.'[18]

Strange though this entertainment was, many of the audience did not wait to sit it out, merely staying to see the *divertissement* in the first act, in which Marie Taglioni, Fanny Elssler, Pauline Leroux, and Albert appeared. The experiment of introducing the Italian style of ballet to London was not repeated. It had run contrary to the trend whereby dancing and mime were drawing closer together. More heightened expressiveness was on the way, but it was to come through the performances of such actress-ballerinas as Fanny Elssler and Carlotta Grisi, who fused the dancing and interpretative aspects of their rôles so that it would be difficult to separate the one from the other.

NOTES TO CHAPTER 7

[1] *Morning Post*, 22nd February 1830.
[2] *Morning Herald*, 18th February 1833.
[3] *The Times, Morning Post, Morning Herald*, 13th April 1836.
[4] *Morning Herald*, 30th July 1836.
[5] *Morning Post*, 22nd April 1829.
[6] Lady Blessington, *The Idler in Italy* (London, 1839).
[7] Léandre Vaillat, *La Taglioni* (Paris, 1942).
[8] *Morning Herald*, 16th April 1832.
[9] *Morning Herald*, 29th April 1833.
[10] *Morning Herald*, 19th February 1833.
[11] *Morning Herald, Morning Post*, 7th March 1836.
[12] *Morning Post*, 3rd April 1843.
[13] *Era*, 27th December 1846.
[14] *The Times*, 6th May 1836.
[15] *The Times*, 19th August 1839.
[16] *Morning Post*, 1st, 4th, 7th, and 14th March 1831.
[17] *Morning Post*, 27th February 1837 and 20th June 1838.
[18] *Morning Herald*, 3rd June 1833.

8

Marie Taglioni, La Déesse de la Danse

'SHE IS A wonderful being, and realizes all that the most sanguine imagination can picture of the poetry of dancing,' wrote the critic of the *Morning Herald* after seeing Marie Taglioni's début in London on 3rd June 1830, in a revival of Didelot's *Flore et Zéphire*. 'She differs from all other artists by the classic simplicity of her style. It has none of the warmth and voluptuousness which do so much discredit to the profession; and she appears to be the Grecian statue animated, and preserving in every movement the purity and delicacy of her first existence. She is all grace. The most rapid execution is accompanied with an inconceivable softness; and exertions which in others are marked by violence, seem to spring from her nature with perfect ease. Though her face is not beautiful, her figure is a perfect model, rather above than beneath the middle size of woman. She has attuned that form to the most delicate harmony, and her neck, her arms, and feet are all inspired by the same elegance.'[1]

Neither the outmoded subject—mythological ballets were very much *vieux jeu* in 1830—nor the clumsy production detracted from the impact which this new dancer made on the London public, an impact all the more remarkable since she could lay no claim to beauty either of form or of feature. The key to her initial triumph, and to her long supremacy, lay in fact in her inherent grace of movement which so concealed her physical imperfections as to give a strong illusion of beauty. So rapidly did she kindle the enthusiasm of the London public that three weeks after her début, when the bills announced her last appearance of the season, a tremendous crowd forced its way into the theatre, and those who could not find a place in the house 'pressed upon the stage from the side scenes, and even seated themselves upon the flowery couches they had usurped from the nymphs' in order to obtain a last glimpse of her.

The intensity of this enthusiasm had not abated when she returned to London the following year. As the moment of her first entrance approached the boxes of the theatre became more crowded, and the audience more animated. 'Everyone appeared to be on the *qui vive* for the moment which was to give them the Terpsichore of Europe,' reported a member of that night's audience. 'At length Taglioni glided in on a sunbeam, as a certain

56

antique macaroni near us swore. She was received with rapturous applause. There was then a general glitter of upraised *lorgnettes*, the old Marquis using small telescopes, with which certain critics in the pit were also particularly intent on observations; one of the ugliest ladies of a certain age who had been attractively noisy during the opera, held her tongue for a while, and there was silence in the Opera House for five seconds.' [2] That season Taglioni appeared in two short ballets, *La Naïade* and *La Bayadère* (a compressed version of Auber's opera-ballet, *Le Dieu et la Bayadère*) (Plate IVb), was rapturously applauded in the *Tyrolienne* and a *Pas napolitain*, and danced a minuet and gavotte with her father.

Proven though her versatility thus was, it was in danger of being forgotten the following year, 1832, when, on 26th July, London first saw her dance in *La Sylphide*. For no other dancer was ever more inseparably associated with a rôle than was she with that of the ethereal, white-clad heroine of this most successful ballet of her father's: it was the sublimest expression of her artistry. As the spirit who falls in love with a mortal Scotsman, and lures him from his betrothed into the forest, there finally to die when her lover places on her shoulders a scarf over which the sorceress has cast her fatal spell, Taglioni was, in the words of the *Morning Post*, 'all that the most poetical imagination could picture of sylph-like airiness, scarcely palpable, it might be conceived, to human touch'. Her performance made the critic of *The Times* proclaim that dancing had become 'an art worthy to rank with poetry and painting', while the *Atheneum* found that 'the terms of praise are almost exhausted on this perfect—this preter-perfect—this preter-pluperfect creature'.[3] Other papers contained eulogies in a similar strain. (Plate VII.)

It was very much of a family affair, this first London production of *La Sylphide* at Covent Garden, with Marie Taglioni in the title-rôle, her brother Paul as James Reuben, and his wife Amalia as Effie. The rôle of the sorceress Madge was 'played . . . and *danced*! with a great deal of character' by none other than the manager of the theatre, Laporte, who was the son of a well-known French harlequin, and a comic actor of some talent. Since the stage at Covent Garden was smaller than that of the Paris Opéra, where the ballet had been created some four months before, Filippo Taglioni had to be content with a relatively modest production. He was, however, fortunate in his collaborators. The 'excellent' scenery was painted by the brothers Grieve, and the mechanism by which Taglioni's flights and glidings were managed was 'wonderfully perfect'. Apparently Schneitzhoeffer's score was adapted by Laporte's young brother-in-law, Adolphe Adam, the future composer of *Giselle*, whose name was joined with that of the original composer on the bills.

Marie Taglioni seldom returned to London without appearing in *La Sylphide*. In 1835 Jules Perrot partnered her in the rôle of James Reuben, their *pas de deux* being described at the time as 'such a masterpiece of dancing as is rarely witnessed', and the honours being 'equally divided between the exquisite grace of Taglioni and the easy activity of Perrot'.[4] It was Perrot, too, who revived the ballet, in a single act, in 1845, the production from which Chalon made his exquisite series of drawings, the *Souvenir d'Adieu*, depicting the great ballerina in her most famous rôle.

'There is a particular charm in her dancing, which no other artist attains,' wrote *The Times* of her performance in that year, 'a garb of elegance thrown about all her movements which gives a poetry to steps which, with other dancers, would be merely insignificant. The neatness with which she executes her *pas* is not merely a mechanical neatness, but indicates a fine feeling for exquisite finish and perfection; the broad ethereal bounds which she takes across the stage are with the easy confidence of a mind perfectly sure that it can regulate every corporeal action. The dancing is not the spontaneous mirthful joyousness of "realism", does not exhibit a wild *abandon*, but it is the calm, graceful exhibition of a poetical conception. It is the elevation of every gesture into an ethereal region that stamps Taglioni as the "idealist" *par excellence*.'[5]

The Sylphide remained her favourite rôle to the end, the last time she played it being on the evening of 7th August 1847, just a fortnight before her last appearance in public.[6]

Filippo Taglioni never produced another ballet to match *La Sylphide*; indeed, many of his later works were mediocre and often escaped oblivion only by the dancing of his daughter. *Nathalie* (1833) was considered 'insipid'; *Sire Huon* (1834), an elaborate ballet on the subject of Weber's opera *Oberon*, created very little impression; *La Chasse des nymphes* (1834) was little more than a *divertissement*; and *Mazila* (1835) failed in London as dismally as it had done, under the name of *Brézilia*, in Paris. More successful, however, were the revivals of ballets which he had staged at St Petersburg: *Miranda* (1838), *La Gitana* (1839), *L'Ombre* (1840), and *Aglaé, ou l'Éleve d'Amour* (1841).

Miranda was apparently inspired by Shakespeare's *The Tempest*, although the resemblance was slight. In the first scene a young Spaniard is cast on to the rocks in a storm and rescued from evil spirits by the nymph Miranda, daughter of the Genius of Good. They fall in love. Here Taglioni performed 'a bow-and-arrow dance, in the course of which she shoots an arrow off the wing, and bounds across the stage waving her bow over her head, as if in the pure recklessness of a child of nature'—a dance whose conception was 'beautiful and poetical in the greatest degree'. The Genius of Good disapproves of his daughter's affection, and in the second scene Miranda is imprisoned in a tent of gauze, and the Spaniard forbidden to touch her. Presently Miranda emerges and strews roses on the ground as a barrier between her and her lover. This gave rise to a *pas de deux*, in which, as the man sprang over to one side of the roses, she bounded over to the other, until at last he removes the roses and she vanishes. Finally, the Genius recognizes the sincerity of the young man's love, and the couple celebrate their betrothal in another *pas de deux*, in which 'all is pure dancing in [Taglioni's] best style'.[7]

There was an aspect of Marie Taglioni's style which was often in danger of being forgotten. She could excel almost equally well in national character dances, as she had shown in 1838 when she had introduced the 'original mazurka . . . composed purposely for her from her own observations during her late residence in St Petersburg', and as her father and Antonio Guerra set out to prove in *La Gitana* the following year. This ballet had been created in Russia the winter before, and was staged in London with dances by Guerra, Filippo Taglioni not having accompanied his daughter to England. The story of a girl stolen as a child from her aristocratic home, brought up as a gypsy, and finally recognized by her parents at a fair and restored to them, was the framework for a lively mazurka, performed 'with the most exquisite lightness', and a *pas* of the *cachucha* type. In this Spanish dance, Taglioni challenged Fanny Elssler on the latter's own ground and 'enchanted the world anew. It could only be done by herself', declared N. P. Willis, 'for there is a succession of flying movements expressive of alarm, in the midst of which she alights and stands poised upon the points of her feet, with a look over her shoulder of *fierté* and animation possible to no other face, I think, in the world. It was like a deer standing with expanded nostril and neck uplifted to its loftiest height, at the first scent of his pursuers in the breeze. It was the very soul of swiftness embodied in a look!' [8]

L'Ombre was a return to the ethereal style. Taglioni's rôle was that of the spirit of a young woman, Angela, who had died shortly before she was to have married Loredano. In a dream, the bereaved Loredano sees how the Grand Duke, desiring that he should marry the Princess Eudosia, had invited Angela to a ball and there caused her death by means of a poisoned bouquet. When he relates this dream to Eudosia, she tells him he is foolish to believe it. The spirit of Angela, however, still haunts him, invisible to all but himself, now alighting on a flower, now on a waterfall, and now coming between him and Eudosia. Finally, as the marriage contract is about to be signed, the spirit wrenches the pen from Eudosia's hand, and pursues both her and Loredano with the fatal nosegay. Both die, and the ballet ends with the spirits of Angela and Loredano united in death, ascending to the realms of light. A large proportion of this ballet was taken up with mime, and despite two exquisite *pas de deux* by Taglioni and Guerra, the work 'wearied full much as pleased'.[9]

Aglaé, though little more than a *divertissement*, was perhaps the most satisfying work that Filippo Taglioni had produced since *La Sylphide*. Staged without any pretensions to splendour, it presented Marie Taglioni in a number of *pas* without being encumbered by an involved plot requiring lengthy passages of mime.

Though her visits to London were neither annual nor very long—only twice did she give more than a score of performances in a season—Marie

Taglioni maintained the supremacy she had won in 1830 until the very evening of her retirement seventeen years later, despite the rivalry of such younger stars as Carlotta Grisi, Cerrito, and Grahn. When, past the age of forty, she took part in the first two of Perrot's grand *divertissements*, the *Pas de Quatre* (1845) and *Le Jugement de Pâris* (1846), her laurels were still secure. 'Although her physical means may in some measure be diminished, and there be some indications of forces partially spent,' wrote the *Morning Herald* in 1846, 'all those traits of grace which made her famous, and which gave an art (until she came, a mere exposition of bodily exercise) dignity and importance, are still strikingly and gloriously visible.'[10]

This magic of hers, which no words could adequately describe, bewitched the public at each performance of *Le Jugement de Pâris*. After Grahn and Cerrito had each completed their *pas* amid storms of applause, she would step quietly forward to play her part in the contest for Paris's apple. This was a wonderful moment:

Who comes like bright Aurora clothed in day?
Pure and unearthly, calm and all serene,
She looks around and knows herself a queen!
She moves—ah! breathe not! will she fade away,
All too ethereal for our common clay?
We fear to see the glorious vision rise,
Spurning base earth, to seek her native skies!
Ah, no!—she smiles—she will not leave us yet,
But will her fairer, fitter home forget,
And stay awhile—to leave, when she is flown,
Laurels unfading, and a vacant throne!
The triumph of the Ideal all her own!
Let others' skill or strength win plaudits vain;
Make but one step, and we are thine again,
And bow before that soft and regal tread,
That would not bend the fragile lily's head.
So it was ever, so we see to-day,
The soul superior to the baser clay,
So Psyche stood, still young, and still divine,
And claimed all hearts—oh! take them, they are thine!
So shall we feel, when future wonders rise,
And smile to see the grace our children prize;
And say that beauties, great and bright as they,
Faded like stars before the approach of day,
When THOU sprang forth and took thy regal place,
As Empress of all art, and of all grace,
So shall we tell of her who will be known
As grace unspeakable, a glory flown.

Marie Taglioni, La Déesse de la Danse

Let no new Idol take the place divine,
For ever vacant TAGLIONI'S shrine,
The apple of the world, oh! Queen, is thine.[11]

The performance of *Le Jugement de Pâris* at Her Majesty's on 21st August 1847 marked the end of Taglioni's career as a dancer, but she was still to make an important contribution to ballet, as teacher and choreographer, at the Paris Opéra from 1859 to 1870. After the Franco-German war, in her old age, she taught dancing and deportment to children at No. 6 Connaught Square, Hyde Park, counting princes of the blood among her pupils. But this was a sad sequel to her years of glory.

As a dancer she had no peer, but so ephemeral is the art of ballet that now, while her fame remains, the quality of her dancing can be little more than guessed at from the descriptions of her contemporaries. For its essential nature eluded the definition of words; only by the use of metaphysical terms and poetic metaphors could an idea, albeit a very inadequate one, of her artistry be conveyed. It was not in any features of her technique—not in her floating bounds, nor in the holding forward of the body with the arms kept rather low, nor yet in what was described as 'those steps with the knee bent forward which are so completely Taglioni's own that no other *danseuse* seems to have adopted them'[12]—that her secret lay, but in the manner of her dancing, in the effort made not by her muscles but by her mind. Hers was the magic that derived from the soul, a magic such as inspires artists.

Fanny Kemble once told her friend, Frederick Rackeman, that Chopin's music always made her think of the great ballerina, and was surprised to learn 'that Chopin had said that he had more than once received his inspiration from Taglioni's dancing; a curious instance of an influence so strong as to be recognized by one who was perfectly unaware of it'.[13] Possibly Fokine, too, was not conscious of this bond when, early in the twentieth century, he conceived *Les Sylphides,* but the strains of Chopin's music may none the less have conveyed to him something of the wonderful movement of the great ballerina who perhaps inspired them, and thus may his choreographic inspiration have captured some of the purest essence of the Romantic Ballet.

NOTES TO CHAPTER 8

[1] *Morning Herald*, 4th June 1830.

[2] *Morning Herald*, 11th April 1831.

[3] *The Times*, 27th July 1832; *Morning Post*, 27th and 31st July 1832; *Athenaeum*, 28th July 1832.

[4] *The Times*, 29th May 1835; *Morning Post*, 1st June 1835.

[5] *The Times*, 27th June 1845.

[6] Other dancers who played the rôle of the Sylphide in London were Amalia Taglioni (Covent Garden, 1832); Élise Varin (King's, 1835); Pauline Duvernay (King's, 1837); Fanny Cerrito (Her Majesty's, 1841); Miss Ballin (English Opera House, Lyceum, 1842); the younger Marie Taglioni (Her Majesty's, 1851); and Regina Forli (Her Majesty's, 1852).

[7] *The Times, Morning Herald*, 15th June 1838.

[8] N. P. Willis, *Famous Persons and Famous Places* (London, 1854).

[9] *The Times*, 17th August 1840.

[10] *Morning Herald*, 27th July 1846.

[11] *Morning Post*, 24th August 1846.   Poem signed 'Adelaide'.

[12] *The Times*, 19th July 1847.

[13] Fanny Kemble, *Records of Later Life* (London, 1882).

9

Fanny Elssler, the Incomparable Dancer-mime

THE ROMANTIC BALLET had two main aspects, the ethereal, represented in its sublimest form by Marie Taglioni, and the picturesque, which found its first great protagonist in the Viennese ballerina, Fanny Elssler. Both played an important part in arousing the enthusiasm for ballet of fashionable London to the pitch even of what later would be termed balletomania. 'We perfectly recollect', wrote a social observer in 1843, 'admiring the emotion of several ancient aristocrats in the stalls, on the recent appearance of the legs of Fanny Elssler. We thought that we observed one aged and respectable virtuoso shedding tears; another fainted in his satin breeks and diamond buckles; one appeared to go mad, and bit his neighbour's pig-tail in half in sheer ecstasy. Oh! the legs of Fanny displaced a vast deal of propriety, and frightened sober men from their prescribed complacency.'[1]

Unlike Taglioni, Fanny Elssler made no sensational impression during her first two seasons in London in 1833 and 1834. With her sister Therese she made her début at the King's Theatre on 9th March 1833. She was well received, and praised by the critics for her neatness of execution, her style being compared to that of Brugnoli, who had so astonished London the year before with her feats on the *pointes*, but both she and her sister were found wanting in 'the lightness and agility of the best specimens of the French school'.[2]

Therese also introduced herself as a choreographer, but neither of the ballets she staged in London obtained any great success. In its incidents *La Fée et le Chevalier* (1833) bore a strong resemblance to Didelot's *Zélis*, although the music, which was possibly by Gyrowetz, was different. The outstanding feature of the choreography was the 'exceedingly complicated and beautiful' evolutions of the *corps de ballet*, for which wreaths and bunches of flowers were used 'with a most happy effect'.[3] Well enough staged, the ballet suffered by being produced towards the end of the season, and there was only time for four performances. *Armide* (1834), a 'meagre' evocation of Tasso's romance, was given only six times, but its choreography was not without merit: the composition of the dances was 'pleasing, if not novel, and the grouping in many instances produced a good effect'.[4]

Though no one yet classed her with Taglioni, or even with Duvernay, Fanny Elssler was making steady progress. In 1834 it was noticed that she had acquired 'a pirouette on tip-toe', and in *Armide* she gave 'a most elaborate and exceedingly clever specimen of her short, rapid, and *staccato* style of dancing'.[5] She was also projecting more of her personality across the footlights, and in this second London season was described as 'one of the most fascinating dancers on the stage'.[4] As yet, however, she had given little evidence of that quality which in later years was to dominate and distinguish her style—her dramatic force. *La Fée et le Chevalier* had in fact drawn from one critic the astonishing statement, in view of what was to come, that 'the Elsslers . . . whatever may be their merit as *danseuses*, are, as actresses, decidedly the least interesting of all the fair leaders of the ballet that we have had here for a long time'.[3]

During these two first visits to London Fanny found two new friends who were to figure largely in her life: Mrs Harriett Grote, who took in her baby Therese—her child by the dancer Anton Stuhlmüller, born soon after her first arrival in London—so that 'that demented Fanny', as she called her, could continue her career, and who made vain attempts at 'making an honest woman of her';[6] and the Marquis de La Valette, who was introduced to her one evening in 1833 and whose mistress she eventually became. Another important event in her life occurred in the spring of 1834, when she was invited by Dr Véron to a banquet at Clarendon's Hotel in Bond Street which in time led to her accepting an engagement at the Paris Opéra, of which her host was then director. As a result London did not see her again until 1838, by which time she had reached maturity as an artist. The technical progress she had made was remarkable. She had 'attained a strength and precision far beyond any other dancer on the stage. Her moving through the most complicated steps on the point of her pretty feet is a wonderful effort', observed the *Morning Post*. 'It is, however, more the result of strength than gracefulness of action, and it will be admired from its difficulty and not from its elegance.'[7] More remarkable still than the skill she evinced in these feats was the development of another feature of her style, which was brought out in her performances in *Le Brigand de Terracina* and *Le Diable boiteux*. Both these ballets had been seen in London before with Duvernay in the principal part, but Fanny Elssler gave them new meaning. 'While Elssler is present', wrote the *Morning Post* of the former ballet, 'we can have no occasion to lament the absence of Duvernay. The dance before the looking-glass was particularly charming. She introduced a playfulness and *abandon* which had an excellent effect. [Plate VIIIb.] The pathetic scene was equally well played, and her unwilling *pas* in the robber's den was admirably managed.'[7] In the latter ballet she danced her renowned *pas de caractère*, the *Cachucha*, which she 'commenced with the sauciest *hauteur*, and concluded as if in quiet rapture at the mazes she had gone through'.[8] Sensitive acting of a quality not hitherto seen in ballet, and the attack with which she performed stylized national dances, particularly those of Spain, were the hallmarks of her style which in its maturity had been brought into full relief.

VII. Marie Taglioni in *La Sylphide*
Lithograph by J. H. Lynch from a drawing by A. E. Chalon

British Museum

VIIIb. Fanny Elssler in *Le Brigand de Terracina*
Drawn and lithographed by Weld Taylor

V. & A. Museum

VIIIa. Fanny Elssler in *La Tarentule*
Drawn and lithographed by J. Bouvier

These two qualities were revealed in later works—*La Gipsy* (1839) and *La Tarentule* (1840), both imported from the Paris Opéra, and *Le Délire d'un peintre* (1843), *Un Bal sous Louis XIV* (1843), and *La Paysanne Grande Dame* (1844)—while her dramatic power was given its fullest and most successful expression in the two greatest ballets to be produced during the Romantic period, *Giselle* and *La Esmeralda*.

Scotland, which held a strong attraction for Romantic artists, supplied the setting for *La Gipsy*, which was first seen in London not two months after *La Gitana,* with which it bore a certain similarity of theme. The principal character, Sarah, played by Fanny Elssler, was a girl who had been stolen by gypsies as a child and brought up by them. The *dénouement* afforded the ballerina a great opportunity to display her powerful mime. Though really innocent, Sarah is accused of theft and brought before the Sheriff. Found guilty, she attempts to stab herself, but is restrained by the Sheriff, who, seeing a scar on her arm, recognizes her as his long lost daughter. He restores her to her lover, but the ballet ends on a tragic note with the latter being shot dead at the instigation of the Gypsy Queen.

Fanny Elssler's extraordinary dramatic power went further than showing itself merely in passages of mime. 'Her *pas* are themselves fine specimens of acting,' wrote *The Times*. 'They are not unmeaning things, stopping the course of the drama when the actress abandons the character and appears to the audience as the professed *danseuse*, but Fanny Elssler gives them a life and a signification which belong to the impassioned girl of the piece, and the whole is one beautiful creation progressively developed.' [9]

Just as choreographically the *Cachucha* had been the centre-piece of *Le Diable boiteux,* so was the *Cracovienne* that of *La Gipsy*. It was danced in a setting representing the market square of Edinburgh, with the castle on its rock dominating the background. 'This', described *The Times,* 'is the perfection of the *pas de caractère. . . .* There she comes with her little military jacket, and her soldier's cap, and her long plaited tails which dangle down her back, and her neat little boots, and the little brass heels which click so prettily to the music—and her *entrée* is a triumph! It is really a dance of character, the talents of the *danseuse* and of the pantomimist being completely blended together. When she first bounds on it is as if she were springing with joy among a circle of admirers. She stops short, she assumes a military stiffness, but it is in the happiest spirit of irony. Now she seems only lazily beating time, and now she rushes along as if seized by the joy of the moment, and not knowing how to contain her delight. Then, when at the conclusion of the *pas* she trots along the lamps in that orderly fashion, and takes leave of the public in right military salute, the impression she conveys is unique. The dance she has been executing is one of the most charming things imaginable —the perfection of art—and yet she contrives to convey a notion that she has merely been playing off some pleasant trick, and is laughing at her audience for their applause.' [10]

E

Fanny Elssler's visit to London the following year, 1840, was brief but very full. She arrived on 6th March, and on the very next day made her first appearance of the season at Her Majesty's in *La Gipsy*. Writing to their mutual friend, the American Henry Wikoff, Mrs Grote told him that the ballet 'had drawn well, and [Fanny] is most frantically applauded, especially in *La Cracovienne*. I think I never saw her look worse', she added, 'worn and haggard. She has been worked like a post-horse to "mount" her new ballet, the *Tarentule*, daily, and even twice a day, returning after dinner to stage slavery!' [11]

Barrez had come over from the Paris Opéra to stage this new ballet, which was first performed in London on 21st March. 'It is unique,' wrote *The Times*, 'and may probably be the first of a new school of ballet. Picturesque effects, elaborate groupings, and *coups d'œil* are less studied than usual, and the design is to represent a little farce by action alone.' [12] The ballet described the adventures of Lauretta, a village girl, who is compelled to give her hand to an old doctor in return for his curing her sweetheart Luigi of a tarantula bite. While Luigi goes to seek the assistance of a lady who is indebted to him for having rescued her from bandits, Lauretta delays her departure with the old doctor by means of a number of ruses. Finally she pretends to be bitten by a tarantula herself, and falls to the ground apparently lifeless. The village is in an uproar. Luigi returns with the lady, who recognizes the doctor as her own husband. Lauretta then jumps to her feet, and all ends happily.

'Fanny Elssler was herself the ballet, its centre and its circumference,' continued *The Times*. 'It was all Fanny Elssler, and the little *pas* without her were merely to give her breathing time. Such a continued flow of animation, such a long deep draught of inspiration, is rarely seen. The manner in which she darted between the two *danseuses* in the first act, and went through one of the wildest figures with almost a ferocity of spirit, was electrifying, it was a complete abandonment of self to impulse during a few moments, and when it was over and she gave her usual arch acknowledgment to the audience, she seemed herself astonished at what she had gone through. The pause was but momentary; off she bounded to a tarantella to the tune well known in concert rooms as *La Danza*, and figured against her companions with all the petulance of this eccentric dance. [Plate VIIIa.] For a few minutes she retired, and returned to describe by actions her lover's misfortune. Here was a new field, she had to illustrate the tarantula bite, and represented the combination of trembling and dancing in a manner quite indescribable. In the second act, where she is supposed herself to be under the influence of the bite, she has an entirely new *pas*—to idealize, as it were, the notion of agony, and render it picturesque, becoming a Philoctetes in a ballet. The lameness gives an opportunity for some elegant movements on one foot, while the other is trembling suspended; the paroxysms, when she drags the doctor about and drives him round the tables and chairs, are a new display of that immense spirit in which Fanny Elssler stands alone.' [12]

66

Time was very short. Little more than a fortnight after the first London performance of *La Tarentule*, Fanny Elssler appeared for the last time before her departure for America. The good-hearted Mrs Grote had agreed to take care of little Therese, who was now about seven, with the words, 'Well, Fanny, send the brat to me; I don't ask you whose child it is, and I don't care, so long as it isn't that fool d'Orsay's, and I'll take the best care of it I can'. She sobbed bitterly when she saw Fanny off at the station. 'I shall be some time getting my mind afloat again,' she wrote to Wikoff the same day, 'for the idea of Fanny has full possession of it, and my heart has gone out with her. . . . She is a precious gem—tend her as one.' On 15th April Fanny and Wikoff watched the shores of England recede as the *Great Western* steamed down the Bristol Channel and into the open ocean, on its journey to the New World.

Mrs Grote was a loyal friend. 'I understand from my friends', she had written to Wikoff some weeks before, 'that my intimacy with Fanny has been the subject of the greatest astonishment, and the general surmise is that I am deceived by her. No one has dared to allude to it to me; but from what I hear, I rather expect it will be tolerated in me as an odd caprice, and is not likely at all to injure me in my relations with society. I shall go on cautiously, and abstain from talking of Fanny, as I feel persuaded no one will believe her to be what *we* know her to be. I believe Lady Blessington's jealousy of d'Orsay's admiration of Fanny Elssler to have been the fertile source of many abominable slanders against her. All my information *ends* in Lady B.'s circle, for each foul tongue seems to take its cue thence. Poor dear Fanny! Well, the venom shall not poison the stream of *my* kind sympathy towards this gifted woman. Long will *I* fight for her, through evil report and good report, so she be but *worthy* of my quixotic devotion, and capable of affection. I will stick by Fanny so long as she will love me and be discreet. If she prove insensible, I droop. Pride and temperament alike forbid a struggle of one side only.' [11]

Poor Mrs Grote was ever seeking—and, as she thought, finding—proofs that Fanny was reciprocating her own feelings, but some years later, in 1844, she was bitterly disillusioned when Fanny snatched her child—'this charming and gifted child whom we had cherished like our own for more than four years'—'without even the decorous formalities of the occasion'. [13]

Fanny Elssler the dancer was absent from the stage of Her Majesty's Theatre for nearly three years. During her absence, news of her triumphs in America found their way regularly into the columns of the London newspapers, and her reappearance was awaited with the most eager expectation. She returned at last in March 1843, and that season danced in *Giselle* and two of Perrot's minor works, *Un Bal sous Louis XIV* and *Le Délire d'un peintre*.

In *Un Bal sous Louis XIV*, dressed in a tunic of white satin, with knee-breeches and stockings to match, and red-heeled shoes, a rapier hanging by her side, she took the part of a noble cavalier of the *ancien régime*, partnering

Adèle Dumilâtre—'the quintessence of prim modishness'—in a sedate and formal *Menuet de la Cour* and *Gavotte*. In this evocation of a former age she 'seemed to perceive a drollery in the antique part she was playing, and she mimicked the sluggish ease of big-wiggism with an archness and mock gravity quite irresistible. She glided about with a diverting self-complacency, and touched the fingers of Dumilâtre with historical indifference'.[14] (Plate XIb.) The following year her partner was Fanny Cerrito, and to mark the occasion she wore a different costume with a brilliant scarlet tunic, said to be copied from one which the Marshal Duc de Richelieu wore in his first campaign.[15]

Le Délire d'un peintre consisted of a mimed scene and a *divertissement*. When the curtain rises, a young artist is found contemplating a picture in his studio, 'pale, dejected, and with the air of a madman'. His mother tries vainly to console him. He is obsessed by thoughts of a young dancer, Blanche, whose portrait he has painted from memory. While he is absent, Blanche learns the cause of his malady and resolves to cure him. On his return he uncovers the portrait and Blanche steps out of the frame. (Plate XIa.) 'Now takes place one of those scenes which only Fanny Elssler . . . can accomplish. It is in fact a repetition of the phantom vagaries of *Giselle*. She drops from the frame and haunts the poor artist in a variety of ways: now peering over him with a languishing gaze, and now floating about the *atelier* like a bird . . . mingling the most sparkling playfulness with the most deep-souled passion as she alone can do.'[16] She returns to the picture, and when he tears aside the veil again, he finds her to be not a dream but reality, and ready to become his wife. A *fête champêtre* followed, which included a *pas de deux*—'the most perfect thing imaginable', particularly 'that portion of it in which she advances towards the lamps with those brilliant tip-toe steps, gracefully waving from one side to the other, and then crosses the stage, her tall and elegant figure slowly revolving on the points of her feet'[17]—and ended with a spirited Spanish bolero, *La Castilliana*.

She possessed an instinctive understanding of the Spanish dance. Another no less successful *pas* of this kind was the *Saragossa*, which she first danced in London in 1843, 'rising and sinking and smiling around her as she cracked [her castanets] merrily to the music'.[18]

La Paysanne Grande Dame, which Perrot arranged for her in 1844, came of the same genus of *ballet-divertissement* as *Le Délire d'un peintre*. Fanny Elssler played a country girl whom a count invites to his mansion and has dressed in a magnificent robe; and her wonderment at this new finery, her discovery that she can ogle from behind a fan, her acquisition of the art of dismissing a gentleman, and her holding up of her train when she throws herself into a rustic dance were the main components of her portrayal. Her acting and dancing—the *pas de caractère*, *La Béarnoise*, did not approach her earlier dances of this kind—redeemed this slight and rather tedious work from failure.

Following her triumph in *La Esmeralda* in 1844, plans were made—and, according to one report, rehearsals even started—for a new grand ballet by Perrot, in which she was to sustain the principal part, *Jeanne d'Arc*. Unfortunately, for some reason, this interesting project never reached fruition. She did not dance again at Her Majesty's after 1844, her only other appearance in London, in 1847, being at the Royal Italian Opera, Covent Garden, where she was seen in two new, but not outstanding, ballets, *La Salamandrine* and *Manon Lescaut*. The latter ballet, with choreography by Casati, contained little of the Abbé Prévost's original story, but Elssler nevertheless gave a moving portrayal and showed that she had lost none of her powers as a dancer.

It was her dramatic insight and the power with which she rendered a character that formed the essence of Fanny Elssler's unique talent. Not only were these qualities apparent in important works such as *Giselle* and *La Esmeralda*, but also in the *pas de caractère* that she performed so inimitably. She never forgot the part she was assuming. Her every look and gesture was instinct with truth and meaning. As a dancer-mime, she had no equal. 'In deep, concentrated tragic expression', wrote a contemporary, 'she excels even Taglioni—also a great actress—and is at an immeasurable distance from any other dancer we have ever beheld.' [19]

NOTES TO CHAPTER 9

[1] *Illustrated London Life*, 16th April 1843.
[2] *The Times*, 14th March 1833; *Morning Post*, 11th March 1833.
[3] *Morning Post*, 12th July 1833.
[4] *Morning Post*, 12th May 1834.
[5] *Morning Herald*, 16th April and 12th May 1834.
[6] For Fanny Elssler's relations with Mrs Grote, see 'Fanny Elssler and her Friends—III: Mrs Grote' by Ivor Guest (*Ballet and Opera*, October 1948).
[7] *Morning Post*, 20th June 1838.
[8] *The Times*, 12th May 1843.
[9] *The Times*, 9th March 1840.
[10] *The Times*, 24th March 1843.
[11] Henry Wikoff, *Reminiscences of an Idler* (London, 1880). For Fanny Elssler's relations with Wikoff, see 'Fanny Elssler and her Friends—I: Henry Wikoff' by Ivor Guest (*Ballet*, November 1947).
[12] *The Times*, 23rd March 1840.
[13] Elizabeth Rigby, *Mrs Grote: A Sketch* (London, 1880).
[14] *Morning Herald*, 7th April 1843.
[15] *Morning Post*, 26th July 1844.
[16] *The Times, Morning Herald*, 4th August 1843.
[17] *The Times*, 19th June 1844.
[18] *The Times*, 7th April 1843.
[19] *Morning Chronicle*, 21st August 1843.

10

Pauline Duvernay, Thackeray's Vision of Loveliness

DOCTOR LOUIS VÉRON, who directed the Paris Opéra from 1831 to 1835, managed his affairs there so successfully that he relinquished his post richer than when he had assumed it, a most unusual accomplishment. He had, it was said, a regular tariff for favours—whether to engage one of his dancers to appear elsewhere during her leave, or to obtain the right of entry backstage, or even to acquire a mistress—and when Alfred Bunn, manager of the Theatre Royal, Drury Lane, wished to engage young Pauline Duvernay he doubtless had to pay Véron's fee, though this—which was said to be 1,000 francs for a month's engagement—was small in comparison with the salary of £500 a month that the dancer herself demanded and obtained.

On the axiom that money spent on ballet was money well spent, Bunn obtained the services of Anatole to stage a spectacular revival of Aumer's *La Belle au bois dormant*, which had been produced at the Paris Opéra in 1829 with Lise Noblet as the Princess Iseult and Marie Taglioni appearing in one scene as a naiad. In the London version, *The Sleeping Beauty*, first given at Drury Lane on 13th February 1833, Pauline Duvernay made her English début in both these rôles, and 'to say that she proved herself equal to the undertaking', wrote the *Morning Post*, 'would be but faint praise. Her beauty, grace, and skill were so conspicuous that everyone appeared anxious to join in acknowledging her merits, and we have never seen a foreigner meet with so flattering a reception'.[1]

This critic was very much smitten with the indisputable charms of the new dancer, with her tall, elegantly shaped figure, her dark eyes, and her 'complexion of a dazzling clearness', and his colleague of the *Morning Herald* was probably more objective in his appraisal of her dancing. 'Mlle Duvernay', he wrote, 'belongs to the school of Taglioni, and, without being equal to her model, is remarkable for finished and unlaboured art, unfaltering precision in all the movements she attempts, and a general easy and pervading gracefulness. Her pantomimic action was in general very expressive. On the whole she is a star, but not one of the first brilliancy.'[2]

Appreciating the great attraction that ballet then had for the London public, Bunn had stolen a march on Laporte by presenting this new ballet three days before the opening of the latter's season at the King's Theatre, and had consolidated this advantage by the splendour of the production, for which the artist Clarkson Stanfield, who painted the scenery, was largely responsible. One of the most successful scenes in what the *Morning Herald* called 'a prodigious conglomeration of dance and spectacle',[2] was a moving panorama showing the banks of a lake passing the hero's boat as he rows towards the castle—a scene, incidentally, which was spoilt for the more nautically minded by Paul's rowing with only one oar and with the boat facing in the wrong direction!

At the end of the first performance, Bunn himself led Duvernay forward to receive the applause, and as he did so two 'garlands of artificial flowers' were thrown from one of the side boxes, one falling among the musicians, and the other landing at the feet of the manager, who bent down, picked it up, and presented it with 'ineffable grace' to the dancer.

Marie Taglioni, who was at no time very charitable towards Duvernay, and was engaged to appear at the rival theatre in April, told a friend that these flowers had been thrown by Duvernay's father, and added that Bunn had complained he had been deceived and had almost rescinded Duvernay's contract. Of Duvernay's performance and reception Taglioni remarked that she had been warmly received on her first appearance, that the public had found her 'graceful but not outstanding' as a dancer, and that the ovation had been 'even somewhat cold'.[3]

A month later, Duvernay appeared in *The Maid of Cashmere*—the English version of the opera-ballet, *Le Dieu et la Bayadère*—and added to her conquests a young writer called Thackeray, who in later years remembered her as 'a vision of loveliness such as mortal eyes can't see nowadays. How well I remember the tune to which she used to appear! Kaled used to say to the Sultan, "My Lord, a troop of those dancing and singing girls called Bayadères approaches", and, to the clash of cymbals, and the thumping of my heart, in she used to dance! There has never been anything like it—never. There never will be—I laugh to scorn old people who tell me about your Noblet, your Montessu, your Vestris, your Parisot—pshaw, the senile twaddlers!'[4] Doubtless it was the expressiveness with which Duvernay rendered her part which so impressed young Thackeray. 'Mlle Duvernay', wrote the *Morning Herald*, 'enacted the part of the Maid with an elegance and feeling scarcely inferior to that of her model [Taglioni]. Her pantomime of jealousy was a mixture of the prettiest pettishness and graceful resignation imaginable.'[5]

Duvernay's charms won her many admirers. One of these, Lord Ranelagh, even followed her to Paris, to be told that he could attain his desire only by marrying her. Bunn, too, was said 'to have attempted a declaration of his attachment by some tender but understood expression of the eye'. For this he suffered doubly since not only did Duvernay indignantly refuse him, but his wife discovered what had happened and rated him soundly for his attempted peccadillo.[6]

The following year, 1834, Duvernay was engaged at the King's Theatre, and appeared there for the first three months of the season. 'She has had here as a dancer', wrote Taglioni to a friend, 'what we call a *succès d'estime*, but as a beauty she has enjoyed an enormous success.' [7] Duvernay, the dancer, took over Taglioni's rôle in *Sire Huon* in the great ballerina's absence, and rose considerably in the estimation of the public, but Duvernay the woman caused an even greater stir.

A young gentleman called Ellice fell deeply in love with her, and to the mortification of Lords Allen and Tullamore and other aspirants for her favours, for a time she seemed to welcome his attentions. To the horror of his father (who very ungallantly called her 'old Brimstone'), Ellice wanted to marry her, and in the ardour of his passion became violently jealous of the Duke of Devonshire, who had conceived a warm but apparently platonic admiration for her. Duvernay, however, had no intention of matrimony, and was glad to escape from this attachment, which had become embarrassing to her, by having to return to Paris at the end of her engagement.[8]

Ned Ellice had plenty of time to allow his passion to cool, for Duvernay did not come back to London until the winter of 1836, when she was engaged by Bunn at Drury Lane at a salary of £600 a month. Joseph Mazilier was engaged at the same time, and it was presumably he who was responsible for the revival of *The Devil on Two Sticks*, which, as *Le Diable boiteux*, had been first given in Paris with Fanny Elssler that June. Based on the romance by Le Sage, this ballet was set in Madrid and contained a number of brilliant scenes, the most striking of which showed the interior of the Opera House, seen from the back of the stage with Asmodeus in the prompter's box and a dissatisfied audience hissing the principal dancer. In reality, of course, Duvernay was well received, particularly in the *cachucha*. (Frontispiece.) 'This curious dance', wrote *The Times*, 'is perfect. Not only is the greatest skill exhibited in the various evolutions, but such spirit and animation are diffused through the whole that, though a result of the most exquisite art, the movements seem to spring from a kind of inspiration.' [9]

After a short illness in January, during which she was replaced by the English dancer Miss Ballin, Duvernay completed the three months of her engagement at Drury Lane on 2nd February. Three weeks later, on 25th February, she appeared at the King's Theatre in Deshayes's *Le Brigand de Terracina*, in which she played the leading rôle, rendering the bedroom scene 'as warm—to say nothing further—as the frequenters even of the stalls can desire. The fashion in which she reclines on the bed . . . inspired the bald-pated part of the audience . . . with intense delight'.[10] Her performance in this ballet, wrote the *Morning Herald*, was 'surely one of the most charming pieces of acting ever exhibited on any stage'.[11] Her feeling for character was brought out again in *La Sylphide*, in which she appeared for the first time on

IXb. Benjamin Lumley
Engraving from a sketch by Count d'Orsay

Coll. of the Author

IXa. James Harvey d'Egville
Engraving by S. W. Reynolds

British Museum

xa. Jules Perrot, Fanny Cerrito, and Marie Guy-Stéphan in Cerrito's *L'Élève d'Amour*

xb. Fanny Cerrito in *Alma*

Pictorial Times

xia. Jules Perrot and Fanny Elssler in *Le Délire d'un peintre*

Illustrated London News

xib. Adèle Dumilâtre and Fanny Elssler dancing the *Menuet de la Cour*
in *Un Bal sous Louis XIV*

xiib. Jules Perrot and Carlotta Grisi dancing the *Truandaise* in *La Esmeralda*

Lithograph from a drawing by J. Brandard

xiia. Jules Perrot and Carlotta Grisi dancing the *Truandaise* in *La Esmeralda*

Lithograph from a drawing by J. Bouvier

11th April. 'She danced like a fairy, the incorporation of a zephyr, and died as a sylph should die, her tiny wings dropping from their place, her gentle form bending like a reed, and her whole frame not struggling but fainting into death.' [12] Another novelty was produced on 29th June, Albert's *Le Corsaire*, 'a very picturesque ballet' with music by Bochsa, in which she played the part of Gulnare.

Of Pauline Duvernay, as she appeared this season, in the maturity of her development, the *Morning Herald* wrote: 'She may justly be considered, and what greater eulogium could we offer her, a sisterly rival of Taglioni, since, to a similar undeviating taste for the essentially graceful and elegant in *la belle science*, and an almost equal accomplishment and power of action, she unites a more versatile and effective dramatic or pantomimic talent. . . . In combining these two sources of fascination, she resembles Heberlé'.[11]

Her appearance in *Le Brigand de Terracina* on 19th August, the final night of the 1837 season, was the last occasion on which she danced in public. She then returned to Paris, having, it was reported, made her fortune and intending to retire, although her engagement at the Opéra had still seven months to run. This sudden decision to abandon her career had been taken as a result of an unexpected development in her private life. When she had gone to London the winter before she had been the mistress of the Marquis de La Valette, who was at that time on a diplomatic mission in Stockholm. In the Marquis's absence there was, of course, no lack of admirers to press Duvernay for her favours, and among these was a certain Stephens Lyne Stephens, to whom she was not at first particularly attracted. Lyne Stephens was determined to possess her, and Count d'Orsay obligingly negotiated a financial arrangement which satisfied both the dancer and her mother. La Valette, as soon as he learnt what was happening, hurried to London, and lost no time in going to the Opera House, where, to his astonishment, he was refused admission to Duvernay's dressing-room by order of Lyne Stephens. His friend, Coulon, then told him what had happened in his absence. Considering himself insulted, La Valette sent his seconds to Lyne Stephens, who accepted the challenge on condition that before the duel the Marquis should have one last interview with the dancer. The two met in Duvernay's dressing-room while Lyne Stephens waited outside with the seconds. After a quarter of an hour La Valette emerged and announced his intention of returning immediately to France.[13]

It was commonly believed, in 1837, that Lyne Stephens had proposed marriage to Duvernay, but that she had refused, preferring to retain a certain degree of independence. After eight years, however, her views changed, and on 14th July 1845 she and Lyne Stephens were married, first, at the Parish Church at Putney, and secondly, at the Catholic Chapel in Cadogan Terrace. This long-delayed event was supposed to have been precipitated by Duvernay's desire to keep an excellent English maid who had given notice on learning that her master and mistress were unmarried!

Lyne Stephens's wealth enabled and entitled him to play an important part in the affairs of his county, Norfolk, of which he was sheriff in 1858. He owned a large estate near Brandon, called Lynford Hall, in the grounds of which stands a small chapel which his wife had built and where masses are still said for her soul; and he also possessed a large property in Roehampton, Grove House. When he died on 28th February 1860 he was worth well over a million pounds. His widow was left the Roehampton property as well as a life interest in Lynford Hall and the residue of his estate.

Though she devoted herself to a 'life of quiet beneficence', Mrs Lyne Stephens did not abjure the world. She continued to pay regular visits to Paris, to see her friends and to order her dresses from Mr Worth, and invariably she would take her own horses with her. Age had not taken from her all her charms, and indeed a rumour circulated the year after her husband's death that she was to marry the Duc de Richelieu. Having no children she dispensed her large fortune liberally for charitable purposes, paying for the building of the Catholic Church of Our Lady and the English Martyrs at Cambridge, donating £20,000 to the Middlesex Hospital, and by her will making further gifts to charities amounting to £24,000.

In her last years she derived much comfort from the devoted friendship of General Edward Stopford Claremont, to whom and to whose children she left the bulk of her disposable estate when she died at Lynford Hall at the age of eighty-one on 2nd September 1894. Her personal estate was valued at more than £600,000, and included valuable paintings by Velazquez, Paolo Veronese, Murillo, Memlinc, Carlo Dolci, Gérard, and other artists. Among the many legacies she left was one of 100,000 francs to her first cousin, the dancer Louis Bretin, and his second wife.[14]

When Mrs Lyne Stephens was laid to rest in a private mausoleum at Roehampton there were still some, though they were very few, who could recall the excitement that reigned in the theatre as Pauline Duvernay danced the *Cachucha*. It was hard, though, to realize that the imperious old lady, with her grey hair parted in the centre and brushed over her ears, was the same person as the ravishing young ballerina who had deserted her admirers so abruptly nearly sixty years before, and of whom the author of *The Ingoldsby Legends* had plaintively written:

> *My Lord Tomnoddy he raised his head*
> *And thus to Tiger Tim he said*
> * 'Malibran's dead, Duvernay's fled,*
> *Taglioni has not yet arrived in her stead;*
> *Tiger Tim, come tell me true,*
> *What may a Nobleman find to do?'* [15]

NOTES TO CHAPTER 10

[1] *Morning Post,* 14th February 1833.

[2] *Morning Herald,* 14th February 1833.

[3] Léandre Vaillat, *La Taglioni* (Paris, 1942).   For a more detailed study of both London and Paris productions of this ballet, see 'An Earlier *Sleeping Beauty*', by Ivor Guest (*Ballet,* April 1952.)

[4] W. M. Thackeray, *Roundabout Papers* (London, 1863).

[5] *Morning Herald,* 18th March 1833.

[6] *Satirist,* 9th June 1833.

[7] Victoria and Albert Museum, Enthoven Collection: Letter to the Marquis de la Maisonfort, 15th March 1834.

[8] *Satirist,* 4th, 11th, and 18th May, 1st and 15th June 1834.

[9] *The Times,* 17th March 1837.

[10] *Satirist,* 5th March 1837.

[11] *Morning Herald,* 14th April 1837.

[12] *Morning Post,* 24th April 1837.

[13] Bibliothèque de l'Opéra, Paris: *Cancans de l'Opéra* (MS. 1836–8).

[14] In the passages relating to Duvernay's later life, I am indebted to Mr G. B. L. Wilson, who has generously supplied me with details obtained from a great-niece of Louis Bretin.

[15] Rev. R. H. Barham, *The Ingoldsby Legends* (London, 1840–7).

II

Fanny Cerrito, the Enchantress of London

IF a dancer of international renown can be said to belong to one city more than to any other, then surely London could have substantiated a claim to the most enchanting of Romantic ballerinas, the Neapolitan Fanny Cerrito.[1] In England's capital she enjoyed her greatest triumphs, and there she chose to dance in public for the last time. She was also, from 1854 until 1857, a rate-payer in Fulham, where she owned No. 21 Stamford Villas,[2] not far from Cremorne Gardens, and in her long retirement—she survived until 1909— she always treasured many pleasant memories of London.

When Laporte first engaged her for the 1840 season, her reputation already extended far beyond the borders of her native Italy and Austria, the only countries in which, until then, she had danced. Her London début came at a very propitious moment, when the public was bewailing the desertion of Fanny Elssler, who had departed for America but a few weeks since. It was originally billed to take place on 30th April, but a riot in the Opera House caused by Laporte's failure to engage the singer Tamburini—the famous 'Tamburini row', immortalized in *The Ingoldsby Legends*—put an end to the evening's entertainment before she appeared, and the test was postponed until 2nd May.

Among those who that evening witnessed her triumphant début were the twenty-one-year-old Queen Victoria, the Queen-Dowager Adelaide, the Duke of Wellington, and Prince Louis Napoleon. Possessed of great feminine appeal, Cerrito at once became the favourite not only of the influ-ential occupants of the Omnibus Boxes but of a very large proportion of the public of every degree. In stature she was considerably smaller than the other great ballerinas of her time, but her figure was most perfectly propor-tioned, and no one could gainsay her striking beauty. It was not, however, so much to her personal charms that she owed her success, as to the unique and remarkable qualities of her style—her languorous grace in *adage*, her astonishing rapidity, particularly in turns, the precision of her *pointe* work, and above all her extraordinary lightness and *ballon*, which at times made her appear to be almost floating through the air, to alight only to rebound once more with the easy spring of a young gazelle. And withal there was ever that bewitching feminine appeal, that power of fascination, which made such a contrast with the ethereal, 'ideal' quality of Taglioni's dancing that people spoke of her as 'the little realist', classing her as in a school apart from that of the *déesse de la danse*.

The key to Cerrito's style lay in her great physical strength, which she knew so well how to control and conceal, and now and then to bring into full play, though always with grace and ease and an absence of effort. Such displays never failed to electrify the audience. In Guerra's *Le Lac des fées* (1840) she performed some *jetés battus* 'so high and so much out of the line of perpendicularity' as to defy description,[3] and in the *pas de quatre* from the same ballet there was a moment which always drew thunderous applause, when she and her partner came rapidly forward from the back of the stage, she displaying 'the most surprising force, advancing more as if she were flying than dancing, and more as if she were impelled through the air by an irresistible force then either'.[4]

Already at the end of this first season she was being hailed by some as 'the rightful successor' to the throne of Taglioni,[5] and in 1841 it might have seemed that she was boldly making her claim before that throne had been relinquished. For on 10th June of that year she made a successful appearance in *La Sylphide*, and on 5th August she not only triumphantly took over Taglioni's most recent rôle, that of the Pupil of Cupid in *Aglaé*, but no less happily performed the Spanish dance from *La Gitana*. By general consent, however, Taglioni was still after this Queen of the Dance, 'although', it was said, 'a very ambitious young rival, to whom the graces are ominously propitious, circles but too closely round the throne'.[6]

The appearance in 1842 of a serious rival in the person of Carlotta Grisi, who danced in the first London production of *Giselle* on the opening night of the season, was counterbalanced by the advantages that Cerrito gained by her association with Jules Perrot, whom Lumley had engaged as dancer and choreographer. During seven successive seasons, from 1842 to 1848, when they were engaged together at Her Majesty's, both Perrot and Cerrito were at the very height of their powers, he as choreographer, she as ballerina. Their first collaboration was in *Alma* (1842), to the choreography of which they each contributed. Later Cerrito created the principal rôles in a number of ballets by Perrot—*Ondine* (1843), *Zélia* (1844), and *Lalla Rookh* (1846)— and had the distinction of being the only dancer to appear in every one of his four grand *divertissements*.

Alma disputed the honours of the 1842 season with *Giselle*. Although the dances were arranged by Perrot and Cerrito, the general production was by Deshayes, who successfully, and in accordance with Lumley's instructions, arranged that Perrot should bear the main burden of the miming, for Cerrito was a far less talented actress than she was a dancer. This division of labour was not unnatural, for in those days the action and the dancing in a ballet were in general still quite separate components.

Perrot's contribution to the choreography included a *pas de fascination* which not only most advantageously displayed the talent of Cerrito but also carried the plot forward by the expressive quality of the dancing without recourse to mime. In Lumley's opinion, however, it was not this but the *pas de trois*, which Cerrito composed, that was the highlight of the ballet. This *pas de trois*, he wrote, 'raised to its height what the colder spirits of the time were pleased to call Cerrito-mania' [7] and according to *The Times*, there was nothing in *Giselle* to compare in effect with either this or the *pas de fascination*.[8]

In her choreography for the *pas de trois*, Cerrito brought out in turn all her voluptuous grace and brilliant attack. The slow movement, in which she evinced 'the most refined perception of the beautiful in the arrangement of groups',[9] threw into strong relief the succeeding *allegro* passage with its culminating sequence of *tours*, of a most dazzling rapidity, in which she was described as 'flying round the stage and whirling as she flies'.[10] (Plate Xb.)

This was not London's first taste of her choreography for she had arranged a *pas de trois* during her first season in 1840, and in 1842 had staged an enlarged version of *Aglaé*, previously produced by her in Vienna, called *L'Élève d'Amour*, which had been greatly praised. (Plate Xa.)

Her popularity was now at its peak. It seemed that London was completely under her spell, and among her warmest admirers she counted no less a personage than Queen Adelaide, who one day sent her equerry with the gift of a jewelled brooch. There were some who dared assert that she had no peer. 'With a vivid recollection of Taglioni and Duvernay,' wrote the *Sunday Times*, 'we maintain that Cerrito is the true goddess of the dance, if dancing be, as we take it to be, a gushing forth of the spirits, exhibited by the irrepressibility of motion. Cerrito appears to us to have been "born to dance". The spirit of gladness is upon her, and she sheds sunshine around her.'[11]

The year 1843 saw the beginning of Perrot's brilliant reign as principal ballet-master at Her Majesty's. *Ondine* (1843), the story of a naiad and her hopeless love for a fisherman, was above all a triumph for him. The qualities of Cerrito's style, though an important consideration, were subordinated in his choreography to the theme of the dances, and for that reason some critics expressed disappointment that she was given less opportunity to display her brilliance than in *Alma*. The *pas de l'ombre*, however, which Ondine, transformed from a naiad into a human being, dances as she steps ashore in the moonlight and sees her shadow for the first time, was both conceived and executed with the most poetic delicacy and became quite as popular as the *pas de fascination*. (Plates XV, XVIa.)

The next grand ballet that Perrot arranged for her, *Zélia* (1844), was a failure through no fault of her own, but his *Lalla Rookh* (1846), founded on an incident in Thomas Moore's well-known poem, gave her a fresh triumph in the *pas de chibouque*, in which she danced 'such a variety of steps as baffles all description—now executing exquisitely small twinkling steps, and the next moment bounding like an antelope'.[12]

Though Saint-Léon scornfully termed them 'steeplechases',[13] Perrot's four grand *divertissements*—the *Pas de Quatre* (1845), *Le Jugement de Pâris* (1846), *Les Éléments* (1847), and *Les Quatre saisons* (1848)—provided Cerrito with successes still greater, for in their devising the choreographer was able to concentrate upon displaying the particular styles of his ballerinas without having to consider the exigencies of a plot.

Fanny Cerrito came of a respectable middle-class family, and during her first few seasons in London was most vigilantly chaperoned by her parents, to whom her achievements were a great source of pride. Her father, a retired army officer, never tired of singing her praises to all within hearing and nearly always carried in his pockets an old ballet shoe or two, garlands, or declarations of love addressed to his daughter, the *divinita*. Many there were, of course, who fell captive to Cerrito's charms and importuned her with offers of protection—among her most assiduous admirers were Lord Macdonald and Alexis Soyer, the chef—but these she consistently and firmly refused. Her virtue, a rare quality then for a dancer—indeed, almost an eccentricity—gained her great respect and even opened a few doors of London society for her. The Countess of Westmorland befriended her; and Lady Dorothy Nevill, as a girl, met her at a social gathering in Grafton Street and thought she looked 'very pretty and demure'.[14]

Cerrito's parents began to entertain hopes that she might make a good marriage and retire from the stage, and when she declared her intention of marrying a fellow dancer, Arthur Saint-Léon, they offered the stoutest opposition. Their blessing, however, was finally obtained when it became clear that Saint-Léon's persistence was not to be overcome. He began to court Cerrito during his first London season in 1843, and they were married in Paris in the spring of 1845.

In many respects Saint-Léon was Cerrito's male counterpart. The male dancer was little more than tolerated in the forties but none the less Saint-Léon conquered all prejudices by his unusual vigour and his astonishing *tours de force*, while his lack of refinement, with which some critics reproached him, perhaps only added to his virile, masculine allure. 'His movements,' wrote one critic after his début at Her Majesty's on 20th April 1843, 'are really gigantic, and he has the uncommon felicity of attracting that attention which is in general awarded exclusively to the ladies of his calling.'[15] *The Times* acclaimed him 'a wonder in his way' and declared that his feats seemed 'to mark him as the founder of an entirely new style of dancing'.[16] 'He flings himself about with the most astonishing force,' the same paper wrote a week later. 'We cannot surmise how many times he goes round in a single spin; it seems as though he had given himself an impetus he could not check. Whirled about as a hurricane, he stops as firm as a rock. Male dancers generally are horrid "bores", but Saint-Léon is a phenomenon, and he had last night the rare honour of being encored in one of his movements.'[17]

The professional partnership of Cerrito and Saint-Léon, which was to last until they separated in 1851, began auspiciously with *La Vivandière* (1844), which was probably a joint creation, for its choreography was attributed to Saint-Léon when first given in Rome in 1843, and to Cerrito when staged in London. Aware of the topical value of the polka which had just then caught the imagination of London, Saint-Léon and Cerrito expanded their ballet by adding 'the *Redowa,* or Original Polka of Bohemia', which by general consent was more effective than that other version of this popular dance which had been performed at Her Majesty's some weeks before by Perrot and Carlotta Grisi. 'A capital thing of its kind,' *The Times* called the *Redowa,* 'full of life, character, and "fun". The gentleman first assumes a kind of awkwardness; he goes lumbering about the stage, and seems indifferent to dancing. Then the lady pats him into compliance, and all sorts of coquetries begin, and are carried on during a pretty sort of stamping movement. Now the pair seem infinitely pleased with each other; now they seem determined to try each other's temper, and the ill-humour of the one is always vanquished by the growing kindness of the other. Cerrito thoroughly entered into the humour of this very amusing dance, and went through all its varieties with admirable *naïveté* and playfulness. Saint-Léon, with his affected awkwardness, kept up the spirit of his part to the life, and was a worthy lover of such a *vivandière.*' [18]

Cerrito's next attempt at choreography was less happy. *Rosida* (1845) was a somewhat obscure and tedious ballet about a young sailor enticed down a mine, and was dropped after only six performances. Considerable invention, however, was shown in the dance passages, and one *pas,* the *Sicilienne,* was deemed too good to discard, being later made use of again by Saint-Léon in his ballet, *Stella,* which he produced for his wife in Paris in 1850.

Cerrito's permanent engagement at the Paris Opéra from 1847 deprived London of the pleasure of seeing her quite so often, but after her breach with the Opéra in 1855 her annual visits were resumed until her retirement in 1857. Although she had passed the crest of her career, and ballet was rapidly losing its popularity in London, she could still command a salary of £200 a month, which was the amount Mr Gye paid her for a four-month engagement at the Royal Italian Opera, Covent Garden, in 1855.[19] During the two following seasons, 1856 and 1857, she was again under contract to Mr Gye, but appeared at the Lyceum Theatre, whither the Royal Italian Opera had migrated after the burning down of the Covent Garden Theatre in March 1856.

During these three seasons, Henri Desplaces, who had once partnered Cerrito at Her Majesty's and was now ballet-master at the Royal Italian Opera—a post he filled from 1853 until 1876—produced two ballets for her —*Eva* (1855) and *La Brésilienne* (1857). *Eva* was performed for the first time, in a curtailed version, at a Gala Performance attended by Queen Victoria and Napoleon III, but—a sad sign of the decline of ballet—it was included last in the programme and the royal party did not wait to see it.

XIIIa. Jules Perrot and Carlotta Grisi in *La Esmeralda*, Scene II

XIIIb. Arthur Saint-Léon, with Adelaide Frassi (left) and Carlotta Grisi (right centre) in *La Esmeralda*, Scene III. *Lithograph from a drawing by J. Brandard*

Illustrated London News

xiva. *La Esmeralda*, Scene V: the Procession of the Fools' Pope

Coll. of Mr Peter Revitt

xivb. Carlotta Grisi and Jules Perrot in *Giselle*, Act I

The Golden Age of the Romantic Ballet was then gone beyond recall, and the *Illustrated London News* found 'something melancholy' in the appearance of this celebrated dancer,

> *Like the last rose of summer blooming alone,*
> *Her lovely companions all wither'd and gone.*[20]

La Brésilienne continued the sad story. It was 'but a sorry affair, a mere excuse, in short, for the *rentrée* of Cerrito', who played the rôle of a Red Indian girl, 'and still', declared a critic, 'invites admiration among the few people who can now be tempted to sit out the Terpsichorean exploits at the Lyceum'.[21] Fanny Cerrito danced in public for the last time a few weeks after her fortieth birthday, on 18th June 1857, when she appeared in the Minuet in *Don Giovanni*.

Twenty-one years later, in 1878, when Mr Thomas Cook visited Paris to find accommodation for the increased number of English tourists who would be visiting the Exhibition under his wing, he entered into negotiations with a lady for the tenancy of a house she owned near the Bois de Boulogne. To his great satisfaction agreement was quickly reached. 'You are an Englishman,' she told him, 'and I love England and the English.'[22] It was Fanny Cerrito, who still remembered with gratitude and pride those evenings of triumph at Her Majesty's.

NOTES TO CHAPTER 11

[1] In England Cerrito's surname was generally spelt 'Cerito', but the correct orthography has been adopted throughout this book.

[2] No. 21 Stamford Villas, later No. 442 Fulham Road, was demolished in about 1909–1910, and its site now forms part of the entrance to Chelsea Football Ground at Stamford Bridge.

[3] *Morning Post*, 18th May 1840.

[4] *The Times*, 19th May 1841. This *pas de quatre* was later transposed by Saint-Léon into a *pas de six* for the Paris production of *La Vivandière* and, as such, fully recorded by him as an example of his system of dance notation, being published in his book, *La Sténochorégraphie* (Paris, 1852).

[5] *Court Journal*, 22nd August 1840.

[6] *Morning Herald*, 23rd July 1841.

[7] Benjamin Lumley, *Reminiscences of the Opera* (London, 1864).

[8] *The Times*, 15th August 1842.

[9] *The Times*, 4th July 1842.

[10] *The Times*, 20th May 1843.

[11] *Sunday Times*, 21st August 1842.

[12] *Morning Post*, 12th June 1846.

[13] Archives Nationales, Paris: AJ[13] 477. Letter from Saint-Léon to Eugène Deligny, written in August 1848.

[14] Lady Dorothy Nevill, *Leaves from the Notebooks of Lady Dorothy Nevill* (London, 1907).

[15] *Examiner*, 29th April 1843.
[16] *The Times*, 21st April 1843.
[17] *The Times*, 28th April 1843.
[18] *The Times*, 24th May 1844.
[19] Information kindly supplied by Mr Walter Toscanini.
[20] *Illustrated London News*, 11th August 1855.
[21] *Era*, 10th May 1857.
[22] George Augustus Sala, *Paris Herself Again* (London, 1879).

12

Benjamin Lumley, the Great Impresario

CERTAINLY the Romantic Ballet would never have reached the standard of perfection that it did in London during the eighteen-forties, had it not been for the presence of Benjamin Lumley at the head of affairs at Her Majesty's Theatre. (Plate IXb.) The chequered history of the Opera House, the management of which had ruined or impoverished many impresarios before him, entered upon a phase of great glory on his assuming control in 1842, and it was with justice that, more than twenty years later in his retirement, he spoke of Her Majesty's Theatre as 'perhaps the noblest lyrical theatre of Europe'.[1] (Plate Ib.) Continuing the policy of Ebers and Laporte of featuring ballet on a scale consonant with the importance of the theatre, Lumley went still further and for a few years succeeded in outshining by the brilliance of his ballet even the fountain-head of the classical dance, the Paris Opéra.

The son of a Jewish merchant from Canada called Louis Levy, Benjamin Lumley early in life assumed the name of Lumley. He was educated at King Edward's School, Birmingham, and was admitted a solicitor in 1832. Three years later, having started practice as a parliamentary agent and studying for the Bar under Basil Montagu, K.C., he was approached by Laporte and asked to assist him as legal adviser at the Opera House.

He soon discovered the importance of his new position. The legal title to the theatre had become indescribably entangled. 'In the history of property', wrote Lumley himself, 'there has probably been no parallel instance wherein the legal labyrinth has been so difficult to thread.' One of his first tasks was to obtain Laporte's discharge from the Fleet Prison, and to advise him while he passed through the Bankruptcy Court. So well did he acquit himself of this that he was then pressed by Laporte to superintend the finances of the theatre, and thereafter he was consulted on every important question with which the harassed manager was faced.

Lumley was quick to learn. He took note of the trends of public taste, including the growing popularity of the ballet among the subscribers, and particularly among the men of fashion; he recognized Laporte's shortcomings, his dilatoriness, his submission to the exacting demands of a cabal of artistes, his sanguine complacency in the face of dilemmas, his failure to impose discipline on his company; and he observed his employer's failing health, aggravated by the tribulations with which he had to contend, though he perhaps little realized on what a slender thread his life hung.

Some weeks after the close of the 1841 season Lumley received the news of Laporte's sudden death in France. His first reaction was to look forward to returning to his legal practice as soon as the financial affairs of the Opera House had been put in order, but this was not to be. From many quarters he was urged to undertake the management himself, and with promises of support from a number of influential people he eventually gave in to their supplications.

Lumley brought to his task an Olympian detachment and reserve, which earned him the epithet, which his artistes bestowed on him, of *l'homme mystérieux*. Added to this was a comprehensive grasp of the legal and financial problems which faced him; indeed, his legal training and natural business acumen were his greatest assets, for without them he could never have succeeded, as he did by 1845, in unravelling the affairs of the theatre and obtaining an unencumbered lease for the first time since the building was erected towards the end of the previous century. His easy charm was another useful attribute, winning him many friends among the aristocracy on whose support he had to rely in the absence of any government subsidy, while his tact smoothed over many a difficulty caused by the clashing temperaments of the singers and dancers under contract to him. These qualities were made doubly effective by the man's confidence in his own abilities.

His vivid imagination enabled him to plan on a bold scale. For his taste and enterprise he was rivalled by no other opera house manager of his day. It was on his suggestion that Perrot set to work to create a ballet out of Hugo's *Notre Dame de Paris*; it was his drive that surmounted the obstacles standing in the way of the fabulous *Pas de Quatre*. Novel ideas, however extravagant, were never dismissed without proper investigation. When the eccentric mathematician Charles Babbage came to him with his plan for a 'Rainbow Dance', Lumley listened sympathetically and gave instructions for a demonstration to be held. After a preliminary experiment with pieces of patent net, the *corps de ballet* performed a dance, lit by powerful limelights emitting red, yellow, blue, and purple light, the stage being encumbered by the presence of two fire engines under the supervision of a section of the fire brigade. The experiment was very successful, and the project—an anticipation of the art of Loie Fuller—was only abandoned because of Lumley's apprehension of the danger of fire.[2]

In his dealings with singers and dancers Lumley was always fair. If his relations with any of them were intimate—as they may have been for a while with Lucile Grahn—he never allowed them unduly to influence him in his official capacity. His first thought was always to add to the brilliance of his theatre's renown.

No sooner had Lumley assumed the management than signs began to appear that Her Majesty's Theatre was about to enter upon an era of great brilliance. On the first evening of his first season he presented a ballet produced in Paris the summer before, *Giselle*, and in June Deshayes, Perrot, and Cerrito combined their talents to stage *Alma*, one of the most popular works in the repertory of Cerrito.

At this time, wrote Lumley in his memoirs, 'the *ballet d'action* still maintained a high prestige with the opera subscribers, though it was never so popular in England as in the gesticulating South, or even in France. It was not till years afterwards that the Lord Dundrearys of the Opera came to regard the ballet as "something that no fellow could understand"; and to set their faces entirely against all pantomimic action, which, in order to follow "the story", required a slight effort of observation and memory'.

Lumley made much capital out of the great vogue for ballet which was at its peak when he assumed his managerial duties. His choice of Perrot as ballet-master assured him the collaboration of one of the greatest choreographers of all time and he supported him manfully by yearly gathering together a galaxy of talent such as had never before been seen, and was to culminate in the supreme achievement of the Romantic Ballet, the *Pas de Quatre*.

But if the ballet was to thrive as healthily in London as it did in Paris, there was need of a school to supply a regular flow of dancers and give a permanent foundation to the company. There had, of course, been a school of a sort attached to the Opera House long before Lumley's time. After the departure of d'Egville, Louis Boisgirard, the *sous-maître-de-ballet*, had taken charge of the instruction, and following his death in 1827 or 1828, the school continued, it would seem, on a somewhat haphazard basis and probably only for six months in the year: Faucher was Master of the Dancing Academy in 1830 and 1831, and Antoine Coulon, Director of the Ballet from 1836 to 1838, probably discharged a similar task. Lumley, however, reorganized the ballet company afresh. To the ballet-master, he added a *sous-maître-de-ballet* (Gosselin, 1842–52) and a *régisseur de la danse* (Coulon, 1842–4; Bertrand, 1845–6; Émile Petit, 1847–52 and 1856–8); in 1856, Petit was *sous-maître-de-ballet* as well as *régisseur*, and Vandris assistant ballet-master. In 1848, Lumley placed the school on a firmer footing, setting aside part of the theatre to house it, and placing it under the direction of Petit. Since the pupils were all, or mostly, English, Petit was known as the Master of the English School of Instruction to distinguish him from his colleague, the Master of the French School of Instruction (Gosselin, 1848–52; Massot, 1857–8), teacher of the more important dancers who were predominantly French.

On Petit's recommendation young girls were articled for three, five, or seven years, and then received free instruction regularly the whole year round; there was apparently no provision made for boys. At the end of the first year these girls were given their first experience of the stage, being paid a small nightly salary commencing at 4s. 6d. a week. After two years, the salary increased until it reached a maximum, for a pupil, of 5s. a night. When the articles had expired, the pupil was at liberty to enter the *corps de ballet* upon the ordinary terms or to leave the Opera House. In 1851, when the school contained between thirty and forty pupils, and the *corps de ballet* numbered about a hundred, it really seemed as if the necessary nucleus of a permanent company of supporting dancers was established.[3]

But influences were at work that were to threaten the very existence of the Opera House. The added importance given to the dance in Lumley's programmes was not received kindly by the singers, and became 'one of the cogent causes' of the rupture which resulted in the setting up of a rival Italian Opera at Covent Garden in 1847. This secession, and the failure some years afterwards of Lumley's venture as manager of the Théâtre Italien in Paris, brought about the closing of the great theatre after the season of 1852 for three successive summers.

The years between his two periods of management were a trying time for Lumley. His attempts to form a joint-stock company with limited liability came to naught, a Royal Charter being refused him and a 'Her Majesty's Theatre Association Bill' being defeated in the House of Commons; and an action of ejectment, brought against him by the ground landlord on the pretext of a breach of covenant in the lease, dragged its way very slowly through the Courts of Queen's Bench and Exchequer Chamber to the House of Lords, before being finally disposed of in Lumley's favour.

This action was still undecided in March 1856, when news of the destruction by fire of the Covent Garden Theatre was brought to Lumley in Paris. He hurried back to London to throw himself into a whirl of negotiations which led to the reopening of the Opera House in May. His financial position no longer allowed him to have full control of the theatre. Lord Ward, later the first Earl of Dudley, had purchased the numerous encumbrances which lay on the title and had taken an assignment of Lumley's lease, granting him at the same time an under-lease expiring at Christmas 1860. Though he had alienated his interest in the property with great reluctance, Lumley comforted himself that he had Lord Ward's word that he would deal liberally with him and not exact his 'pound of flesh'.

Once more the ballet formed an important element in the season's entertainment. In 1856, a grand *ballet d'action*, *Le Corsaire*, was staged on a lavish scale, but its reception was disappointing. It was only, said Lumley, a 'demi-success. . . . The majority of the male supporters of the ballet (as a mere display of dancing) had long decided upon eschewing all pantomime. They disliked the trouble of understanding a "story", however lucidly set forth in mute action before them. They shut their eyes and said, "We *cannot* understand it"; when the fashion of the day simply meant to say, "We *will not* understand it". They wanted only dancing, not acting, they said. They should, to tell the truth, have said, "We only want legs, not brains". And so it was that the mere *divertissement* obtained an undue position on the great choreographic stage of London'.

Defying public opinion, Lumley engaged a strong ballet company for the following season, 1857. 'It strikes me,' remarked Lord Ward, who now, as creditor, landlord, and patron, considered himself justified in tendering advice to Lumley, 'it strikes me you have an enormous ballet. I do not know how you will place them all.' But place them Lumley did, in a curtailed revival of *La Esmeralda,* and the production of extracts from the latest Paris Opéra success, *Marco Spada.*

Relations between Lumley and Lord Ward, harmonious though they had been at the outset of their association, deteriorated suddenly just before the opening of the 1858 season. Despite his assurance given two years before, Lord Ward did demand his pound of flesh, and after the close of the season, obtained full possession of the theatre. Lumley's career as manager was over. He accepted the disappointment with philosophical resignation, sustained, he said, 'by the absence of all self-reproach in retracing the memory of the past, as well as by the consciousness of the great things I had been able to achieve as director of the first theatre of the kingdom—may it not be added the first in Europe?'

The final phase of his life—he died at his house in Kensington Crescent on 17th March 1875—he devoted to his legal practice and to literature. His writings reveal the man: his clear-sighted and enterprising direction of Her Majesty's Theatre could have had no better memorial than his *Reminiscences of the Opera,* while ample proof of his fecund imagination is to be found in his two novels—*Sirenia,* a story of the sirens, and *Another World,* an evocation of Utopia on the planet Mars.

NOTES TO CHAPTER 12

[1] Benjamin Lumley, *Reminiscences of the Opera* (London, 1864). All quotations in this chapter are from this work.

[2] For a full account of Babbage's ballet, largely based on the mathematician's papers in the British Museum, see 'Babbage's Ballet' by Ivor Guest (*Ballet,* April 1948).

[3] *Morning Chronicle,* 20th March 1851.

13

Jules Perrot, the Flaxman of the Ballet

WHILE MUCH credit was due to Lumley for the part he played as impresario in the brief but astonishingly brilliant renaissance of ballet in London during the forties, the contribution of Jules Perrot, his ballet-master from 1843 to 1848, was immeasurably greater. Perrot is one of the greatest figures in the whole history of ballet, and these six seasons at Her Majesty's contain a large proportion, certainly very much more than half, of his total choreographic output. Such a flood of great works—made possible by the co-operation of Lumley, who liberally provided the means, in dancers and in money, for their realization—for a short time raised the ballet in England to a position of eminence where it stood unrivalled even by the ballet at the Paris Opéra.

London had seen some of Perrot's early essays in choreography during the management of Laporte, and had not been unimpressed. In July 1835 he had danced in a *pas* of his own composition, in which, according to *The Times*, he 'was certainly never seen to better advantage'.[1] This may have been the same *pas*, perhaps his first creation, which he had staged at Bordeaux earlier that year. The following year he brought Carlotta Grisi with him to London, and this afforded him the opportunity of arranging several *pas de deux*, including a sprightly tarantella, the fruit of his recent visit to Naples. These beginnings, though successful, were small, but before his next visit to England in 1842 he had experimented on a larger scale in Vienna and Naples, and gained much profit by the experience.

Perrot's share in the first London production of *Giselle* at Her Majesty's in 1842 was undoubtedly greater than that of Deshayes, with whom he shared the credit, for he had collaborated—to an extent which is now a matter for conjecture—in the original production in Paris the summer before. It was, however, his contribution to *Alma* later that same season, and particularly his *pas de fascination*, that induced Lumley to fix upon him as his future ballet-master. The *pas de fascination* was a dramatic *pas* in which the design of the dance was subordinated to the action which it had to convey. It was truly a danced scene, a *pas d'action*. 'There was Cerrito, in her compact fitting bodice, hung with gaily coloured streamers, tambourine in hand, flitting airily before the astonished burghers, and laughing their prohibitions to scorn. And then there was Perrot, the mysterious, sardonic

Periphite, who lures maidens to dance with him against their will, tempts grave citizens to drink goblets of fire, and melts awfully into nothing when they fain would seize him.' [2] Further examples of expressive dances were to be given in the five important grand ballets he produced in London: *Ondine* (1843), *La Esmeralda* (1844), *Éoline* (1845), *Catarina,* and *Lalla Rookh* (1846).[3]

In these five works Perrot showed himself to be the most Romantic in thought of all the choreographers of his day. Few choreographers, working on a theme taken from literature, have so captured the spirit of the original as he did when staging his greatest masterpiece, *La Esmeralda.* Whether his canvas portrayed the mediaeval as in *La Esmeralda,* the supernatural as in *Ondine* and *Éoline,* the Oriental exotic as in *Lalla Rookh,* or the *couleur locale* of Italy as in *Catarina,* he was equally successful. His works, in short, present an almost complete survey of the Romantic Ballet in all its aspects.

Many elements went to make up the force behind the impact that Perrot's grand ballets made on the audiences which saw them. One of these was his great sympathy with humanity, which showed itself in the delineation of his characters. These were never cardboard figures. Often, his heroes were not conventional princes or nobles, but men of quite humble origin—Matteo, the fisherman, in *Ondine,* for example; and Pierre Gringoire, the itinerant poet, in *La Esmeralda* (the hero of the piece despite his failure to win the heroine) —while his most captivating heroine was surely the gypsy beggar-girl, Esmeralda. That these characters were so convincing was a measure of the sincerity of his democratic sympathies, which he had occasion to prove in 1848. He was in Milan when the revolution broke out, and was reported to have led the waiters of his hotel into battle against the Austrians [4]—hardly a very courteous act, perhaps, since he had only just staged *Faust* at the Scala for Fanny Elssler, who was herself an Austrian!

Then there was the completeness of the picture which his arrangement of the stage always presented. In devising mass movements and mass dances he had no equal: he could compose the movements of a crowd so subtly that the design was felt rather than seen, and the resulting realism was unforgettable. In *Ondine* the company broke into a tarantella in a manner so true to life that a spectator declared that it might have been 'danced on the *chiaja* by the real *contadini* when the *lacryma Christi* is getting into their noddles'; [5] while the scene of the Cour des Miracles in *La Esmeralda* was as vivid a representation of Hugo's descriptive pages as could have been put on the stage.

The most important innovation which Perrot introduced in his ballets was the closer alliance of the mime and dance passages. 'Every portion of the action is danced,' wrote the *Morning Post* in 1844, 'which avoids the tedious gesticulations and mimicry between the *pas,* which the public had formerly to endure, and avoids those sudden transitions that mar the illusion. Our present ballet-master is of opinion that this portion of a ballet should bear the same relation to the grand feats of dancing which the *récitatifs* do to the *bravura* in an opera.'[6] Of course, this innovation did not amount to an abandonment of mime. Rather, it was a more subtle approach to the problem, the gestures used being probably not so much a speechless and exaggerated imitation of everyday action, as artistically designed rhythmical movements which followed one dance passage and led to the next without any abrupt change of mode. It was noticed that in Perrot's grand ballets the ratio between dance and mime, which had formerly been greatly in favour of the latter element, was reversed.

All Perrot's ballets, too, possessed an aesthetic value greater than those of any other choreographer in his day. This was shown not only in his treatment of the action, but also in his no less masterly arrangement of the *pas*. 'In all his compositions of this kind,' wrote the *Morning Herald* of *Ondine*, 'Perrot evinces a fine sense of the beautiful, and independently of the characteristic properties they have as pantomimic illustrations, they are frequently constructed with a classic feeling which, in another sphere of art, would be estimated by a much higher standard. Many of his configurations are worthy of being arrested and made permanent. Pity they are so fleeting! They come like shadows and so depart, but they leave a distinct impression on the mind of a novel and ingenious form of beauty. Perrot is the Flaxman of the ballet; he would compose admirable *bas reliefs* for the frieze of a temple; and in olden times he would have wielded the mallet of the sculptor rather than the baton of the ballet-master.'[7]

The achievement of this superior aesthetic value was admittedly not wholly obtained by Perrot, though his contribution was the most important; credit was also due to his collaborators, William Grieve and Charles Marshall, the stage designers, and the musician Cesare Pugni. Pugni was a very prolific composer who often had to write to order at very short notice. For that reason, his work doubtless varied greatly in quality, but his finest scores were superior to most ballet music of his day. He sometimes introduced a descriptive element which greatly enhanced the effect of the scene, as, for example, his suggestion of the rippling of the water in *Ondine*, and the *Morning Post* once wrote that *Ondine* and *La Esmeralda* surpassed in melody many of the most inspired operas.[8]

Perrot's first important work, *Ondine*, at once established his renown as a choreographer. Seldom had London seen a more splendid production. William Grieve, the designer, had conceived some truly magical scenes which Perrot peopled and animated with rare genius: the rising of Ondine, like Botticelli's Venus in her shell, from the lake—the Festival of the Madonna, a reproduction on the stage of Léopold Robert's painting—the appearance of the naiads beneath the lake, across which the hero and his earthly betrothed are seen rowing—and the moonlit shore where Ondine dances with her shadow. Choreographically, *Ondine* was a revolutionary work. None of its dances was unrelated to the theme, but each developed quite naturally out of the action. The *pas de l'ombre*, for example, was expressive of Ondine's wonderment and delight at the first sight of her shadow, an exquisite creation which was danced in London long after the ballet itself had been forgotten. (Plate XVIa.) The Festival of the Madonna was another danced scene, in which, as the peasants are kneeling in prayer, Ondine appears to the infatuated Matteo, who pursues her through the worshippers until recalled by his betrothed to his devotions.

Ondine and *La Esmeralda*, which was produced the following year, were in their time without doubt the most perfect examples of ballet construction to have been seen. *Éoline, Catarina,* and *Lalla Rookh,* though they did not quite attain the same excellence, were also works complete in themselves, bearing the unmistakable stamp of Perrot's genius. The heroines of *Éoline* and *Catarina* both met tragic ends, and both were originally played by the Danish dancer, Lucile Grahn, who was a very strong mime. Éoline, half-mortal and half-dryad, dies when Rubezahl, Prince of the Gnomes, in his jealousy at her betrothal, sets fire to the tree upon which her life depends; while Catarina, the bandit chief, sacrifices herself by receiving the thrust intended for her lover, the painter Salvatore Rosa, by his rival. (Plate XVIIb.)

The great danced scene in *Éoline* was the *mazurka d'extase,* 'one of the most extraordinary creations of the genius of Perrot'. Rubezahl mesmerizes Éoline to dance with him, despite her loathing, and finally, when the girl's lover and brother come to her rescue, vanishes down a trap. In this *pas,* Lucile Grahn combined 'the most graceful dancing with the most soul despairing pantomime'.[9] 'She is animated', wrote the *Morning Herald,* 'by an unnatural energy, which relaxes at each successive touch of the malicious Gnome, who catches her in his arms as she whirls *tipsily* before him; she recoils convulsively as his evil fingers press and collapse her heart, until bewildered and paralysed by his insidious power, she sinks down motionless at his feet. All this is described with consummate skill. Perrot's personation of the Gnome is a finished bit of demonianism; the glance of his eye is fiendish, and the poor dryad, all light-heartedness and innocence, seems to be benumbed as she comes under its withering influence. The dancing of Mlle Grahn is remarkable for its firmness: it is not wonderful—there are none of the vigorous bounds of Cerrito, nor the twinkling impossibilities of Elssler—but there is the neatness of the latter and the genial impulse of the former.'[10]

Catarina contained nothing to compare with this *mazurka d'extase.* Its principal dance was the *pas stratégique,* in which Catarina instructs her brigands in musket drill and military evolutions, and which ended with the *corps de ballet* climbing up the rocks, then rushing down fiercely towards the audience, pointing their muskets at the unfortunate M. Nadaud, who was conducting the orchestra. (Plate XVIIa.) There was also a well arranged combat between the troops and the bandits.

Atmosphere was an important feature of Perrot's ballets. It was the logical accessory to the more concentrated dramatic content. In *Ondine* there was

91

the moonlit mystery of the *pas de l'ombre*, and the colourful splendour of the tarantella; in *La Esmeralda*, mediaeval Paris was portrayed with unusual fidelity; in *Éoline*, a tragic tale of dryads and gnomes, 'the sense of the shadowy and uncertain [was] preserved throughout';[11] and *Catarina* captured something of the picturesque quality of Salvatore Rosa's canvases. *Lalla Rookh*, the last grand ballet to be staged by Perrot in London, showed a marked departure from the strongly dramatic texture of the earlier works. Based on the section of Thomas Moore's poem describing Lalla Rookh's journey to Cashmere to marry the King of Bucharia, it contained little dramatic interest. (Plate XVIb.) Two scenes indeed were devoted to representing the caravan crossing the desert, and the emphasis was here on the creation of atmosphere: a storm, nightfall, daybreak, and the call to prayer formed the theme, with a *pas* for Cerrito introduced almost incidentally. The highlight of Perrot's choreography in this ballet was a *pas de neuf* in the final scene which was remarkable for the beauty of the grouping. It was, wrote *The Times*, 'an attempt to introduce into a ballet a principle new to the English, to rely more upon the effect of an *ensemble* than on that of isolated dancing',[12] a principle which Perrot had also been developing in his other genre, the grand *divertissement*.

One of the many debts owed by ballet to royalty is that due to Queen Victoria for giving the initial impetus whence derived the *Pas de Quatre*, *Le Jugement de Pâris*, *Les Éléments*, and *Les Quatre Saisons*, those four fabulous spectacles in which the talents of the greatest ballerinas in Europe were combined. It had been decided in 1843 that the Queen and Prince Albert would pay a State Visit to the Opera towards the end of the season. While Lumley was making the necessary arrangements for this event, a notification reached him from the Palace that it would please Her Majesty if the programme could include a *pas de deux* danced by Elssler and Cerrito. The wish was natural enough, but its fulfilment presented a most difficult problem. Both ballerinas were inordinately proud: Elssler was still aflush with the triumphs of her recent American tour, and Cerrito was very consciously the favourite of fashionable London. As neither would agree to starting the *pas* alone, since that would, to their minds, imply inferiority to the other, Perrot, on Lumley's suggestion, arranged the opening movement with both ballerinas dancing identical steps. To the confusion of the pessimists, the *pas de deux* was duly performed on the evening of the Queen's visit, and on many evenings thereafter. For the last few weeks of the season a furious and happily undecided battle was waged between the respective partisans of the two dancers, each of whom apparently realized that far from favouring one at the expense of the other the *pas de deux* greatly enhanced the prestige of both.

This was only a foretaste of the miracle which was to follow two years later. The year 1845 marks the *apogée* of the Romantic Ballet, for it was the year of the immortal *Pas de Quatre,* danced by Taglioni, Cerrito, Carlotta Grisi, and Grahn, a simple *divertissement* so perfect in its choreography and execution that it dealt the more cumbersome *ballet d'action* a blow from which, in England, it never recovered. It is not without significance that, with two exceptions, Perrot's future work in London was limited to creating works of a similar nature.

In the following year, 1846, Perrot repeated this choreographic triumph on a larger scale, with *Le Jugement de Pâris,* featuring Taglioni, Cerrito, and Grahn as the Goddesses, Saint-Léon as Paris, Perrot as Mercury, and seven other *danseuses* in secondary rôles. (Plate XVIIIb.) The original plan had been to open with a scene showing a harassed ballet-master in the throes of arranging such a *divertissement* and to close with the finished product, but at the final rehearsal the introductory scene, although it was very amusing, was so outshone by the brilliance and beauty of the *divertissement* itself that it was suppressed. The critics, when they saw it, were again carried away: all hailed it as a masterpiece, and some boldly asserted that it was even superior to the *Pas de Quatre.* Once again Perrot succeeded in evenly distributing the gems in his choreography, and the public and the dancers gave him full credit for what he had done. After the first performance, seeing him modestly holding back, Cerrito dragged him forward, and with the assistance of Taglioni and Grahn, pushed him to his knees and crowned him with a wreath of flowers. This 'coronation and apotheosis' thereafter became a regular event, and was always greeted with applause and laughter, applause in recognition of the ballet-master's genius and laughter at his blushing modesty.

The year 1847 was critical in the history of ballet in England. It was then that London first heard Jenny Lind and was immediately conquered. The awakened interest in opera that the Swedish Nightingale aroused coincided with a growing public distaste for the *ballet d'action* which had been apparent for some time past. The grand *divertissement,* however, was still very much in favour, and towards the end of June, Perrot produced his third essay in that genre, *Les Éléments,* featuring Cerrito, Grisi, and Rosati, and introducing some brilliantly contrived stage effects.

Carlotta Grisi thought it 'one of the best works that Perrot has devised. Cerrito represents Air, Rosati Water, and I Fire', she explained in a letter to the critic Fiorentino. 'We have each a separate entrance, after which there is a scene, short but very pretty, in which Water tries to extinguish Fire; then follow the *pas.* For my own entrance, I emerge from the flames, which is very effective because it happens so quickly that no one can understand how I appear on the stage. Here I have a very brilliant *variation* which gives me a magnificent success at the outset. Regarding the *pas,* if I am not mistaken and from what everyone is saying, it is I who had the greatest success of the three. I dance a good deal with Cerrito, which she does not like very much, though it pleases me. We have a *variation* together in the *allegro* movement of the *pas* which we are always made to repeat. This *divertissement* has contributed much towards the success of the ballet, for even without Lind we have had two magnificent houses, and the Queen has honoured us with her presence.'[13]

The last and longest of Perrot's grand *divertissements* was *Les Quatre saisons*, which he staged with Cerrito, Grisi, Rosati, and the younger Marie Taglioni, after only about a fortnight's rehearsals, in the summer of 1848. The *Morning Post* hailed it as 'a composition which marks the utmost limit of perfection to which choreography has ever reached'.[14] But the tide had already turned. A few weeks after its first performance Perrot left London, never to return. The hey-day of the Romantic Ballet was over.

Despite their success and renown, not one of these *divertissements* was revived at Her Majesty's in after years. Their revival, in fact, was unthinkable without the participation of the great Romantic ballerinas, whose stars had then set or were setting; unthinkable, too, without the guiding hand of Perrot. Unique of their kind they crystallized the quintessence of Perrot's choreographic genius and expressed at its most sublime the glorification of the Romantic ballerina. They were the supreme achievements of the Romantic Ballet.

NOTES TO CHAPTER 13

[1] *The Times,* 17th July 1835.

[2] *Morning Herald,* 17th May 1844.

[3] The plots of all these ballets are to be found in Cyril W. Beaumont's *Complete Book of Ballets* (London, 1937). The version of *Catarina* given there, however, is that of the Russian production for which a happy ending was substituted for the tragedy with which the London production ended.

[4] *Satirist,* 23rd April 1848.

[5] *Morning Post,* 23rd June 1843.

[6] *Morning Post,* 25th June 1844.

[7] *Morning Herald,* 23rd June 1843.

[8] *Morning Post,* 12th June 1846.

[9] *Morning Post,* 10th March 1845.

[10] *Morning Herald,* 17th March 1845.

[11] *The Times,* 10th March 1845.

[12] *The Times,* 19th August 1846.

[13] Victoria and Albert Museum, Enthoven Collection: Letter from Carlotta Grisi to Pier Angelo Fiorentino, 1st July 1847.

[14] *Morning Post,* 10th July 1848.

I4

Two Giselles, Grisi and Elssler

CONSECRATED as a classic by more than a century's existence, *Giselle* is to-day regarded by public and dancers alike as a test of a ballerina's talent, a yardstick by which her worth as an artist may be gauged. Londoners acquired the habit of comparing dancers in the title-rôle of this ballet very early. Indeed, they were treated to an experience which was denied even to the Parisians, at whose opera house the ballet had been created. There the rôle belonged exclusively to Carlotta Grisi; at Her Majesty's Theatre, on the other hand, no such proprietary right could be claimed, and the year after Grisi had introduced the ballet there, Fanny Elssler appeared in the same rôle. The contrast between the two ballerinas was most striking. Each played the rôle to perfection in her own individual style, yet how different were their interpretations!

Giselle was first performed in London on 12th March 1842, nearly nine months after its creation in Paris. It was produced by the veteran ballet-master Deshayes with the assistance of Perrot, and was at once acclaimed as a masterpiece. The enthusiasm mounted even to the throne: at a ball in Buckingham Palace in April, the popular composer Jullien was charged by the Lord Chamberlain, acting on the Queen's command, to arrange a quadrille, galop, and waltz based on Adam's score for the ballet.

The stage of Her Majesty's Theatre being somewhat restricted in depth by opera house standards, the production could not be on the same lavish scale as in Paris. For the Vicomtesse de Malleville, who wrote a weekly article in the *Courrier de l'Europe*, this was a bitter disappointment. Having seen the ballet at the Paris Opéra, she complained of cuts—the peasant *pas de deux* in Act I was one of the passages omitted—and forecast 'an inevitable fiasco', so skimpy was the staging.[1]

The gloomy prophecy of the Vicomtesse was far from fulfilled. Carlotta Grisi was called for twice at the end of the first performance—'a new proceeding', commented *The Times* [2]—and before she returned to Paris at the end of April, *Giselle* had been performed thirteen times, and the Queen had seen it twice. The public and the critics penetrated the superficial details of the production which had produced such an unfortunate effect on the

95

Vicomtesse. That the dancing formed an essential part of the drama, and was not a 'mere casual illustration' of it, was noted with appreciation, although *The Times* remarked that the idea of the heroine being charged against her will to lure her lover to destruction was not entirely new, having been used in *Le Diable amoureux*.[2] The *Era* recorded that the ballet 'produced such profound emotion that it had been compared to one of the fantastic creations of Shakespeare'.[3]

Carlotta Grisi, the first Giselle, had a style which was remarkable for its 'graceful ease' and 'complete "naturalness"'.[2] She betrayed no sign of exertion in her *tours de force*. Delicate in her movements, she approached the school of Taglioni, with its flowing grace and ethereal manner—the 'ideal' school, as it was called—rather than the 'realistic' school personified by Cerrito, who conquered by agility, speed, and brilliance. When she brought *Giselle* to London, she was supported by Perrot in the rôle of Albert, Coulon as Hilarion, Gosselin as the Prince of Courland, and Louise Fleury as the Queen of the Wilis.[4] (Plate XIVb.)

From her very first entrance, when she bounded from her cottage, Carlotta Grisi set the illusion of being a happy carefree peasant. Her trust in her lover was illustrated, in her *pas de deux* with Perrot, by the 'easy voluptuousness' with which she fell into his arms. After her crowning as queen of the vintage festival, the drama developed. The disappointed Hilarion reveals that Albert is a nobleman and betrothed to another. Giselle, unable to bear the shock of her lover's infidelity, loses her reason and dies. With Grisi, the culmination of the first act was more a danced than a mimed scene. 'Exceedingly well devised was the dance previous to the death of Giselle,' wrote *The Times*. 'In her distraction, the love of dancing takes possession of her. The fling of the arms, the joyless movement, was supernatural; it was an anticipation of the ghostly scene of the second act.' [2]

The second act created a greater sensation than the first, partly because of the Romantic vogue for the supernatural, and partly, perhaps, because it was more suited to Grisi's style. It was significant that, while the entire ballet was always given when Elssler played it, Grisi often appeared in the second act alone.[5] The scene of the second act showed a lake overgrown with reeds, with the tomb of Giselle in the foreground; the lighting was dim, giving a haunting *chiaroscuro* effect. The Queen of the Wilis, spirits of maidens who have died before their wedding day and are condemned for ever to dance in the glades of the forest, rises out of the ground and summons her phantom subjects. Their heads veiled, they appear, some from the wings, a few from beneath the stage. The use of traps at this point was not wholly successful: one unlucky Wili was noticed to extricate herself only after a struggle. Giselle is then raised from her tomb in the same manner. Her initiation as a Wili contained an inspired moment of choreography which has been preserved to this day. 'It was the sudden paroxysm of unearthly joy which took possession of the hitherto quiet spectre . . . by the imposition of a

xv. Fanny Cerrito in *Ondine*

Lithograph by W. H. Mote from a drawing by E. Smith

xvia. Fanny Cerrito dancing the *Pas de l'Ombre* in *Ondine*

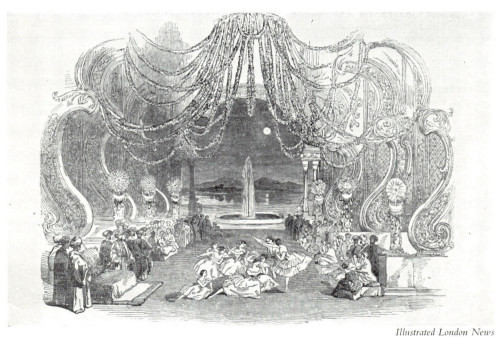

xvib. *Lalla Rookh*, Scene I: the *Pas symbolique*

crown on her head. One rapid whirl marked the transition from the inhabitant of the grave to the reckless sprite.' [2]

Shortly afterwards the stage empties and Albert enters to pray by the grave. He suddenly sees Giselle before him, 'now suspended in the air, now balancing herself on the flowers, at one time alighting on the water's brim, at another skimming along the heath like a rapid flash of lightning' [3]—'sometimes delighting him by throwing flowers over him, sometimes tantalizing him by evading his grasp'.[2] After she has vanished, Albert sees Hilarion driven into the lake by the Wilis, then is himself caught in their power. As he clings for protection to the cross of the tomb, Giselle is commanded to dance before him that he might join her and perish. But the Wilis' power ends with the coming of dawn, and Albert is saved. Giselle lingers behind after her companions have vanished. But she too must join them. 'The earth opens under her feet, she slowly inters herself in the abyss, and her wretched betrothed cannot retain her. She gradually disappears, and now nought but the arms slowly sinking are discernible, and now the hands which appear to implore him. At length all is over; the brightness of the morning has entirely dispersed the vision. This scene is heart-rending, nor is it easy to describe the profound impression it produces on the spectators. The drama is melancholy as a souvenir of death, but beauteous as a dream of love.' [3]

Lumley was unable to engage Carlotta Grisi the following year, and, loath to omit so popular a ballet as *Giselle* from his prospectus, arranged that Fanny Elssler should take over the leading rôle. Elssler had recently returned from her fabulous tour of North America, and her prestige was at its zenith. Vivid imaginations were strangely stirred when she appeared for the first time on the opening night of the season, and one nobleman was heard to cry out in a tone of reverent awe, 'Those are the feet that conquered America!'

She danced in *Giselle* for the first time on 30th March 1843, in the following cast:

Giselle	– –	Fanny Elssler
Berthe	– –	Mme Copère
Bathilde	– –	Elisa Scheffer
Myrtha	– –	Adèle Dumilâtre
Principal Wilis	–	Mlles Camille, Bénard, Galby, Plunkett
Albert	– –	James Silvain
Hilarion	– –	Antoine Coulon
Prince of Courland		Louis-François Gosselin [6]

Her rendering of the rôle was very different from Grisi's, and more like the usual interpretation of to-day, in that she shifted the emphasis from the sentimental mood of the second act to the tragedy at the end of the first, making the rôle a vehicle for a mimetic *tour de force* of astonishing power. 'From what we have long known of Fanny Elssler's talents as a pantomimist, we had expected a remarkable interpretation,' wrote *The Times*, 'but certainly we did not anticipate such a *chef d'œuvre*, such a grand conception and perfect execution.' Where Carlotta had given the impression of 'melancholy sweetness, a sort of unearthly sentiment that could not be surpassed', Elssler marked the part 'with bold lines as a high tragic character'.[7] Comparing the mad scenes of the two dancers, there was no doubt that Elssler's was vastly superior. 'The acting of Carlotta Grisi in this scene of delirious frenzy was of a totally different kind,' wrote the *Morning Herald*. 'It excited only occasional pity, with a passing admiration for the agility and cleverness of the dancer. Fanny Elssler does more. The situation in which she is placed exacts the sympathy, but the art—emphatic, classic art—with which she surrounds it demands the cool and deliberate respect due to original genius.' [8]

She began by bringing out the innocence and the artless impassioned tenderness of the character, so that when her mind gave way at the discovery of her betrayal, the tragedy was brought home in all its horror. The air then became charged with the force of her acting. For a moment she seemed to recover from the abysmal grief which had first taken possession of her and to have found a strange peace, as though in resignation to death and in the realization that she must soon join the ghostly band of Wilis. It was as if she had passed for a moment into 'a sort of intermediate existence', as if she had 'half become a Wili, while yet wearing a mortal frame'.[7] Then, momentarily, her reason returned; her heart was wrung afresh, and she threw herself weeping upon the ground. In the *danse de folie* which followed, wrote the *Morning Post*, 'her movements were so wildly and still so gracefully eccentric, that at a distance she did not appear as if she were dancing, but as if, her form being too light to resist the currents of the air, she were whirled about in the eddies of the wind'.[9]

Thanks to the observant eye and retentive memory of the anonymous critic of the *Morning Herald*, the mad scene of Fanny Elssler has been preserved in a detailed and vivid description.

'Her scene in the first act,' he wrote, 'when she becomes apprised of her lover's rank, and suspects the purity of his intentions, is a masterpiece of expression: her acting—for it amounts to acting of the highest kind—is, we believe, quite unparalleled in the annals of the pantomimic art. The guileless, trusting girl, just now so sprightly and good-humoured, changes in an instant; her vivacity gives place to the intensest anger; her frame swells with dignity and wounded pride, and the tightened lip, the lifted brow, the dilated nostril, and the erect figure, denote the scorn and indignation which consume her. Presently her countenance blanches with apprehension, and she becomes weak and tremulous with horror. A smile lightens her features—but it is the smile of a gathering insanity, the fitful and unearthly calm of an unhinged mind. She is seized with the Wili fever, and dances wildly and incoherently, mingling with her motions many little touches of feeling eminently beautiful and pathetic. She regards her lover with a glance of admiration and devotion, and caresses him with a playful tenderness—then she repulses him as a serpent; and then, with a seeming interval of consciousness, fondles him anew, and scatters imaginary flowers on his path. A moment of gloom succeeds, and she walks about lonely and dejected, as if engrossed in some horrible reverie. Her mother in wretchedness and despair embraces her fondly, but she knows her not—she is cold, insensible, and heart-stricken. Impelled by some mysterious power she attempts to dance again, but her steps falter, her eyes become fixed and lustreless, and you *feel* the chill which is creeping over her heart. The grip of death is there, and she sinks with a marble insensibility into her mother's arms.' [8]

Elssler's genius was no less telling in the second act—'the most soul-stirring phantasmagoria ever produced on the stage as a ballet', as the *Morning Post* called it. [9] The vestiges of the sorrow which had destroyed her were still visible when she was raised from her tomb, but vanished at the very moment that the Queen touches her with her wand. Wings then sprang from her shoulders and she whirled round 'with a maniac delight'. [7] Her personality began to melt away as she assumed the spectral state of a Wili, yet still she retained her love for Albert, though powerless to resist her Queen's command to destroy him. The *pas de deux,* in which she 'executed a succession of rapid *pas*, her feet coruscating millions of quaint, delicate steps', [10] was far from being solely a display of technique; not for a moment did she step outside the character she was portraying.

'No smile of recognition animates the face of the poor phantom,' described the *Morning Herald*. 'The features are pale and immoveable, wearing an air of placid resignation, yet sad, inconsolate, and deathlike. She executes the malign bidding of the Wili Queen with involuntary readiness, but the sentiment of earthly love still clings to her, although the outward manifestations of dismay and repugnance are obliterated from her countenance. The spectre maiden unconsciously binds fresh chains around the sympathies of her lover; she lures him to his doom with the bewitching phrases of her dancing, with her fanciful flittings in the pale glimmer of the moon and her erratic flights through the air—but more so by those fascinating evidences of love which she practised when living, and which even the grave cannot utterly suppress.

'In this silent pantomime Fanny Elssler is most eloquent and pathetic. The opposite characteristics of the forlorn spirit are strongly marked, and the touches of art, which give form, substance, and elevation to the conception, are so manifold that admiration can scarcely find terms in which to vent itself. Such a complete expression of a dramatic sentiment has never before been evolved by the merely imitative means of the ballet. It has been left for Fanny Elssler to show the full eloquence of bodily gesture, and what a forcible significance and intensity may be given to it when genius and feeling are the prime movers. The performance of *Giselle* proves the influence she can exercise at will over the sympathies of an audience. . . . It is a study worth the contemplation of every lover of elevated and refined art.'[8]

NOTES TO CHAPTER 14

[1] *Le Courrier de l'Europe*, 16th April 1842.
[2] *The Times*, 14th March 1842.
[3] *Era*, 17th April 1842.
[4] The hero of *Giselle* was, in the original London production at Her Majesty's, as he has always been and is still at the Paris Opéra, named Albert; in modern English versions, following Gautier's description in *Les Beautés de l'Opéra* (Paris, 1845) rather than the original scenario, he is known as Albrecht. His prospective father-in-law was originally the Prince of Courland, but is now, even at the Paris Opéra, given the title of Duke, again following *Les Beautés de l'Opéra*.

[5] PERFORMANCES OF *GISELLE* AT HER MAJESTY'S, 1842–50

	1842	1843	1844	1845	1847	1849	1850	Total
Entire	11	8	6	—	—	—	—	25
Act II only	2	—	—	2	4	1	2	11

Elssler danced Giselle eight times in 1843, and twice in 1844, always in its entirety. All other performances were by Carlotta Grisi.

[6] PRINCIPAL DANCERS IN *GISELLE* AT HER MAJESTY'S, 1842–50

GISELLE: Carlotta Grisi ('42, '44, '45, '47, '49, '50); Fanny Elssler ('43, '44).
ALBERT: Jules Perrot ('42, '45); James Silvain ('43); Arthur Saint-Léon ('44); Louis Dor ('47, '49); Charles ('50).
MYRTHA: Louise Fleury ('42); Adèle Dumilâtre ('43); Marie Guy-Stéphan ('43); Elisa Scheffer ('44); Joséphine Petit-Stéphan ('45); Caroline Beaucourt ('47); Marie Taglioni II ('49); Rosa ('50).

[7] *The Times*, 31st March 1843.
[8] *Morning Herald*, 17th July 1843.
[9] *Morning Post*, 31st March 1843.
[10] *Morning Herald*, 31st March 1843.

15

La Esmeralda

OF ALL Perrot's grand ballets—with the exception of *Giselle*, of which he was but part author—*La Esmeralda* alone has survived, having outlived *Alma* and *Ondine* despite the prophecy that *The Times* made at the time of its creation in 1844, that it would not become so popular as either of these two earlier works, though dramatically superior to both.[1]

Just as the choreographers of *Giselle* had worked to a scenario founded on a fancy of the great Romantic poet, Théophile Gautier, so, in *La Esmeralda,* Perrot derived his inspiration from another, and greater, giant of Romantic literature, Victor Hugo. Hugo's novel *Notre Dame de Paris* had appeared in 1831, and from it there had already derived two operas and at least one ballet before Perrot staged his choreographic version. The first choreographer in the field was Antonio Monticini, whose ballet *Esmeralda* was staged at the Scala, Milan, in the spring season of 1839. As was common in Italian ballets of that time, the functions of the mime and the dancer were rigidly separated, the principal rôles being played by mimes, while Cerrito, the prima ballerina, appeared only in the dances.

The germ of Perrot's masterpiece originated in the brain of Benjamin Lumley. When the subject was first suggested to him, Perrot rejected it as impracticable, but eventually Lumley was able to convert him to his own way of thinking, and, while the ballet-master was working out the scenario, would often sit up with him well into the early hours of morning assisting and encouraging him in his task. To compose the score Cesare Pugni, then a comparatively unknown musician, was brought over from Paris, and worked in close collaboration with Perrot, 'ready to seize any idea that might suggest itself for a "situation" or *pas*', and producing a score 'highly descriptive and characteristic'.[2]

Early in the summer of 1843 Perrot had made sufficient progress to enable him to select a ballerina to play the part of Esmeralda. His choice fell on the tall, raven-haired Adèle Dumilâtre, whom he introduced to London at the opening of that season in March. But in the course of their *grand pas de deux* in the *divertissement, L'Aurore,* he twisted his foot, and this painful accident confined him to his room for some weeks. When he was well enough to resume his duties Cerrito had arrived, for whom a new ballet had to be staged. *La Esmeralda* was perforce put aside, but only to be taken up again at the earliest opportunity. The following season, 1844, Lumley succeeded in engaging Carlotta Grisi, and it was with her that Perrot resumed rehearsals at Her Majesty's towards the end of February, five or six weeks after Coulon, the *régisseur de la danse*, had begun the task of organizing and drilling the *corps de ballet*, which was to have an important part to play in the new work.

Preparations went ahead smoothly, and all was ready by the opening night of the season on 9th March. The success of *La Esmeralda* was complete. 'As long as the ballet mania prevails,' wrote the *Morning Post* the day afterwards, 'vain are our protests in favour of the superior rights of the lyrical drama. If, however, thousands out of the operatic exchequer and the talents of first-rate composers are bestowed on ballets, it is but just to confess that the results are incalculably superior to all we beheld in our early days. At that period the dancing department presented scarce anything but the most inane and affected mythological absurdities. One very striking circumstance in the ballets in former days was that all the general dances and all the pantomime portions of the performance were intolerable, or only borne by the public because they allowed the chief dancers to rest, whilst the dancers of lesser note were beyond measure offensive. In the present ballet the secondary *dramatis personæ* are admirably grouped; their motions are full of life and spirit, and the intricate dances which they execute most justly draw down, from time to time, the loudest applause.

'It is rather singular to observe that in the working out of a ballet, once deemed a very lax style of dramatic composition, all the beauties of a celebrated novel have been elicited, whilst all its impurities and horrors have been eschewed.'[3] In other words, the plot was modified to suit the requirements of early Victorian taste. The only serious liberty that Perrot took with Hugo's characters was to transform Phoebus from a handsome but licentious Lothario, callously counting Esmeralda as one of his conquests, into a hero of the conventional type whose intervention finally saves her from the scaffold. Claude Frollo, the archdeacon, whose unhallowed passion for the gypsy girl turns into a sadistic hatred and, in the novel, brings about her death, necessarily played a somewhat lesser part in the ballet, although his character was not fundamentally altered. Considerable simplification was also necessary to reduce the plot of the novel to the required proportions of a five-scene ballet: the secret of Esmeralda's birth was discarded, as also was the torture scene at her trial, her rescue by Quasimodo and her sojourn in the sanctuary of the cathedral, the storming of Notre Dame by the truands and Quasimodo's desperate defence, and the awful fate of Claude Frollo, who in the novel is pushed by the hunchback from the roof of the cathedral while Esmeralda's body still swings from the gibbet. For the macabre final pages of the novel, a happy ending was substituted 'without the slightest loss of interest'.[3] 'A perfect model of ballet building,' *The Times* described it. 'Never did we see those parts of a long story that might be dramatically effective selected and arranged with such skill as in this new ballet.'[1]

The action of the ballet was set in Paris towards the end of the fifteenth century. After the overture the curtain rose to reveal the Cour des Miracles, the haunt of beggars, thieves, and gypsies. It is sunset and the stage is thronged with a crowd of vagabonds, known as the truands, gaming, drinking, dancing, and fighting. In their midst is Clopin, their acknowledged king. Suddenly Pierre Gringoire, a struggling poet, appears, pursued by a body of thieves. He throws himself at Clopin's feet, imploring his protection. But his only possession is a volume of poems, and Clopin, in his indignation and disappointment at the victim's poverty, orders Gringoire to be hanged. Crazed with fear, Gringoire seeks to take advantage of the beggars' law by which he will be spared if he can find a woman to marry him. But no one will accept him. At that moment, followed by her pet goat, Esmeralda, 'the loveliest of vagrants', approaches, dancing gaily and heedlessly, 'her head tossing from side to side'. At once she realizes Gringoire's plight, and touched with compassion, she consents to marry him. Their marriage is celebrated by the breaking of a pitcher, and the crowd give themselves up to dancing.

After a *Valse de vieux Paris* danced by the *coryphées*, came the famous *Truandaise*, a *pas de deux* by Carlotta Grisi and Perrot, 'delicately imagined, novel, and eccentric', expressive of Esmeralda's pity for Gringoire and at the same time her amusement at his plight. It was 'a compound of good humour and a mild sort of malice'. Carlotta circled the stage with wonderful rapidity and lightness, tempting her partner to follow her, 'now dipping towards him, now avoiding him, now peeping at him archly under her arm, always within two paces of him, and yet eluding his touch until he becomes almost tipsy with delight'.[4] (Plate XIIa and b.)

When it was over, the whole *corps de ballet* surged into movement in a *bacchanale*. Their evolutions were 'new and striking', wrote the *Morning Herald*, giving a rare indication of the choreographic pattern of such a scene. 'Some crosses are formed by them, which are bisected by moving lines at right angles very ingeniously; the effect of which, when seen from above, is excellent.'[4]

Suddenly the mood of the music changes, and a plaintive note is struck. The curfew sounds and the crowd disperses. Esmeralda leaves, but not before noticing the sinister glance of the priest Claude Frollo (Gosselin). When she is gone, Frollo seeks the aid of Clopin in his desire to possess her. For a bribe Clopin reveals that she will shortly recross the square, and Frollo and Quasimodo (Coulon), the hunchbacked bellringer of Notre Dame, lie in wait for her. They seize her, but are disturbed by the approach of the patrol. Frollo makes his escape, but the hunchback is arrested. Struck by the girl's beauty, the captain of the patrol, Phoebus (Saint-Léon), questions her and learns that she is an orphan and alone in the world. She plays with the end of his scarf which he gives to her. Then she intercedes for Quasimodo, and Phoebus orders him to be released. At his demand for a kiss in exchange for the scarf, she recoils and asks him to take back the scarf. When he refuses, she slips from his grasp and disappears into the darkness.

The second scene, set in Esmeralda's humble lodging, opened with a *pas scénique, La Nuit des noces*. Gringoire enters to find Esmeralda gazing sadly and lovingly at the scarf and at the word 'Phoebus' which she has formed with ivory letters on the floor. He places his arm round her waist, but she frees herself and draws a dagger from her belt. Pity alone induced her to marry him, she tells him, and she shows him into an adjoining room. (Plate XIIIa.) Her solitude is soon interrupted by the appearance of Frollo and Quasimodo. Frollo declares his passion and, meeting with a refusal, tries to violate her, but Esmeralda succeeds in making her escape through a secret door.

The scene changed to the garden of a mansion: 'an exquisite Watteau picture on a large scale'. Festoons of flowers hang from the trees, and the green foliage glows with the light from innumerable lamps. Celebrations are about to begin for the marriage of Phoebus and his high-born *fiancée*, Fleur-de-lys de Gondelaurier. The girl observes that her betrothed is pensive and distant, and that he is no longer wearing the scarf she had given him. Soon the guests arrive, the women all dressed in silver-embroidered white satin, and the dancing begins. A *pas des fleurs* introduced, as a dancer, Adelaide Frassi, who was playing the part of Fleur-de-lys: a well-formed girl with a style somewhat in the manner of Cerrito, possessing an unusually fine *port de bras* and able to 'drop upon the point of her toe, and lodge there with extraordinary decision'.[4] Then followed a *pas de trois* by Saint-Léon and the two *coryphées*, Adeline Plunkett and Elisa Scheffer, who were already at that time the talk of the town on account of their rivalry for the affections of Lord Pembroke; and it was in this dance that Saint-Léon, who possessed a phenomenal elevation, executed what the *Morning Post* described as 'an extraordinary saltatory artifice', leaping into the air like the flying Mercury in the well-known painting by Pietro da Cortona.[5] (Plate XIIIb).

Meanwhile Esmeralda has been invited to dance at the festivities, and she has arrived in the company of Gringoire. Phoebus asks if he may dance with her, and Fleur-de-lys becomes apprehensive at the sight of her betrothed so absorbed by the fascinating gypsy. When the dance is over she chides him gently. Esmeralda, dancing now with Gringoire, produces Phoebus's scarf to show that she still loves him. At this proof of her lover's infidelity, Fleur-de-lys reproaches him bitterly and is borne away fainting. The guests threaten Esmeralda, who is protected by the faithful Gringoire.

A drop-cloth was then lowered, representing a cabaret by the Seine. It is night. Frollo and Quasimodo enter and hide. Soon Esmeralda appears with Phoebus, who declares his love for her. 'Nothing can be more exquisitely managed than her pantomime' in this scene, wrote *The Times* of Carlotta Grisi. 'The timidity with which she recoiled from him, and which gradually gave way to the overpowering effects of her love, the contest between two feelings, which gradually subsided, was most beautifully managed. Those

xviia. Lucile Grahn dancing the *Pas stratégique* in *Catarina*

xviib. Louis-François Gosselin, Lucile Grahn, and Jules Perrot in the final scene of *Catarina*

xviiia. Marie Taglioni, Fanny Cerrito, Carlotta Grisi, and Lucile Grahn in the *Pas de Quatre*

xviiib. Fanny Cerrito, Marie Taglioni, and Lucile Grahn in *Le Jugement de Pâris*,
with Arthur Saint-Léon (Paris) and Jules Perrot (Mercury)

XIX. Adeline Plunkett. *Oil-painting by R. Buckner*

xxa. The Danseuses Viennoises in the *Pas des fleurs*
Lithograph from a drawing by J. Brandard

xxb. Manuela Perea (La Nena) and her Company of Spanish Dancers

who have read the novel itself, and know what the scene in the cabaret is in the original, can alone appreciate the delicacy with which a situation so critical was preserved without the slightest offence, while all the emotions were retained.'[1] Esmeralda is kneeling before Phoebus, her head resting on his arm, when Frollo leaps from his hiding-place. To protect her, Phoebus draws Esmeralda into the shadows. There is a flash of steel, a groan, and the sound of a body falling. Frollo leaps through the window, while Esmeralda sinks to the floor in despair. A crowd enters, and Esmeralda, denounced as the murderess of her lover, is carried away protesting.

The stage then opened out to show the gates of the prison by the banks of the Seine, with the twin towers of Notre Dame stretching above the roofs in the distance. Esmeralda is led to the prison, followed by Gringoire, who attempts to stir up the populace in her defence. Suddenly the stage is invaded by the procession of the Fools' Pope. Quasimodo, in mock papal robes, is borne upon a chair, followed by a crowd of truands. (Plate XIVa.) The tolling of a bell interrupts their revelry, and Esmeralda emerges from the prison on her way to the scaffold. She lingers to bid a last good-bye to Gringoire. Frollo then steps forward. He can still save her, he says, if she will only yield to him. Scornfully she refuses. At this moment there is a stir in the crowd and Phoebus pushes his way to the front. His wound was only superficial, and he denounces Frollo as his assailant. Maddened with fury, Frollo tears himself free from the guards who hold him, and rushes, dagger in hand, at Esmeralda. Quasimodo snatches the weapon from his grasp and plunges it into the villain's heart.

Carlotta Grisi's portrayal of Esmeralda was so perfect an impersonation of Hugo's heroine that one critic declared that it could only be the result of a diligent study of the novel. The emphasis lay not so much on the tragic implications of the character, as on its softer qualities, on Esmeralda's tenderness and her devotion to Phoebus, her 'merriment, sprightliness, love, and benevolence'. In the dances, her style was such as almost to defy description. One could recognize the characteristics which stamped the styles of her rivals—the innocent playfulness of Cerrito, the arch coquetry of Elssler, the quiet poetry of Taglioni—but there was a quality above all this which endeared her to the hearts of all who beheld her as well as to most of those who danced with her.

She had to return to Paris in time to dance in *Giselle* at the Opéra on Monday, 6th May. Persuaded by Lumley to remain in London until the latest minute, she took her benefit at Her Majesty's on the preceding Thursday evening. With the cheers and applause which greeted the final curtain of *La Esmeralda* still ringing in her ears, she ate a hurried supper and made her way through a throng of admirers to a waiting carriage. Lumley had ordered a special train to take her to Folkestone, where a steamer was waiting to carry her across the Channel to Boulogne. She was in Paris nineteen hours after leaving London.

The arrival of Cerrito put *La Esmeralda* temporarily out of the programme, but it was revived in the last weeks of the season with Fanny Elssler in the title-rôle. It afforded an interesting comparison. Where Grisi's portrayal was 'sensitive and affectionate, waggish and passionate, full of archness and amiability, waywardness and *espiéglerie*', Elssler's was less delicate but more intense and more in the grand tragic manner.[6] In an attempt to analyse the difference, *The Times* wrote that Elssler looked down upon the character and its capabilities as an artist, while Grisi identified herself with its joys and sorrows by a sort of unstudied sympathy. The difference in the two dancers' interpretations, however, was less marked than it had been in *Giselle*, where Elssler had seized upon the 'terror' as the dominant element, and Grisi on the 'pathos'. Elssler's Esmeralda was a studied portrayal, coming from the intellect; Carlotta's 'far more native and unsophisticated'.[7]

With Elssler, therefore, it was the dramatic moments in the ballet which stood out in greatest relief. The sudden touch of pity at the plight of Gringoire in the Cour des Miracles was so cleverly expressed as to make the impulse to marry him seem quite logical. Her encounter with Frollo in the same scene 'was worked up into an incident of terrific importance by the skill of the actress. The attitude she assumed, expressive of fear and horror, was startling: the cold shiver that seemed to pervade her frame, the fixed uplifting of her arms, and the apprehension depicted on her countenance, presented altogether a picture of mental uneasiness and womanish timidity not often realized on the stage; and it may easily be imagined that the subsequent struggle with the infuriate ravisher was elaborated strongly and effectively'.[6]

In the fourth scene, however, where her passion for Phoebus contends against 'the momentary upbraidings of conscience', she was 'grand and classical—effective, but not engaging'. Carlotta had been more moving with her portrayal of the 'yielding feebleness of a lovesick maiden'. But, at the end of this scene, when Esmeralda is accused of murdering her lover, Elssler was truly magnificent. 'At first she is overcome with terror, but presently she swells with pride and innocence, and indignantly confronts her denouncers, until, becoming sensible of her weak and forlorn condition, her courage forsakes her, and she droops into dejection and submissiveness.'[6]

Another wonderful moment came in the final scene: to some it was 'the most consummate of all her dramatic efforts in this ballet. Her prayer to heaven, her resignation to her fate, mingled with her remembrance of her lover, and her sorrow at parting with her friends, are all expressed in a few seconds with marvellous truth'.[8]

The achievements of Carlotta Grisi and Fanny Elssler did not, however, detract from the credit given to Perrot as choreographer, who in no other work demonstrated more effectively the underlying truth of the precepts of Noverre, which he studied so carefully. The audience's interest was not allowed to flag: the ballet was played through without any long intervals, the second and fourth scenes being probably enacted before a drop-curtain to the fore of the stage while the succeeding scene was being prepared behind. Great care had been given to each one of the characters, who carried on the drama by means of gestures much more natural than were ordinarily seen, and the movements of the *corps de ballet* in the first and last scenes contributed to give the ballet an element of impressive realism.

With *Giselle* and the *Pas de Quatre*, *La Esmeralda* was one of the great achievements of the Romantic Ballet, a triumph of choreography and a triumph of interpretation by the two renowned ballerinas who played the principal rôle. In England, this rôle was afterwards played by Francesca Auriol at the Princess's Theatre in 1848, by Victorine Legrain during a tour of the provinces in 1851, by Carolina Pochini in a revival at Her Majesty's in 1857, and by Lydia Thompson, in the first act only, at the St James's Theatre in 1860. But these dancers were but pale reflections of the brilliant stars who had preceded them. 'Mlle Pochini', wrote a critic of the 1857 revival at Her Majesty's, 'is a spirited, airy, quaint little *danseuse* . . . but oh! Carlotta Grisi!—*quanto minus est cum reliquis versari quam tui meminisse,* which, being translated, means—it is pleasanter to throw oneself into an armchair and, amid the fumes of a pipe, to recall that dreamy, voluptuous, graceful witchery, which marked thy every movement, thou queen of ballerinas, than to go and see any dancer of the present day.' [9]

Albert Smith, author of the *Natural History of the Ballet Girl,* also grew nostalgic when he allowed his memory to dwell upon the ballet of *La Esmeralda,* and wrote:

> *Carlotta! Carlotta! we think of the days*
> *When bright* Esmeralda *set up such a blaze*
> *In our pulses and hearts; and thy lov'd tambourine*
> *Gave the note of approach, as you flash'd on the scene.*
> *That pose above all—you and Phoebus together—*
> *When you blew from his cap the light morsel of feather.*
> *Oh! e'en had we known of the priest at the portal,*
> *To spurn thy allurements was not for a mortal;*
> *Carlotta!*

> *I've not yet quite done with that ballet—by all*
> *That tore out our heart as we gazed from our stall;*
> *By all those sweet smiles—sunny facial rays—*
> *By the nods that you gave in the sly* truandaise—
> *By that soul-charming music of Pugni—confess'd*
> *Of all ballet-music, the lightest and best—*
> *Carlotta! Carlotta! we beg—we implore—*
> *Come back, dear, and play* Esmeralda *once more,*
> *Carlotta!* [10]

NOTES TO CHAPTER 15

[1] *The Times,* 11th March 1844.
[2] Benjamin Lumley, *Reminiscences of the Opera* (London, 1864).
[3] *Morning Post,* 13th March 1844.
[4] *Morning Herald,* 11th March 1844.
[5] *Morning Post,* 11th March 1844.
[6] *Morning Herald,* 5th August 1844.
[7] *The Times,* 5th August 1844.
[8] *Morning Post,* 5th August 1844.
[9] *Illustrated Times,* 25th April 1857.
[10] *Musical World,* 24th October 1846.

16

The Pas de Quatre: *the Romantic Ballet at its most Sublime*

THE IDEA of a *divertissement* of all talents did not originate with Lumley, although it was he who was first able to realize it. In 1841, the last year of the management of his predecessor, Laporte, a 'new grand ballet' called *Le Jugement de Pâris*, in which Taglioni, Elssler, and Cerrito were all to appear, had been announced, but never produced. Two years later, Lumley succeeded in presenting Elssler and Cerrito together in a *pas de deux*, and their apparent willingness to dance side by side caused the manager's ambition to take a further step forward. In February 1845 it was announced that Taglioni, Cerrito, and Carlotta Grisi might all appear in a single ballet during the forthcoming season—'a collision', commented *The Times*, 'that the most carelessly managed railroad could hardly hope to equal';[1] and the success of that season's *débutante*, the Danish dancer Lucile Grahn, transformed what had been projected as a *Pas de Trois* into a *Pas de Quatre*.

Before a task such as that confronting Lumley, it was said that a statesman of the calibre of Metternich or Talleyrand might well have quailed. Having soothed as best he could the animosities of the four dancers by much coaxing, flattery, and supplication, Lumley succeeded in warming his idea into life. Perrot then set to work. The greatest care had to be taken not to wound the ballerinas' susceptibilities, and Lumley had given instructions that 'every twinkle of each foot in every *pas* had to be nicely weighed in the balance, so as to give no preponderance. Each *danseuse* was to shine in her peculiar style and grace to the last stretch of perfection; but no one was to outshine the others—unless in their own individual belief'.[2]

But almost at the last moment, a quarrel broke out between Cerrito and Grisi. All were agreed that Taglioni should be given pride of place and dance the last variation, but both Cerrito and Grisi claimed precedence over the other for second place. According to Taglioni it was Cerrito who started the quarrel. Grisi stamped about the stage in a violent rage, calling Cerrito 'a little chit',[3] and Perrot fled to Lumley's office in despair. '*Mon Dieu!*' he exclaimed, '*Cerrito ne veut pas commencer avant Carlotta—ni Carlotta avant Cerrito—et il n'y a pas moyen de les faire bouger; tout est fini!*' Lumley's decision was worthy of Solomon. 'The question of talent must be decided by the public,' he said. 'But in this dilemma there is one point on which I am sure the ladies will be frank. Let the *oldest* take her unquestionable right to the envied position.'

The effect was miraculous. 'The ballet-master', wrote Lumley in his memoirs, 'smote his forehead, smiled assent, and bounded from the room upon the stage. The judgment of the manager was announced. The ladies tittered, laughed, drew back, and were now as much disinclined to accept the right of position as they had been before eager to claim it. The ruse succeeded. The management of affairs was left in Monsieur Perrot's hands. The order of the ladies being settled,[4] the *grand pas de quatre* was finally performed on the same night before a delighted audience, who little knew how nearly they had been deprived of their expected treat.'[2]

There were, however, many in the fashionable audience at Her Majesty's on that memorable evening of Saturday, 12th July 1845, who doubted even after the bell had rung whether the curtain would really rise on the promised *Pas de Quatre*, for rumours of the quarrel had penetrated the Opera House walls. But rise it did, to reveal a sunny landscape—'the well-known *divertissement* bower'—before which a number of *figurantes*, dressed in muslin and pink hose, were arranged in picturesque groups. Then, from the wings, the great four appeared, hand in hand, in a simple straight line, all clad in pale pink, adorned by a rose or two in the hair and on the bodice: Taglioni, Cerrito, Carlotta Grisi, Grahn. Amid a tumult of cheering and clapping and stamping of feet, they advanced slowly in a line to the front of the stage and curtsied to the audience.

Then, as the musicians began to play, the house was suddenly stilled. The four dancers began with a series of groupings, picturesque and elegant in design and of an exquisite effect, all being executed with the most perfect precision, and with no apparent exertion nor struggle for effect. Taglioni formed the centre of these groups, with the others surrounding and overhanging her with outstretched arms, as though in homage; in the most striking of all, she appeared in their midst, her head thrown back, apparently reclining in their arms. These groupings were in time succeeded by a 'quick transverse movement', which led to a brilliant solo by Grahn, then to a *pas de deux* by Cerrito and Grisi, and at length to a series of broad aerial *jetés* across the stage by Taglioni, such as only she could do. Each display culminated with a storm of applause, a rain of bouquets, and a curtsy; and as time went on, the boards of the stage became almost lost to view under a layer of freshly fallen petals.

Now, to an *allegro* variation, there appeared Lucile Grahn, revolving with 'dainty semicircular hops' on the *pointe*, as light as 'a feather in a current of wind', yet vigorous and, in her poses, astonishingly firm. Then followed an *andante* movement for Carlotta Grisi, performing 'tip-toe flights' and 'lightning gyrations' of 'equal dexterity and number, mingled, however, with a world of little sprightly steps, which multiplied her feet into thousands': a piquant, coquettish *variation*, in which she brought her youthful grace and fascination into fullest play. A romantic note was now struck, as the tempo changed to a slow, expressive *andantino* movement danced by Taglioni and Grahn. But this mood was only momentary. Cerrito, who had been calmly contemplating her rivals from the back of the stage, burst upon them with a sequence of revolving steps, taken diagonally across the stage, followed by voluptuously buoyant boundings and balancings, all performed with such vigour and suddenness as to draw forth from the audience a shower of bouquets which fell all around her . . . and some, indeed, on top of her. Flushed and exhilarated by her exertions, the Neapolitan dancer surveyed the tributes at her feet with mingled gratitude and confusion before beginning to pick them up. There were more wreaths and nosegays than she could hold in both arms, and Taglioni came forward to help her, and handed her a chaplet with a kindly smile of congratulation. It was now the turn of the greatest dancer herself, and it was a tribute to her own peerless artistry that, despite the triumphs which had gone before, she could yet raise the enthusiasm of the audience to still more frenzied heights. Hers was an *allegro variation*, gentle and languid in mood, in which she 'displayed all her commanding manner, relying much on that advancing step, of which, we believe, she was the inventress, and astonishing by some of her bounds'; she introduced 'steps with the knee bent forward', which were so completely her own that no other dancer seemed to have adopted them; and it was observed that her 'line of dancing was always maintained nearer the perpendicular' than that of her companions.

Then followed the *coda*, in which all four vied with each other in performing 'steps of various and dazzling complexity', 'flying with a rapidity the eye could scarcely follow, mingled in beautiful evolutions and presenting a moving picture of which no description can give any idea' (Plate XVIIIa); and finally coming together with precision to form a 'sculpturesque' group as yet more bouquets were thrown from the boxes, and the curtain descended.[5]

The appearance of the four dancers before the curtain was the signal for fresh enthusiasm which mounted to a frenzy as Cerrito placed a crown of white roses upon Taglioni's head. There were shouts for Perrot, who was to be seen during the performance from the left-hand side of the house, conducting the *divertissement* from the wings, beating time, fuming and fidgeting in an agony of zeal. But now his worries were all over as he came forward to acknowledge his share of the triumphant ovation.

The *Pas de Quatre* was performed only three times more during July 1845—on the 15th, the 17th (when Queen Victoria and Prince Albert saw it), and the 19th—before Carlotta Grisi left London; and was revived two years later, in 1847, for just two performances, on 17th and 20th July, with Carolina Rosati taking the part originally played by Lucile Grahn. Even had it been given but once, instead of six times, the renown of this fabulous *divertissement* would have been no less. 'There are more than ten ballets of the calibre of *La Esmeralda* in this new effort of Perrot's,' wrote the Vicomtesse de Malleville.[6] 'Never was such a *pas* before,' said *The Times*; 'it was the greatest Terpsichorean exhibition that ever was known in Europe.' [7] It 'shook one's soul to the very centre', added the *Era*.[8] It marked 'an era in the records of the ballet-master's art', concluded the *Morning Herald*, 'and those who saw it chuckle to this day with satisfaction, and talk boastingly to those who did not'.[9]

NOTES TO CHAPTER 16

[1] *The Times*, 19th February 1845.

[2] Benjamin Lumley, *Reminiscences of the Opera* (London, 1864).

[3] Frederick Gale, *The Old Ballet* (*Globe*, 1899, and *Dancing Times*, August 1940).

[4] The youngest, Grahn (1819–1907) danced first; then Carlotta Grisi (1819–99); then Cerrito (1817–1909); and finally Taglioni (1804–84).

[5] This description of the *Pas de Quatre* is based on contemporary accounts to be found in the following papers: *The Times*, 14th and 18th July 1845; *Morning Post*, 14th and 16th July 1845; *Morning Herald*, 14th and 18th July, 20th August 1845; *Morning Chronicle*, 14th July 1845; *Era*, 20th July 1845; *Court Journal*, 19th July 1845; *Illustrated London News*, 19th July 1845.

[6] *Le Courrier de l'Europe*, 19th July 1845.

[7] *The Times*, 14th July 1845.

[8] *Era*, 24th August 1845.

[9] *Morning Herald*, 20th August 1845.

xxɪa. Manuela Perea (La Nena)

xxɪb. Petra Cámara

XXII. Monsieur Charles. *Oil-painting by R. Buckner*

17

Some Pages of Scandal

SCANDALS MAY occur even in the best regulated establishments. In the days of the Romantic Ballet, they were liable to break out at any time in those theatres which presented ballet, for these places were one of the favourite fields for the sowing of wild oats by young men about town. At Drury Lane, under Bunn, the more influential patrons were allowed the run of the *coulisses*, and Sir Charles Shakerley, Lords Dupplin, Suffield, and Chichester, and many men of fashion and Guards officers enjoyed the favours of the dancers, the less important of whom may sometimes have been glad of an opportunity to augment their meagre salaries. For it was notorious, as the *Satirist* wrote in 1845, 'that the female part of the *corps de ballet* are harder worked in every way and worse paid than any other class of damsels in London—needlewomen not excepted'. Also, procuresses of the worst type were able to penetrate back-stage at Drury Lane, among those being the woman who became notorious in the sixties as Madame Rachel, the black-mailing beauty specialist.

At Her Majesty's the picture was perhaps a little more pleasant, although it was far beyond even Lumley's powers to prevent his more important subscribers, and particularly those gentlemen who occupied the omnibus boxes on either side of the stage, from associating with the dancers. The most he could do was to ask Mme Copère to give the girls a lecture, a proceeding which probably had little effect, since everyone suspected her to be the mistress of her 'spiritual adviser', a clergyman related to one of the noble families, with whom she had been on terms of close friendship for many years, and there was thought to be a discernible likeness between this reverend gentleman and her son.

Early in the season of 1845 a curious scene was enacted in the Opera House. Mme Copère, who was in charge of the Wardrobe Department, 'summoned some of the nymphs of the ballet, whom she thought a lively and excitable temperament might lead into mischief, to the little room on the left hand of the hall for the purpose of pointing out to them the morality and propriety of conduct which she deemed fit to be observed during the season. She remarked, as we are given to understand, that the noblemen and gentlemen who crowd behind the scenes between the opera and the ballet, came

H

like roaring lions seeking whom they may devour; but after the warning she had given her feminine hearers they would know how to repulse them. She said she had been a member of the Opera House during the lesseeships of Ebers, Benelli, Laporte, and others, and though she knew that a large *douceur*—(here the parson whispered in his sleeve, "*Omnia bona bonis*")—had been sometimes given for the surrender of what a foolish young nobleman thought a great prize, she was happy to say that during her long experience (loud cries of "*Hear, hear*")—yes, during her *very* long experience, she had always found that the citadel of virtue might be rendered impregnable if they would only follow her example. (Here some of the girls began to titter.) They beheld her the Pantomimic Queen of the Ballet, the Mistress of the Robes, a housekeeper, and, moreover, surrounded by her family, who had been well provided for; and all because she had relied more on her merits than her person, and could always afford to despise unworthy patronage. After a prayer from the parson, and "Amen" from her son, she dismissed the troupe. In passing out through the little room at the back into the long dark passage which leads to the stage, one of the *corps,* more skittish than the rest, said, we think very improperly, that the old dame, having left off running herself, wished to keep the young fillies from proper exercise; but that she was determined to have a good start, let her be entered for what stake she might'.

This homily was no doubt prompted by the scandal which had been the talk of the town all the previous season and for some months afterwards, and had been brought to a head by Lumley's dismissal of Adeline Plunkett (Plate XIX) and Elisa Scheffer.

These two dancers had first been engaged for the season of 1843, and had made a favourable impression on the public. By the following year they had become implacable enemies, as a result of a bitter contest for the protection of the Earl of Pembroke, which everyone knew—from the ostentatious manner in which Scheffer paraded the change in her fortunes, even on the stage, where she appeared as the Queen of the Wilis in *Giselle,* her costume blazing with diamonds—had ended in her favour. For some weeks Pembroke had enjoyed the favours of both dancers, but in time his passion for Scheffer completely absorbed him, and Plunkett had to console herself as best she could by accepting the protection of Henry Baring, a member of the well-known banking family, and a Lord Commissioner of Her Majesty's Treasury.

She was slow to forget. Like a storm-cloud, her fury gathered in intensity until the evening of Saturday, 11th May 1844, when the ballet of *Ondine* was billed. The two dancers were both to appear dressed alike, and, by an unfortunate mistake, they had been given each other's costumes. Plunkett, who was the smaller of the two, had her dresser sew a few stitches in the costume she had been given to make it fit her, but the other costume was much too small for Scheffer, who flew into a rage and demanded that her own be restored. Plunkett refused. A violent scene then followed, both dancers and their protectors reviling each other with 'the blackest words', and to avoid an unpleasant incident in the presence of the public, their *pas de deux* had to be omitted.

Their hostility had still not abated when the time came for Fanny Cerrito to dance the *pas de l'ombre*. In the wings Plunkett observed Scheffer facing away from her and aimed a savage kick at her. Scheffer bounded aside and deflected the blow, which broke the cord holding up the lamp supplying the light for the moon. There was a resounding crash, and the public, deprived so abruptly of its anticipated pleasure, strongly voiced its disapproval. A corpulent gentleman in black vainly tried to make himself heard, and an ugly scene seemed to be brewing, when Jules Perrot, with a disarming smile, stepped forward and said: '*Mesdames et messieurs, un accident impossible à prévoir a dérangé la machine de la lune. . . . C'est une éclipse complète.*' The tempest was at once quelled. The audience broke into peals of laughter, and the ballet was allowed to continue.

There was a further incident on 25th July when Plunkett and Scheffer were to have danced a new *pas de deux*, arranged by Gosselin to music by Nadaud, in *La Paysanne Grande Dame*. The two dancers had asked that their skirts should be fringed with gold and their bodices made of crimson velvet, and the management had agreed to their request. But on seeing their costumes for the first time, they discovered that Mme Copère had had the bodices made of common cotton velvet, instead of silk velvet. Their indignation knew no bounds, and they flatly refused to go on in such inferior material. Lumley's patience was now at an end. He considered it imperative to put a stop to such scenes as this, which were beginning to have a serious effect on the general discipline of the company, and neither Lord Pembroke nor Henry Baring could dissuade him from cancelling the engagements of their mistresses. Pembroke took great offence, and was not seen at the Opera for three successive performances.

By now the Earl was completely in Scheffer's thrall. He forsook his friends, spending nearly all his time with his mistress, whom he had installed with her mother over the premises of a well-known firm of military cap-makers at No. 14 Piccadilly. His assiduous attentions were observed with considerable surprise and amusement, for he had the reputation of being the gayest of Lotharios. Soon, however, this charming idyll was to be interrupted. Pembroke's friends were very disturbed at the sudden change which had come over their companion and which deprived them of all opportunities of taking advantage of his lavish generosity, and when he fell ill, they found it convenient to surmise that he had been poisoned. On its becoming clear that his health was not seriously affected, it was suggested, and generally believed, that he had been given a love philtre by Scheffer and her mother to stimulate his waning passion, and that this had disagreed with his constitution, but his indisposition was probably the result of a more natural cause. The suspicion, however, afforded some of the Earl's friends with the excuse to effect a rescue, and once having him in their hands they urged him to abandon his mistress.

Bewildered, Lord Pembroke went to Paris to think matters out. Soon afterwards, Scheffer, desperate at the thought of losing him, followed and finally ran him to earth in the Rue de la Paix. To the amazement of the passers-by, she threw her arms round his neck with a cry of joy and relief. The embarrassed Pembroke hailed a *fiacre*, hurriedly pushed her inside, and ordered the *cocher* to drive around the centre of the city until told to stop. They were soon reconciled, and from that moment Scheffer's influence over Lord Pembroke was never again in doubt. Her career was quite forgotten in her happy and prosperous concubinage. Known as Mme Montgomery, she lived with the Earl in Paris until his death in 1862, bearing him three children for whom he provided as handsomely as he could; and when she died early in 1873, she was laid to rest by his side in the Cemetery of Père Lachaise, where their impressive stone tombs stand as a monument to their love.

An American friend once asked Lord Pembroke why he had lavished a quarter of a million pounds on this girl. 'Do you think her beautiful?' he asked.

'Certainly not,' Pembroke replied.

'Clever?'

'No, she's a fool.'

'Voluptuous?'

'Good heavens, no!'

'Well made?'

'No; flat as a pancake, and hands and feet like a stable-boy.'

'What then?'

Lord Pembroke considered for a moment. 'Well,' he said, 'I think it must be because she has got rather nice shoulders.'

Scheffer's triumph rankled in Plunkett's breast for months, and everyone knew that she only accepted the blind attachment of Henry Baring and the pressing attentions of the Comte de Biron to console herself for the disappointment she had suffered. She continued her career as a dancer, visiting England again only a few weeks after her dismissal from the Opera House to dance at Drury Lane. In the years that followed she returned several times to London, but it was always at Drury Lane or Covent Garden that she appeared. She never again trod the boards of Her Majesty's. Lumley would not forgive her for her indiscretion.

NOTES TO CHAPTER 17

The principal sources for this chapter are the *Satirist*, 1844–6, and *Le Courrier de l'Europe*, 1844. Further details are to be found in Léandre Vaillat, *La Taglioni* (Paris, 1942); Benjamin Lumley, *Reminiscences of the Opera* (London, 1864); the anonymous *More Uncensored Recollections* (London, 1926); and the *Maestro*, 18th May and 10th August 1844.

18

The Viennese Children

THE VIENNESE, during the Romantic Period, had a great taste for children's ballets. In the years following the Congress which reshaped Europe after the Napoleonic wars, Friedrich Horschelt presented a number of ballets of this kind which became known as much for their excellence of composition as for the talents of the young persons who appeared in them, at least two of whom—Therese Heberle and Fanny Elssler—afterwards became internationally famous. A generation later another troupe of dancing children made its appearance in Vienna, a troupe which was to gain universal renown and to count among its many conquests that of London in the very year of the *Pas de Quatre*.

The founder of this troupe was the ballet-mistress of the Josephstadt Theater, Vienna, Frau Josephine Weiss, who, to restore the fortunes of that establishment, had gathered from the lowest and poorest classes of society about twenty children, in whom she had proceeded to instil the rudiments of dancing. The result was phenomenal. Crowds began to flock to the theatre to see these charming and remarkably disciplined children, and before very long parents of quite respectable station were confiding their offspring to the charge of Frau Weiss.

When Frau Weiss's contract with the Josephstadt Theater expired, she became her own impresario and took the children on tour. Everywhere—in Pest, Brunn, Berlin, Frankfurt, Cologne, Hamburg—the children were received with enthusiasm. Notwithstanding the artistic and financial triumph of her enterprise, however, Frau Weiss was beset with many troubles. Pressure was continually being applied by the children's parents for a larger share of the profits, and while the troupe was appearing at Frankfurt, the authorities would have sent them back to Vienna on account of an alleged passport irregularity, had not Frau Weiss quickly spirited the children from the city. By way of Brussels, they eventually reached Paris early in 1845, and there, at the Opéra, caused something of a sensation with their youthful appeal and their extraordinary precision. As soon as he heard of this success Lumley lost no time in coming to terms with Frau Weiss.

The engagement of the Danseuses Viennoises at Her Majesty's was due to commence on the opening night of the 1845 season but 'unexpectedly', as

Lumley afterwards wrote, 'the most untoward difficulties arose'. Acting on orders from Vienna, the Austrian Embassy in Paris, without giving any reason, refused passports and threatened to have the children sent back to Vienna, under police escort if necessary. Negotiations were then opened at diplomatic level. Lord Cowley, the British Ambassador in Paris, tried to intercede with his Austrian counterpart, Count Apponyi, but the latter was obdurate. The mystery further deepened when Léon Pillet, the Director of the Paris Opéra, successfully claimed that his engagement still had some time to run, and the demand for the immediate return of the troupe to Austria was then apparently abandoned.

Meanwhile, being informed that the Austrian Embassy in London had approached the Lord Chamberlain with a request that the troupe should be restrained from performing in England, Lumley obtained a personal interview with the Ambassador, Count Dietrichstein, but was unable to discover what objections the Austrian Government had to his engagement of the children. All he was told was that the Ambassador was acting under orders from Vienna. At the same time, negotiations were continued in Paris by the legal counsellor of the British Embassy, and obviously with some reluctance certain objections were specified. First, it was alleged that the children's morality and health might be endangered, and this Lumley met by submitting documents showing the contrary. Then it was put forward that some of the parents desired their children to return, which Lumley promptly countered by concluding an agreement with the parents.

The real reason for the refusal of passports was quite different. The ultramontane party in Vienna, led by the Empress, had become alarmed at the thought of these children, who were all Catholics, being exposed to the heretical opinions held in Protestant England, and in Paris Queen Marie-Amélie had lent her powerful support to the conspiracy to prevent the visit to London. As soon as this became known, the London press raised a great clamour, inveighing against the Jesuits in a self-righteous surge of anti-Catholic feeling and giving Lumley and the troupe some welcome publicity.[1]

At last—'by what connivance, or what secret arrangement with the French authorities, does not appear'—Frau Weiss reached England with thirty-five little girls and one little boy. They landed at London Docks one evening early in April, and were at once conveyed to their residence in eight carriages. 'These pretty votaries of Terpsichore', wrote an onlooker, 'were accompanied by some of their parents, and appeared to enjoy the happiest flow of health and spirits, and their chatter and laughter rang merrily in the ears of the astonished witnesses of the disembarkation.'[2]

The Austrian authorities, who now wisely desisted from further measures to prevent the children from appearing in public, had no need to fear for their welfare, for Frau Weiss was a most conscientious guardian. During their stay in London, the children were kept from all improper contact, and always retired under her wing as soon as the performance was over. Despite the very plebeian origin of many of them, they were models of good behaviour, in itself sufficient proof of the control which worthy Frau Weiss exercised over them.

The Danseuses Viennoises were seen for the first time on the stage of Her Majesty's on 8th April. Appearing between the acts of the opera, they danced in three numbers: a *Pas allemand*, 'wherein they all figured in pink satin'; a *Pas hongrois*, 'wherein one half . . . appeared as little Hussar officers, and danced with the other half attired in Sclavonic Amazon style'; [3] and finally a *Pas des fleurs*. This last dance created a great sensation. 'Watteau', wrote the *Morning Post*, 'would have gone on his knees at such a sight—would have transferred their effigies to the frescoes of his voluptuous sovereign's Marly or Trianon.' In their smart peasant costumes, with straw hats on the side of their heads and wreaths of flowers in their hands, the children bounded from one group to another with 'the precision of clockwork' and yet 'the appearance of the most unrestrained freedom'. 'Now they assume the pyramidal form with one or two leading figures towering above according to the rules of pictorial grouping, and anon the elders hold above their heads hoops of flowers, forming a bower through which the gay little forms below career with lightning speed.' [4] (Plate XXa.)

As the season wore on they introduced other *pas*. There was the *Pas des moissonneurs*, introduced into Perrot's ballet *Kaya*, which ended with the children smothering each other with straw; the *Pas rococo*, danced in court costume of Louis XV's reign, with its acceptance of snuff by the ladies (to the well-known theme from Haydn's 'Surprise' Symphony) and the resulting explosion of sneezing which preceded 'the liveliest coranto we ever beheld'; [5] the *Pas des amours*, in which they appeared among clouds all dressed in white; and, perhaps the most striking of all, the *Pas du miroir*, which was so perfectly performed that many failed to penetrate the illusion of the gauze curtain behind which eight little girls followed with great precision the movements of a similar number in front of it.

When they were dancing, the evening's amusement never ended with the last note of music from the orchestra. This was the signal not only for applause and for bouquets, but for a shower of bonbons which dropped from all sides on to the stage amidst laughter and cheering. All the renowned discipline of the children was then at an end, and a general scramble followed. Good Frau Weiss's precepts, however, were never entirely forgotten. It happened once, for example, that one little girl, in search of a packet of sugar-plums which had rolled towards the footlights, was shut off from her companions by the fall of the curtain, and delighted the audience by the self-possession with which she retrieved her prize, tripped off towards the wings, and then stopped and curtsied before disappearing from view.

Whenever Queen Victoria was in the Royal Box—and she paid several visits to see them—the curtain would rise again after their performance to reveal the children formed in a diagonal line facing Her Majesty, and they would then bow gracefully with the same precision they had displayed in their dancing. They were no less appreciated by the Queen-Dowager Adelaide, who invited them to appear at a fête given at Marlborough House for the Royal Children,[6] and was so pleased that she afterwards presented Lumley with a snuff-box in acknowledgment of his 'obliging attention and ability'. The public too was charmed by the original feats of 'these exquisite little marvels', by their rapidity and their precision. Never before had such a disciplined troupe of dancers been seen in London. Their performance, wrote the *Morning Post*, 'proves . . . most positively . . . that the ballet *corps* of all theatres are woefully neglected and mismanaged, and the *maîtres de ballet* have to begin a new course of study to redeem the stage from the slow mechanism of their awkward squadrons'.[4] This was the lesson of the Viennese Children, but it was not, alas, to be fully appreciated.

Despite the stir they caused at the time, the Danseuses Viennoises enjoyed but a brief triumph, for the novelty having passed, their attraction was greatly diminished. They returned to London only once more, being engaged by Bunn for a few performances at Drury Lane in the summer of 1846, but they had nothing new to offer and caused no such stir as they had done the year before at Her Majesty's.

NOTES TO CHAPTER 18

[1] For the difficulties in engaging the Danseuses Viennoises in London, see Benjamin Lumley, *Reminiscences of the Opera* (London, 1864), and also *Illustrated London News*, 19th April 1845, which gives details of their early history.

[2] *Morning Post*, 5th April 1845.

[3] *The Times*, 9th April 1845.

[4] *Morning Post*, 9th April 1845.

[5] *Morning Post*, 16th May 1845.

[6] This was probably the first experience of professional dancing of the Prince of Wales (afterwards Edward VII), who was then aged three and a half.

19

Visitors from Spain

A STRIKING instance in the development of ballet of that quest for *couleur locale* which was so important a factor in Romantic art in all its forms, was the vogue for national dances. And of these dances none were more consistently popular during the period of the Romantic Ballet than the Spanish. A bolero, *cachucha*, or *guaracha* was certain to please, and choreographers would insert them in ballets and *divertissements* irrespective of locale: there was a *cachucha*, for instance, in Aumer's *Fête hongroise*, and Duvernay once danced her *cachucha* in *Beniowsky*, a ballet with a Russian setting.

Many of the favourite *pas de caractère* of the great Romantic ballerinas were derived from the dances of Spain. Fanny Elssler's *Cachucha*, and the bolero, *La Castilliana*, in which she was partnered by Perrot, Marie Taglioni's *Gitana*, and the *Double Cachucha* of Cerrito and Perrot, were but a few examples of such dances adapted and stylized for performance by classical ballerinas. No country is richer in its dances than Spain, but it was not only the abundance of material that made Spanish dances so popular, nor merely their exotic appeal and their half-Latin, half-Eastern fire; it was also their technical construction, which enabled a classically schooled dancer to put her prowess to use with only a small modification of the original dance.

The form of Spanish dancing which is termed 'classical' was developing in the latter half of the eighteenth century. Technical innovations from the French and Italian schools of ballet were then being grafted on to the older forms of regional dances, and new dances were emerging, such as the bolero, developed about 1780 by Antonio Boliche and Sebastián Cerezo and their disciples, which took its place with the voluptuous and impetuous *fandango*, the *cachucha*, and the many forms of *seguidillas*. Elevation, *batterie*, pirouettes, *pas de bourrée*, and many other borrowings from classical ballet gave Spanish dancing a wider vocabulary and a sophistication possessed by the dances of no other nation.

While these influences were enlarging the horizons of Spanish dancing, the French dancer Charles Le Picq visited that country. Shortly afterwards, in 1783, he was engaged as ballet-master at the King's Theatre in London, where he produced a very successful ballet, *Le Tuteur trompé* (based on

121

Beaumarchais's *Le Barbier de Séville*), which became the setting for two Spanish dances, *seguidillas* performed by himself and Mme Rossi, and a *fandango* by Mme Rossi. Both the ballet and the dances were revived in several later seasons, the latter being eventually merged into a *pas de trois* known as *Les Folies d'Espagne*; Charles Didelot, Madeleine Guimard, and Duquesney danced it in 1789, and Auguste Vestris and Mlles Hilligsberg and Mozon in 1791. Deshayes, who was principal dancer in Madrid in 1799, revived it in 1807 for himself, his wife, and Mlle Parisot, and again in 1810; and it was last performed in 1814, thirty-one years after Le Picq and Mme Rossi had first danced it.

During the Napoleonic wars the management of the London opera house found great difficulty in securing the services of foreign dancers. Many of those who succeeded in reaching England from the Continent came by way of Lisbon, and it was from there that Armand Vestris, son of Auguste, and Fortunata Angiolini arrived to make their London début in 1809. Their first-hand knowledge of Spanish dancing was soon put to good use when they danced a bolero in d'Egville's *Don Quichotte*; and in later London seasons Armand Vestris often appeared in a classical dance of Spain and on occasions produced Spanish *divertissements* which never failed to please.

He and Signora Angiolini also imparted their knowledge to others, and in 1811 the critic of *The Times* was enraptured by the grace with which Mlle Mori, a pupil of the latter, danced a *guaracha*, a grace which showed itself principally in the expressive carriage and poise of the body, in the movement of the arms, shoulders, and bust; for footwork, in those days, was quite a secondary element in female Spanish dancing. Mlle Mori, this critic described, 'wore a long light scarf with the centre fastened to her hair behind, and the ends to her wrists. The tune was melancholy and slow, sometimes accompanied by the castanets; and the dance was chiefly attitude. There were some periods at which the feet were scarcely moved, and all the effect was in waving the figure, and wreathing the scarf around the head and arms. The tune was still slow and wandering, and the dancer, sometimes touching the castanets, sometimes giving herself up to the delight of gesture, seemed to sport with the variety and expression of her movements. We never felt the beauty of motion more deeply. There were attitudes that might have been taken from the model of a Grecian statue'.[1]

If one ignores the visit of Luengo and the Señoras Ramos to Covent Garden in 1816 and the brief appearance of Maria Mercandotti, who was classically trained, it was not until 1834 that London saw its first Spanish dancers of any real distinction. In that year there arrived Dolores Serral, who is supposed to have taught Fanny Elssler the *cachucha*, Mariano Camprubí, whom Manet painted in later years, Francisco Font, and Manuela Dubinon. They were first seen in a bolero, 'their lower extremities being all the while thrown about with a graceful independence in stamp and scrape and swerve, and featly footed step, the upper extremities emulating them in all manner of gyrations and implications, and the body swaying all the while upon the waist as upon a pivot, and rising or sinking in sympathy discreet'. Another of their dances was a *zapateado,* which contained a great variety of movements, 'some being very bold, such as shooting the leg frequently, if we may so call a very brisk motion; some very neat, as the heel and toe step; and all more or less graceful—the *señoras* alternately waving the scarf or winding the eloquently chattering castanets, and their partners beating, thrumming, and jingling the tambourine'.[2]

During his management of Her Majesty's Theatre Benjamin Lumley did not overlook the appeal of Spanish dancing, although the first Spanish dancer he presented turned out to be of somewhat dubious origin. This was Lola Montez, who was billed as having come from the Teatro Real, Seville, when she made her début at Her Majesty's on 3rd June 1843, in the dance *El Olano.*

'There was a solemnity in the whole affair,' reported *The Times.* 'There was a gloominess in the music which accompanied the dance; we could fancy the melody such as might have served for the recreation of Philip II, or the great Duke of Alba; it might have been played without impropriety pending an *auto-da-fé.* The few bars that preceded the rising of the curtain sounded forebodingly; and when the curtain was removed, we saw indeed a few little ladies of the *corps de ballet* on each side of the stage; but the principal object was a mysterious folding-door in the centre of the scene at the back. This opened slowly, and a figure completely muffled in a black mantilla stepped forward. A few moments and the mantilla was cast aside, leaving visible the tall and commanding person of Doña Montez, attired in a black bodice, the skirt terminating in dark red and blue points. In the most stately fashion she wound round the stage, executing all her movements with the utmost deliberation. These movements were such as have been often seen in the various Spanish *pas* which are danced before us—there was the bending forward and drawing back, the feat of dropping on the knees, the haughty march forward. But in the style in which Doña Montez went through these movements there was something entirely different from all that we have seen. As a finished dancer she would not bear comparison with [Taglioni, Elssler, Cerrito, or Guy-Stéphan], but there was nevertheless a kind of national reality about her which was most impressive. The haughtiness with which she stepped, the slow play of the arms, the air of authority with which she once stepped with the hands resting on the hips—all gave an air of grandeur to the dance. For the qualities to which the *danseuses* are generally indebted to favour she cannot be highly commended. Her dance is not characterized by buoyancy, by remarkable grace, but it may be said to have much intensity. The whole soul of the artist seems worked up to a stern purpose—we do not believe Doña Montez smiled once throughout. As she retired from the stage showers of bouquets were thrown, but the proud one of Seville did not deign to return to pick them up, and one of the gentlemen in livery was deputed for

123

that purpose. She had evidently adopted the maxim of one of Calderón's heroines:

> *Cuanto es noble accion el dar,*
> *Es bajeza el recibir.*

When, however, her dance was encored, she alighted from her pinnacle, and actually condescended to come forward and pick up the additional bouquet that was thrown.' [3]

To judge from the press her début was little short of a triumph, and there was some mystification when she did not make a second appearance. Lumley had engaged her in the belief that she was the leading dancer from the Teatro Real in Seville, and was only enlightened as to her antecedents on the night of her début. It appeared she had been born in the barracks at Limerick, the daughter of an ensign called Gilbert, and his wife, whose maiden name was Oliver. But though she had probably never seen Spain, it is difficult to believe that she could have deceived all the theatre critics of London. Her mother probably had more Spanish blood in her veins than her name implied, for Lola was baptized with Spanish names, spoke Spanish well, and certainly had a considerable knowledge of Spanish dancing. With the story of her imposture gaining currency in society, Lumley realized it would be inviting a disturbance to allow her to appear again. Piqued, the dancer wrote protesting to *The Times*, appeared once at a benefit performance at Covent Garden, then left the country to try her fortune in other lands.

Lumley was much more fortunate with his second Spanish dancer. Manuela Perea, known as La Nena, an exquisite little creature, had gained great renown in her own country both as a dancer and as a beauty. (Plate XXIa.) Reports preceded her to London that she had 'made roast meat of the hearts' of General Narvaez, the Duc de Glücksberg, Don José Salamanca, and Henry Bulwer; and the statesman-poet, Lord Francis Egerton, penned the following verses under the inspiration of her beauty and artistry:

> *Once more my anchor swings above the brine,*
> *Yet, to what shore so e'er I plough the main,*
> *One page in memory's album shall be thine,*
> *Seville, the flower of all the realms of Spain.*
>
> *And though, sweet Nena, when that page I scan,*
> *With many an outline of fantastic grace,*
> *With Moorish arch and Arab tracery's lore,*
> *Thy gentle vision there shall find a place.*
>
> *If sages rightly to the dancer's skill*
> *Have given the name of motion's poetry,*
> *I ask no other Lesbos than Seville,*
> *No fairer Sappho, gentle child, than thee.*

To thy young ear time has not struck the hour
   For aught but gay guitar or castanet;
Nor breath of lover stirred the jasmin flower
   Which decks thy locks of Andalusian jet.

Oh! may some sylph, commissioned from above,
   Still haunt that flower, and, with Ithurial spear,
Deny to all but truth and honest love
   Access and entrance to that maiden ear.

Thou art not all thou shalt be, more than Spain
   Is what she was. That eye, half dew, half fire,
Can but provoke some livelier music's strain,
   Some nameless wanderer's verse like mine inspire.

Time was when charms like thine matured had warmed
   To triumphs, not of dancing, but of war;
And partners in the seguedille *had armed*
   To onslaught on the Arab's Alcazar.

When such approving glance as thine to meet,
   Towns had been sacked, and Emirs had been slain;
And at the lively Nena's nimble feet
   The spoils of slaughtered infidels had lain.[4]

Some days before her début, she was seen seated in a box at Her Majesty's, 'a floating mantilla attached to her braided raven locks', and there could then be no wondering at her conquests.

She made her first appearance with her partner and teacher, Felix Garcia, on 10th April 1845. 'As stars ought to glisten,' wrote *The Times*, 'so did she as she came forward . . . in a dress unrivalled for splendour, and dazzling the eyes of all beholders by its radiations. Placing herself with an air of almost defying primness opposite a stoutish young gentleman named Felix Garcia, she started off in a *bolero cachucha*, which she executed with amazing spirit. Her Spanish dance is not like the idealized versions of Fanny Elssler or Taglioni, but a much more native affair, and it is the native *gusto* with which it is danced that is its recommendation. The intricate steps are given with a sort of bustling rapidity, and with a pretty appearance of decision . . . La Nena bounds through her intricacies with the greatest possible good humour, and with the swiftness of a flash of lightning, to which, in her sparkling costume, she bore no small resemblance as she darted about the stage. Also, she has the advantage of a very pretty face, and elicits from castanets a sonorous music, such as is seldom produced by that national instrument.'[5]

Her second dance, the *Seguidillas Manchegas*, was less brilliant in form, and its effect was further reduced by the simpler red and black costume into which she had changed. Later, she introduced *El Olé de Cadiz* ('more intricate in its steps than any other she has hitherto executed'),[6] *Las Mollares de Sevilla*, and the *Bolero de la Caleta*.

La Nena became a great favourite in London in the eighteen-fifties. From 1854 to 1856, and again in 1858, she and her company drew large houses to the Theatre Royal, Haymarket (Plate XXb), and the whole town was humming the air of her *Jaleo de Cadiz*. Her popularity encouraged Lumley to engage her a second time in 1857, when she appeared in the title-rôle of *Acalista*, a ballet by Pierre Massot, who had come to London from the Teatro de Oriente in Madrid.

By the fifties London had become so accustomed to Spanish dancing that Lumley dared to devote a whole evening to a performance by Petra Cámara and her company of twenty-eight, who had arrived fresh from a triumphant season in Paris. (Plate XXIb.) It was the year of the Great Exhibition, 1851, when the town was full of foreign visitors, and Her Majesty's Theatre was playing five nights a week instead of the customary two or three. On 7th July, the night of the company's début, the programme consisted of three *divertissements*, *La Feria de Sevilla*, *Curra la Gaditana o los Toreros de Chiclana*, and *La Gitana in Chamberi*; and among the dances presented were *El Vito*, *La Manola*, *El Jaleo de Jerez*, *La Fantasia Española*, *Las Seguidillas Gitanas*, *La Jerezana*, *El Jaleo de la Pandereta*, and 'the celebrated' *Danza Valenciana*.

'Certainly the first burst of the spectacle is exciting enough,' wrote *The Times*. 'The whole stage is peopled by a number of persons picturesquely clad, who go through the most violent movements, as if actuated by a natural impulse, while the sound of infinite castanets rolls on with the precision and perpetuity of a succession of waves breaking on the shore. Then, when the twenty and odd minor celebrities disperse and leave a clear field for . . . Doña Petra Cámara, her evolutions are most extraordinary. She will enter as a village coquette, and her coquetries will be of a most *prononcé* character. She dances, and her suppleness of limb is astounding. Those bold gestures which the French and Italian *danseuses* seem to have acquired by art have apparently been bestowed upon her by some peculiar nature. The dance, moreover, is not only remarkable for its vigour, but for its strange eloquence. The artiste seems restless with an inspiring passion, to which her movements, hurried as they are, can scarcely give an adequate expression. Now she will snatch a hat, and, dashing it on the ground, execute her *pas* around it, as if it were a fallen enemy; now she will do the same kind office for a cloak; now she will execute the boldest steps upon a small table, regardless of the chance of tumbling. These evolutions are effected not only with the legs, but with the arms, the bust, the head—every muscle of the artiste will be dancing, and as she comes to the end of her *pas*, she shakes her petticoats to extend the sympathy.'[7]

After five performances the company issued a statement to the press informing the public that although the house had been 'extremely crowded' whenever they appeared they had received no payment, that they had therefore refused to perform again, but that as the Queen was to visit the theatre on the 17th, they had offered their services so as to have the honour of appearing before her. Another unfortunate experience was to befall them in Manchester, where the manager of the Theatre Royal considered unreasonable their demand to be paid half the receipts from Monday to Friday and the whole of the receipts on Saturday, but at Liverpool the public made ample amends by its enthusiasm and 'one gentleman actually threw his hat upon the stage'.

To have inspired such transports in the breast of a phlegmatic Lancastrian (if such he was) was surely an artistic triumph of the greatest magnitude and a most eloquent testimony to the popularity of Spanish dancing in the days of the Romantic Ballet.

NOTES TO CHAPTER 19

[1] *The Times*, 20th May 1811.
[2] *Morning Herald*, 17th May 1834.
[3] *The Times*, 5th June 1843.
[4] *Morning Post*, 21st April 1845.
[5] *The Times*, 11th April 1845.
[6] *The Times*, 9th May 1845.
[7] *The Times*, 8th July 1851.

20

Alfred Bunn and the Ballet: Clara Webster, Fuoco, Blasis

POSTERITY has dealt somewhat harshly with poor Alfred Bunn. To-day he is generally only remembered when a revival of *The Bohemian Girl* provides amusement with its curiously laboured libretto which recalls to mind the derisive epithet of 'Poet Bunn'. Yet in the history of English ballet he deserves honourable mention, for he was for some years the only theatre manager whom Lumley might regard as a rival, albeit an inferior one, in the presentation of ballet.

Bunn first grasped the reins of the Theatre Royal, Drury Lane, in 1833, and was quick to exploit the current vogue for ballet by engaging Pauline Duvernay and presenting her in Aumer's *The Sleeping Beauty*. For a short time he attempted to direct the fortunes of both Drury Lane and Covent Garden, and at certain hours of the evening dancers could be seen scurrying from one theatre to the other. Far from being economical, however, this double management was one of the causes which led to his first bankruptcy in 1840. Within three years, the resilient Bunn was back at Drury Lane, succeeding the 'eminent tragedian' Macready in the summer of 1843. He relinquished his management again in 1847, turning up about a year later at Covent Garden. From August 1851 to May 1852 he directed the fortunes of Drury Lane for a third time.

It was during his second period of management at Drury Lane that Bunn made his greatest contribution to ballet. *The Peri*, with Carlotta Grisi and Lucien Petipa in the rôles they had recently created in Paris, opened his first season and drew immense half-price houses in the autumn of 1843, and this was followed by *The Devil in Love* (*Le Diable amoureux*) (1843) with Pauline Leroux and *Lady Henrietta* (1844) with Lucile Grahn. More importations from Paris were billed in the seasons that followed: *The Devil to Pay* (*Le Diable à quatre*) in 1845, *Paquita* and *The Wags of Wapping* (*Betty*) in 1846, and *Vert-Vert* in 1852. *Giselle*, too, found its way into the programmes with a succession of interpreters: Maria, Adèle Polin, Louise Weiss, and Louise (an English girl who had appeared at the King's Theatre in the twenties as Louisa Court) in 1845, and Giovannina Sali in 1846.

128

XXIII. Marie Taglioni the younger, Carlotta Grisi, and Amalia Ferraris in *Les Grâces*
Water-colour by A. E. Chalon

xxiva. *Les Métamorphoses*, Scene II

xxivb. *L'Île des amours*

Appealing to a wider and less cultured public than Lumley, Bunn generally announced his ballets with English titles. His *corps de ballet* was almost entirely English, as also were many of the dancers who took supporting rôles: among these were George Wieland, Tom Matthews, W. H. Payne, all famous as pantomimists, Howell, O'Bryan and his sister Adelaide, and Clara and Arthur Webster. Only the principal dancers were foreign. Bunn appreciated as well as anybody the exotic attraction of a star from Paris, Vienna, or Milan, and for this very reason was slow to discover the potential talent of Clara Webster, the most promising English dancer of the Romantic Ballet.

The daughter of a dancing-master of Bath and half-sister of Benjamin Webster, manager of the Theatre Royal, Haymarket, Clara had entered Drury Lane in 1841, under Macready's management, and remained with the company when Bunn succeeded him. Though only about twenty-one, she was already an experienced artiste, having made her first stage appearance at Bath before she was seven, been *première danseuse* for two seasons in Dublin, and appeared in support of Cerrito in Liverpool and Manchester. Her progress in little more than a year was extraordinary. Though no doubt hastened by the experience of dancing with such ballerinas as Carlotta Grisi, Pauline Leroux, Lucile Grahn, and Adèle Dumilâtre, it was none the less a natural development of her talent. Contemporary critics likened her style to that of Cerrito, whose particular qualities were a dashing attack, brilliant turning, speed, and withal a fascinating charm.

On the opening night of Bunn's second season in the autumn of 1844, Clara, who was playing a secondary rôle in Albert's *The Corsair,* was immediately greeted with 'the most enthusiastic cheering', and not long afterwards *The Times* described her as 'perhaps the only English *danseuse* who has attained that firmness, freedom, and confidence which distinguish the artistes of the Continent'.[1] Adeline Plunkett, whom Bunn engaged that winter, was almost put in the shade by the brilliance of the young English dancer. Rather hesitatingly Bunn tried Clara in a principal rôle, that of Louise in a revival of *The Deserter of Naples*, but the experiment was not repeated. Bunn never realized the true value of the native gem which lay within his grasp.

It was, alas, soon to slip from his fingers. During a performance of *The Revolt of the Harem* on 14th December 1844, Clara's skirt touched the naked flame of an oil-burner, and the audience rose to their feet in horror as she rushed panic-stricken about the stage, her costume blazing. It was a stage carpenter who eventually caught her and put out the flames, but it was then too late. She was driven to her lodgings accompanied by a doctor and her distraught lover, a young officer in the Guards, and there lingered on in agony and delirium until the early morning of the 17th when she was at last released from her terrible sufferings. Such accidents as this were all too common in those days of gas-lighting and insufficient fire precautions, but seldom was the toll so heavy as when Clara Webster was snatched from English ballet.

Bunn was happier when purveying foreign talent, and several historic names adorned the casts of the ballets he presented, not the least among them being those of Sofia Fuoco and the great pedagogue of the dance, Carlo Blasis.

Puffed by Bunn as 'the most celebrated *danseuse* in Europe', Sofia Fuoco was above all a technician, the most skilled exponent of *pointe* work of her time. The period of the Romantic Ballet was one of rapid technical development, and this was most particularly evident in the exploitation of the *pointe*, which had been introduced in its rudimentary form about a quarter of a century earlier. Such was the technical progress made within quite recent memory that the *Morning Post*, writing in 1843 of Plunkett and Camille, neither of whom were dancers of the first class, could remark that they were nevertheless greatly superior in taste, style, and execution to Fortunata Angiolini, who had danced in London from 1809 to 1814, and Maria Mercandotti, the favourite of the early twenties.[2] This technical progress was maintained throughout the century. In 1872, Marie Taglioni, then an old lady, was sitting in a box at Covent Garden watching Henriette Dor dance in *Babil and Bijou* when she turned to her companion and remarked, 'We could not dance like that in my day'.[3]

Fuoco made her first appearance in London on 16th November 1846, in *The Wags of Wapping*, which, as *Betty*, had been created at the Paris Opéra four months before. She was then a slight but well proportioned girl of sixteen, not strictly beautiful, although very attractive when a smile lit up her features. As an actress she was not remarkable; but her technique as a dancer was prodigious. 'The salient points of her execution', wrote the *Musical World*, 'are the pirouette and the *pointe*, which she achieves with greater facility and with greater variety of position than perhaps any dancer extant. At any rate she equals Elssler in the pirouette and Carlotta in the *pointe*, and perhaps her fault is that she makes too frequent a display of her mastery of both these essentials.'[4] 'She glides, revolves, and poises herself on tiptoe with as much ease as ordinary mortals walk on the soles of their feet, and she accomplishes these feats with surpassing grace,' added the *Morning Post*.[5] Her *grand pas de deux* with Eugène Huguet was, as several critics remarked, performed from beginning to end on the *pointes*, and the neatness and precision of her 'short incidental revolutions under the upraised hand of her partner (movements in which Cerrito is so superbly dexterous)'[6] drew thunders of applause night after night.

Not long after Fuoco had returned to Paris, Carlo Blasis, the great teacher from Milan, arrived in London with his young pupil, Marietta Baderna. As a dancer he had appeared at the King's Theatre during the 1827 season, and had made no great impression. Now, on his second visit to London in February and March 1847, he displayed his talent for choreography, producing two new ballets, *The Pretty Sicilian* and *Spanish Gallantries,* and for Bunn's benefit the *divertissement La Pléiade de Terpsichore.* The choreographer's father had collaborated in the two ballets as composer of part of the score of the former and the whole of the score of the latter, but his music failed to earn the same measure of praise as was given to his son's work.

The choreography of Carlo Blasis was judged to be very pleasing, the groups being picturesque and the dances 'well composed, novel, and graceful'.[7] Though neither of his ballets was remarkable for its plot—*The Pretty Sicilian* possessed very little, and *Spanish Gallantries* erred rather to the opposite extreme—their action was well sprinkled with dances, and in the latter ballet Blasis displayed his knowledge of the Spanish dance by arranging a *Minuet à Fandango, Seguidillas Manchegas,* and a *Nouvelle Cachucha.* Both these ballets contained a male rôle played in travesty. From the indications of the London critics it would appear that Blasis was more successful in arranging dances than in producing dramatic action.

His principal claim to fame, however, is as a teacher, and it was just that he should be judged also by the performance of Marietta Baderna. At the time of her appearance in London she was still very young. She was small, pretty, and wore her hair 'in that most trying of all fashions—the Chinese'. There was nothing very astonishing about her style. There were moments indeed when she seemed to be lacking in strength, and her attitudes, though 'struck readily', were not always held with firmness. None the less, her movements were generally neat and finished, she had 'an admirable *pointe*', and she was always 'most graceful, especially in the position of that most difficult portion of the human frame divine—her arms'.[8]

Though it would be misleading to class him with Benjamin Lumley, the part played by Alfred Bunn in the development of the Romantic Ballet in London was one of some importance. While he did not nurture a choreographic genius of the stature of Perrot, he presented a succession of great foreign ballerinas, some of whom were seen in England for the first time under his aegis, and imported a number of the most recent productions from the Paris Opéra. To quote only two instances, *La Péri* and *Le Diable à quatre* were both given their first London performances on the stage of Drury Lane during his management. He was a great showman—indeed, one of the first of his kind—and aimed at giving the public what it wanted. Yet out of his managerial ventures he made very little profit for himself. He died, a convert to the Catholic faith, in the last days of 1860 at Boulogne-sur-mer, the haven of many an impoverished or bankrupt exile from England.

NOTES TO CHAPTER 20

[1] *The Times*, 2nd October 1844.

[2] *Morning Post*, 30th March 1843.

[3] Information kindly supplied by Mr P. J. S. Richardson, who was told the story by Mme Léon Espinosa, the person to whom the remark was made.

[4] *Musical World*, 21st November 1846.

[5] *Morning Post*, 17th November 1846.

[6] *Morning Herald*, 17th November 1846.

[7] *Morning Post*, 5th March 1847.

[8] *Morning Post* and *Morning Herald*, 6th February 1847; *Era*, 7th February 1847.

21

Some English Dancers

ENGLISH DANCERS played a modest part in the development of the Romantic Ballet in their own country, effacing themselves—not by choice, but as a result of the fashionable vogue for the foreign ballerina—either in the *corps de ballet* of the more important theatres or in the companies on the lesser stages. Few emerged from the anonymity of the *corps de ballet* at the Opera House, those that did merely doing so momentarily, to return almost immediately afterwards to the herd whence they had come. It was often only when they appeared out of season at one of the other theatres that the public were able to put a name to them: as when, in the autumn of 1827, Hullin staged Didelot's *Flore et Zéphire* at the Adelphi with Miss Davis as Flore, and a number of other English dancers, who were named as 'of the King's Theatre'. Of the few English names on the Opera House bills in the time of the Romantic Ballet, the most frequently met was that of Adelaide O'Bryan, who was a member of the company for a number of seasons between 1823 and 1843. Another Englishwoman who was featured was Caroline Forster, but she was a *sujet* of the Paris Opéra and so possessed that all-important foreign allure. In the list of the 1852 company figured a Mlle Lydia, a talented young English dancer who had graduated from Émile Petit's class, and was to become known in later years as Lydia Thompson, but who, on this first rung of her career—she was only fourteen years old at the time—had probably been advised that it was necessary to conceal her very ordinary-sounding surname.

The lot of the English male dancer was no better. The days when Slingsby could rival the younger Vestris were long past. Nevertheless, an occasional Englishman still attracted notice. In the decade before Ebers injected a strong stream of French talent into the Opera House ballet, the name of Oscar Byrne often appeared on the bills. The son of the great Harlequin and ballet-master, James Byrne, Oscar Byrne was brought up in the atmosphere of the theatre from his earliest childhood. He had already obtained some stage experience when in 1809 he made his début at the King's Theatre, where he remained a not very important member of the company intermittently until 1820. His ambition was high enough to make him try his luck at the Paris Opéra, but his début there in 1816 was not successful. After leaving the

King's Theatre he became First Dancer at Drury Lane, and later devoted himself to choreography, being ballet-master at a number of London theatres, notably the Olympic, Covent Garden, the Princess's under the management of Charles Kean, and finally Drury Lane again. He died in 1867 at the age of seventy-three.

Ellen Terry was a child in the Princess's company when Oscar Byrne was ballet-master, and acknowledged the debt she owed to his teaching. He had a theory that 'an actress was no actress unless she learned to dance early', and used to teach his pupils the minuet, and drill them by making them walk along long planks at increasingly greater speeds without deviating from the straight line. 'I can hear the dear old man shouting at us as if it were yesterday,' Ellen Terry wrote in her autobiography, 'and I have learned to see of what value all his drilling was, not only to deportment, but to clear utterance. It would not be a bad thing if there were more "old fops" like Oscar Byrne in the theatres of to-day.'[1]

During the *apogée* of the Romantic Ballet in England, when Lumley was directing the affairs of Her Majesty's, two men of British origin were engaged there as principal dancers, but both took the wise precaution of disguising the unfortunate fact of their birth. These were James Silvain and Monsieur Charles.

James Silvain had danced at the King's Theatre under his real name of Sullivan in 1824 and 1826. He then went to Paris where he eventually obtained an engagement at the Opéra from 1831 to 1833, having adopted the more elegant name of Silvain. In the thirties he obtained three London engagements—at Drury Lane in 1833, at Covent Garden in 1834, and at the St James's in 1839—but it was not until 1843 that he reappeared at the Opera House. He had then recently returned from accompanying Fanny Elssler during her fabulous tour of America, and became for the season her regular partner, playing Albert to her Giselle. His dancing, wrote *The Times*, evinced 'much strength and excellent taste'.[2] In later years Bunn engaged him twice at Drury Lane: in 1844, to partner Grahn in *Lady Henrietta*; and in 1846, to stage, and partner Carlotta Grisi in, *Paquita*. He danced at Covent Garden in 1848, and again appeared at Her Majesty's in 1851. He died in Paris on 12th April 1856.

Monsieur Charles belonged to a younger generation. He made his first appearance at Her Majesty's in 1848, and was one of the principal male dancers there almost to the end of Lumley's management. He danced with Carlotta Grisi in *Les Cosmopolites*, the *divertissement* staged to commemorate the Great Exhibition of 1851, and also partnered Rosati and Ferraris, played Albert to the Giselle of Carlotta Grisi in 1850, and James to the Sylphide of the younger Marie Taglioni in 1851. 'It has lately been unfashionable to applaud male dancers,' wrote *The Times* in 1856, 'but M. Charles, who combines the Alcides with the Hermes, seems likely to change this order of things, if we are to judge from the hearty approbation he obtained last night.'[3] Despite this public favour, however, Charles was a plain Englishman, his real name being Charles Edward Stacey, as became known in 1850 when the *Era* reported a public-house brawl in which he was outfought by a powerful Irishwoman and received 'a frightful blow on his mouth, which split his lip and made it bleed for some time'.[4] (Plate XXII.)

It was at the Opera House that the public first appreciated the talent of another excellent English dancer, George Gilbert, whose career, however, was mainly spent on other stages. He was the Zéphire in the Adelphi production of *Flore et Zéphire* in 1827, being announced as from the King's Theatre, where he had appeared as Monsieur George the season before. In 1833 he joined Bunn's troupe at Drury Lane, playing the rôle of Gannelor in *The Sleeping Beauty*, and dancing a *pas de deux* with a young English girl called Ballin. 'The improvement which Gilbert has made is extraordinary,' commented the *Morning Post*, 'and whether it was a feeling of rivalry which induced him to put forth all his strength on the occasion, we know not, but certain it is he has proved himself superior to all the male dancers with whom he was associated. His vaulting exceeded anything of the kind we have witnessed; and, if his pirouetting was less rapid than that of others, in gracefulness he was not exceeded.'[5]

Eliza Ballin became his regular partner on the stage, and also in the home. Indeed, their careers ran parallel to one another almost from the beginning. She probably began, like him, in the *corps de ballet* of the Opera House, though her name did not appear on a bill until 1828 when she was dancing at Drury Lane. Slowly her merits were recognized. When Gilbert became ballet-master at Drury Lane in 1836 she began to assume important rôles. Early in 1837 she took over the part of Florinda in *The Devil on Two Sticks*, and in November of the same year she played Fleur des Champs in her husband's production of *The Daughter of the Danube*. Between 1840 and 1842 they were dancing at Covent Garden, where Oscar Byrne was ballet-master.

After a brief engagement at the Lyceum in 1842, during which Gilbert produced *La Sylphide*, they joined the company at the newly built theatre in Oxford Street, the Princess's, where they remained from 1843 until 1846. These years mark the culmination of their careers. Assisted by Mme Védy, who arranged the dances, Gilbert produced a number of ballets: *Giselle* (1843), *Leola* (1844), *La Fête des pêcheurs* (1845), *The Spirit of the Air* (1846). At the end of their engagement at the Princess's Gilbert retired, but Miss Ballin reappeared in 1850 and 1851 to play the mime rôle of Fenella in *Masaniello* at the Royal Italian Opera, Covent Garden. Hers was a competent and creditable performance, though not, it was universally admitted, of the same order as that of the great Italian mime, Paolina Monti, whom Lumley engaged in 1851. Of the later life of George Gilbert and his wife nothing is recorded, unless the dancing mistress, Eliza Ann Monk, professionally known as Mrs Eliza Gilbert, who died in the Waterloo Road in her sixty-sixth year in January 1873, and was buried in the Brompton cemetery, was the former Miss Ballin.

There was no lack of talented English dancers to appear at the secondary theatres, or even to appear as principals on one or other of the important stages when there were no foreign luminaries to hand. Christmas was the season when they came into their own, and the story of most of them belongs perhaps more to the history of pantomime than to that of ballet. Tom Matthews, George Wieland, Dicky Flexmore, W. H. Payne, and many other Clowns and Harlequins of the period were all trained as dancers, and possessed two qualities in particular which set them apart from their foreign counterparts. They were experienced comedians, and their dancing was often grotesquely and brilliantly acrobatic. Among the women, Rosina Wright—'our clever English Taglioni', as the *Era* called her [6]—was a great favourite in the fifties; and other popular artistes were Caroline Barnett, Clara Gibson, Carlotta Leclercq, Caroline Parkes, Fanny Wright, Annie and Therese Cushnie (the latter became the wife of the ballet-master, John Milano, and died in 1857), Louise Blanche, Eliza Gates, and Rose Edouin.

If it could be said that there was then an English school of ballet, it was a very minor one, and certainly almost negligible historically.[7] Ballet, as it was seen in London during the Romantic period, was primarily a foreign importation, and what efforts were made by native artistes were little more than a pale reflection of the glories to be seen at the Opera House. Whether Clara Webster, had she not met with her accident, would have broken through the prejudice that certainly existed in favour of the foreigner, and paved the way for others of her compatriots to follow her, must remain a subject for conjecture. But to oust the foreign dancer from her pedestal of supremacy was a most formidable task, and one which could perhaps only have been accomplished by a carefully and imaginatively planned programme extending over a period of many years, a programme aimed at creating an English branch of the Academic French school, fostering not only dancers but teachers and choreographers as well. It was a task for an impresario, an organizer, a man of vision, and that Lumley himself apparently never considered it is an indication that conditions were not at that time propitious for such an undertaking to succeed.

A century later, the fashionable preference for foreign dancers would be passing, public sympathy for native artistes would be growing, and state assistance in supporting a National Opera House, together with a resident ballet company, would be somewhat belatedly granted; the enterprise, impossible to accomplish in Lumley's day for lack of these very factors, would then be accomplished at last, and a National Ballet worthy of its name established.

NOTES TO CHAPTER 21

[1] Ellen Terry, *The Story of my Life* (London, 1908).
[2] *The Times*, 13th March 1843.
[3] *The Times*, 16th June 1856.
[4] *Era*, 12th May 1850. 'Knight's' was the Feathers, No. 50 Hart Street, Covent Garden. Hart Street has since been renamed Floral Street.
[5] *Morning Post*, 14th February 1833.
[6] *Era*, 20th July 1856.
[7] More details about English dancers of the Romantic Ballet will be found in George Chaffee's *The Romantic Ballet in London* (*Dance Index*, Sept.–Dec. 1943).

22

The End of an Era

THE HIGH NOON of the Romantic Ballet in England coincided with the years when Perrot was ballet-master at Her Majesty's. With his departure, the light began to fade, and to fade so rapidly that before a dozen years had elapsed the Romantic Ballet was little more than a memory: a great era in the history of ballet was ended.

Perrot's successor, Paul Taglioni, younger brother of the famous ballerina, was a choreographer of outstanding qualities, but he was unfortunate to lack those advantages which had assisted Perrot in his first years at Her Majesty's. Perrot had arrived in London when the popularity of ballet was at its height, and with Lumley's backing had been able to stage his works on the grandest scale; advancing from triumph to triumph, he had gathered inspiration on the way from the warm enthusiasm of a public not yet grown tired of the art that he served. He also had the inestimable benefit of being able to shape his ballets and *divertissements* to the measure of Taglioni, of Cerrito and Carlotta Grisi in the full vigour and freshness of their youth, of Fanny Elssler and Lucile Grahn. Paul Taglioni had to be content with working on a smaller scale, and with a somewhat less brilliant palette.

In his ballets, the qualities of the dancer were brought into play much more than those of the mime. There were no great dramatic rôles of the order of Giselle and Esmeralda. For this, the choreographer could not be reproached, for he was only taking account of the growing public distaste for the ballet-pantomime that began to make itself felt in the late eighteen-forties.

Paul Taglioni's most ambitious production at Her Majesty's, and indeed the only work which he staged there that could truly be termed a grand ballet, was his first, *Coralia* (1847), a faithful transcription of La Motte-Fouqué's romance of *Undine*, which introduced to London both Carolina Rosati, one of the most expressive *danseuses-mimes* of her time, who played the principal rôle, and the choreographer's daughter, the younger Marie Taglioni. Skilfully arranged and lavishly produced, with a culminating transformation scene showing a garden dissolving into a scene beneath the waters, *Coralia* met with a triumphant reception which, Lumley thought, 'seemed to have restored for a time the ancient prestige of the lately-discredited ballet-pantomime'.[1]

Most significantly, however, Paul Taglioni's next work, *Théa* (1847), pleased the public still more. One of the merits of this 'little gem', as *The Times* described it, was its economy of plot, which served merely to lead to the *divertissement* of animated flowers; in this, Rosati established her reputation in London with a wonderful *variation*, containing a brilliant passage of *batterie*, which earned her a double encore. *Théa*'s success set the model for its choreographer's future work at Her Majesty's. The elaborate ballet-pantomime developing a strong theme and affording the ballerina the opportunity for a profound character study was now clearly out of favour. 'Let a simple new thought be caught up,' advised *The Times* at the end of the 1847 season, with the scene of the animated flowers in *Théa* in mind, 'let it be adorned with picturesque effect, and illustrated by the highest choreographic art, and the spectators will be more pleased than by an intricate plot in dumb-show, overlaid by processions.' [2]

Whether consciously or not, Paul Taglioni took heed of this advice and in future years drastically reduced the amount of plot in his ballets. Thus, with the exception of *Coralia*, all those that he produced in London were minor works. *Fiorita* (1848) was only very lightly burdened with a plot, just sufficient to justify the inclusion of national dances and the introduction of ethereal beings in a scene which was slightly reminiscent of the second act of *Giselle*. A somewhat similar contrast was achieved in *Electra* (1849), which contained Norwegian peasant dances and *pas* of a more classical nature danced by the personified stars, the most brilliant of which was played by Carlotta Grisi.[3] Even *La Prima Ballerina* (1849), based on a supposed adventure of Taglioni's when she was kidnapped by brigands and allowed to proceed on her way only after paying the ransom demanded of a few dances, was a *divertissement* built around an anecdote rather than a ballet. Creation of atmosphere was the keynote of *L'Île des amours* (1851), which *The Times* described as 'a bold, novel and successful attempt to found a ballet on an entirely new principle—the reproduction of a certain school of painting', that of Watteau.[4] (Plate XXIVb.)

From such works as these to the pure *divertissement*, unencumbered by plot, was a short step. One of Paul Taglioni's most popular works was *Les Plaisirs de l'hiver* (1849), in which, as *The Times* observed with obvious pleasure, 'story there is none, not even so much as to attempt to represent a little flirtation'.[5] Its highlights were the skating scene by the *corps de ballet*, in which roller skates were used and occasional falls introduced to provoke amusement, and the *pas*, *La Hussarde*, which was danced by Carolina Rosati and the choreographer;[6] and it ended with 'a fall of snow and a general pelting with snowballs'.[5]

It was not difficult to see that Paul Taglioni was a master at producing *divertissements*, and the simultaneous presence of Carlotta Grisi, the younger Marie Taglioni, and a new star, Amalia Ferraris—'a *ballerina di forza*', as Lumley described her, 'remarkable for her grace and rapidity of execution'[1]

—was the excuse for a grand *divertissement, Les Grâces* (1850), similar in conception to those works that Perrot had produced some years before. In the *variations*, Paul Taglioni succeeded, as Perrot had done, in bringing out the qualities of each ballerina's style: the 'vigorous broad bounds' of the younger Taglioni, the remarkable *équilibre* of Ferraris in 'sudden pauses on the point', and the poetry that Carlotta gave to her every movement. The *divertissement* was received with the greatest enthusiasm, and one critic dared the opinion that 'in grace and groupings' it even surpassed the *Pas de Quatre*.[7] But, alas! it was but a last brilliant flicker of a flame that was already dying. (Plate XXIII.)

The glory of the Romantic Ballet was very much a matter of personalities: of Perrot, the master-choreographer, and that wonderful pleiad of ballerinas —Marie Taglioni, Fanny Elssler, Fanny Cerrito, and Carlotta Grisi, whom Providence chose to allot all to the same generation. In doing so, Providence was perhaps too prodigal, and neglected to provide for the inevitable coming of their retirement. For though the spark of their genius may have seemed divine, their frames were only human. Marie Taglioni danced no more after 1847; the same year marked Fanny Elssler's last visit to London; soon afterwards, becoming star of the Paris Opéra, Cerrito was only seldom able to cross the Channel; and in 1851 Carlotta Grisi appeared to a London audience for the last time. Farewells are always sad events, but the farewells of these great ballerinas were doubly so, for they passed at once into legend, like the giants they were, leaving only artistes of common stature to take their place.

Two of Carlotta Grisi's last creations in London were in Paul Taglioni's *Les Métamorphoses* (Plate XXIVa) and in Halévy's opera, *La Tempesta* (1850), in which, as Ariel, a mime rôle, she made a perfect foil for the massive, uncouth Caliban of Lablache, the celebrated bass. A glimpse of her personal magic, which enthralled all who saw her, can be gleaned from the *Morning Post*'s appreciation of her performance in this work:

'The divine Carlotta . . . moved upon the stage, a thing of light and beauty. . . . In Ariel [she] has carried pantomimic art to its highest perfection; and this admitted, can we say too much in honour of the consummate artiste? Is she not a living embodiment of the most exquisite beauties of form which the mind can conceive? Is not hers the spirit which must animate a Phidias or a Raphael? To their conceptions they can give an enduring form, while hers are transient. But is she for this reason to be less prized, or the claims of her art to a high poetical influence to be denied? Observe the wonderful intelligence of her gestures, the purpose and meaning of her every movement, the eloquent limbs, the speaking eye! Her whole body talks to you! She is all truth, all nature; but nature expressed in such exquisite forms as only ideal loveliness could suggest.

'We have spoken of Phidias and Raphael, but we doubt that even such artists as those could produce in a whole life as many and as various forms of beauty as the fair Carlotta gives to the world in one hour. After what we have already said, it will be needless to dwell upon the perfect delicacy and womanhood of her performance, even in the wildest moments of her enthusiasm. These qualities will be understood; for the slightest approach to coarseness would break the charm, degrade a great and poetical artiste to a mere vulgar jumper, and falsify the praise we have bestowed.' [8]

The history of the ballet in the last years of Lumley's management is a story of his vain struggle to restore it to its one-time popularity. By importing the latest grand ballets from the Paris Opéra—*Le Corsaire* (1856) and *Marco Spada* (1857)—and reviving *La Esmeralda* with Pochini in 1857, he hoped to revive interest in the elaborate ballet-pantomime, but not even the dramatic Rosati could alter the trend of public opinion. Only a dozen years had passed since the vogue for grand ballet had reached its peak, and yet in 1856 *The Times* felt it necessary to preface its notice of *Le Corsaire* with an apologia for the ballet-pantomime, as though it were a form of art resuscitated from the distant past.

'To many of the younger patrons of operatic entertainment', it was explained, 'a grand ballet, on the old scale of magnificence, will seem a phenomenon of a completely novel kind. Some years ago the London season would not have been treated with customary respect if it had been allowed to pass away without the production of a stately Terpsichorean spectacle— a combination of gorgeous scenery, picturesque costume, sparkling music, and, above all, transcendent dancing, that should draw all the world to look at it, and, when its glories had set, should leave all the world talking about it till some new marvel had expelled it from memory. Lately, however, there has been a great change in this respect; dancing has become a mere supplement to the vocal part of an operatic performance, and, under the compound name of *ballet-divertissement*, a slight sort of piece, with just enough plot to distinguish it from the *divertissement* properly so called, but utterly devoid of that concentration of varied effects that belongs to the *grand ballet*, has been allowed to supplant its more august predecessor.' [9]

Nevertheless, so long as Her Majesty's Theatre remained an opera house, so did ballet continue to hold a place, albeit increasingly more modest, in its programmes. After Lumley had retired at the end of the 1858 season, a number of well-known Italian ballet-masters tried their hands, but it was clear that the popularity of their art in London had waned almost to insignificance. The public showed little interest in the productions of Borri, Rota, and Diani. In 1867 the theatre was destroyed by fire, and when rebuilt, once again, though for a few years only, became the home of opera and, on a very minor scale, ballet.

The meteoric fall of the popularity of ballet in England so soon after a Golden Age was due partly to the lack of great artists, both choreographers and dancers, to succeed the giants of the preceding generation, and partly to the passing of a vogue. For the ballet had been accepted in London as a fashionable entertainment, and it happened that, as the stock of opera rose, so, like the other arm of a pair of scales, did that of ballet fall. Being, in London, only an imported entertainment, the management of Her Majesty's could, and did, drastically curtail the ballet, with the result that it could no longer adequately survive in the Opera House; an economy that was not so easy to bring about at the Opéra in Paris, which had its permanent, elaborately organized troupe, and where ballet therefore maintained much of its former importance, though suffering a rapid artistic decline.

Ballet never died out in London. Its centre merely shifted from the opera house to the music hall; and with this shift, there necessarily came a lowering of artistic standards, for the public that filled the Alhambra and later the Empire lacked the refinement of the *haut ton* that formed the greater part of the audiences at Her Majesty's. By the end of the century, a great change had taken place in the art of ballet. 'The new Terpsichore', wrote the author of an obituary notice of Carlotta Grisi in 1899, 'is a resolutely prosaic young woman, abounding in muscle, but devoid of charm. "High kicking" is her forte, and when she is not inviting applause by the height of her kicks, she is inducing *ennui* by the monotony of her attitudes. Her movement is an affair of leaps and bounds, and the rest of her performance is mere posturing "in her tracks". If she calls the skirt to her aid, the beauty which evokes our admiration is in the waving folds of the garment, and not, as of old, in the gliding movements of the wearer. The sylph, the fay, the creature of air and fire, who floated light as thistledown across a stage, which no more felt her weight than the springing corn felt the footsteps of Camilla, has vanished like the dream she seemed. She has vanished, and left behind her nothing but a topic for the reminiscences of the old, and a challenge to the incredulity of the young.' [10] The tradition thus was lost and the vital chain snapped, so that when eventually a National Ballet was formed in Britain, it was to the Russian Ballet that it turned for its foundations. The Golden Age of the Romantic Ballet in London, except for what had been transmitted by way of Russia, had long before passed into legend.

NOTES TO CHAPTER 22

[1] Benjamin Lumley, *Reminiscences of the Opera* (London, 1864).

[2] *The Times*, 4th August 1847.

[3] It was in the final scene of this ballet that electric light was used for the first time in a ballet, though not for the first time in a theatre. That distinction belonged to the Paris Opéra, the first performance there of Meyerbeer's opera *Le Prophète,* in which electric light was used to simulate a rising sun, preceding by one day that of *Electra* at Her Majesty's.

[4] *The Times*, 24th March 1851.

[5] *The Times*, 6th July 1849.

[6] The music title by Brandard to Jullien's waltzes from *Le Prophète* probably depicts Paul Taglioni (certainly not Charles, as has been hitherto assumed) and Rosati in this dance, which occurred in the second scene of the *divertissement*. Rosati and Charles danced a *pas de deux* in the first scene, in which a Polish marriage is celebrated in a Winter Garden.

[7] *The Times*, 3rd May 1850; *Era*, 5th May 1850.

[8] *Morning Post*, 10th June 1850.

[9] *The Times*, 9th July 1856.

[10] *Daily Telegraph*, 24th May 1899.

Appendices

Appendix A

BALLET-MASTERS AT THE KING'S (LATER HER MAJESTY'S) THEATRE,
1770–1881

Year	Ballet-Master	Year	Ballet-Master
1770–1	Galeotti	1826–7	J. d'Egville
1772	Lépy	1828	Anatole
1773	D'Auvigne	1829	Deshayes
1774	Pitrot	1830	Deshayes / Léon
1775	Lany		
1776	Bouqueton	1831	Deshayes
1777	Simonet / Vallouy	1832	Albert
		1833	Deshayes
1778–9	Simonet	1834	F. Taglioni
1780	Favre-Guiardel	1835–8	Deshayes
1781	Simonet	1839	Guerra
1782	Noverre	1840	Barrez / Guerra / F. Taglioni
1783	Le Picq		
1784	Dauberval		
1785	Le Picq	1841	Guerra / F. Taglioni
1786	P. d'Egville / Giroux	1842	Deshayes
1787	Hus	1843–6	Perrot
1788–9	Noverre	1847–8	P. Taglioni / Perrot
1791	G. Vestris		
1793–4	Noverre	1849–51	P. Taglioni
1795–6	Onorati	1852	Cortesi
1797–8	Gallet	1856	P. Taglioni
1799–1802	J. d'Egville	1857	P. Taglioni / Ronzani / Massot
1803	Gallet		
1804–5	J. d'Egville		
1806–7	Rossi	1858	Massot
1808–9	J. d'Egville	1860	Borri
1810–11	Rossi	1862	Petit
1812–14	Didelot	1863	Diani / Rota / Borri
1815–16	Armand Vestris		
1817	Léon		
1818	Favier	1864	Petit / Magri
1819	Guillet		
1820	Hullin	1865	Diani
1821	Deshayes	1866	Petit
1822	Anatole	1867	Lauri
1823–5	Aumer	1877–81	K. Lanner

147

Appendix B

BALLETS GIVEN AT THE KING'S (LATER HER MAJESTY'S) THEATRE,
1772–1881

Date	Title of Ballet	Choreographer	Composer	Revivals
10 3 1772	Admete and Alceste	Noverre (1789)	Mazzinghi	1789
12 5 1772	Le Triomphe de la magie			1776
14 5 1772	Le Jaloux sans un rival			
11 6 1772	La Clochette			
2 2 1773	L'Île déserte	D'Auvigne		
1 4 1773	La Fête du village			
1 4 1773	Les Sauvages			
6 5 1773	Les Tartares			
20 11 1773	La Bagatelle			
30 11 1773	Orfeo e Euridice			
29 1 1774	The Adventures of the Harem of Ispahan			
19 4 1774	The Tempest			
5 5 1774	L'Embarras du choix			
12 5 1774	La Bouquetière du village			
12 5 1774	Les Faunes vainques			
8 11 1774	Pirhame et Thisbée			
8 11 1774	Le Ballet des fleurs			
3 12 1774	Silvie			
17 12 1774	Le Bal masqué			
7 2 1775	La Fête de Flora			
7 2 1775	Les Méxicains			
23 3 1775	La Mascherata			
25 5 1775	Oreste et Electre	Vallouy		
31 10 1775	Apollon et Daphne			
31 10 1775	Le Triomphe d'Euthime sur le génie de Libas			
31 10 1775	Pigmalion amoureux de la statue			
16 11 1775	Il Filosofo amoroso			
9 1 1776	Les Événemens imprévues			
9 1 1776	La Générosité de Scipion			
3 2 1776	Les Deux sœurs rivales	Bouqueton		
24 2 1776	La Fête du village	Bouqueton		
12 3 1776	Diane et Endymion			
12 3 1776	Astolphe dans l'île d'Alcine			
19 3 1776	Le Retour des matelots			
25 4 1776	Les Moissonneurs distraits			
2 11 1776	Les Amants heureux			

Date	Title of Ballet	Choreo-grapher	Composer	Revivals
2 11 1776	Les Amusements champêtres			
12 11 1776	Les Chasseurs			
7 12 1776	La Force de l'Amour	Zucchelli		
21 1 1777	L'Épouse persane			
15 3 1777	La Clochette			1778
8 5 1777	Le Culte d'amour	Vallouy		
20 5 1777	La Paysanne distraite			
4 11 1777	Le Devin du village			
4 11 1777	La Polonaise favorite			
16 12 1777	Les Bohémiens	Banti		
24 2 1778	La Sérénade interrompue	Simonet	Noseri	1779, 80
31 3 1778	La Surprise de Daphnis et Céphise	Simonet, Banti		
4 4 1778	Les Amants unis par l'Hymen			
19 5 1778	L'Amour en vendange			
24 11 1778	Annette et Lubin	Noverre (1789)	Federici (1789)	1789
24 11 1778	La Noce hollandaise			
24 11 1778	Les Nymphes de Diane	Simonet		1781
22 12 1778	Les Moissonneurs		Paisiello	
23 1 1779	Les Oiseleurs			
23 3 1779	Hippomene e Atalante			
23 3 1779	La Fête du ciel			
15 4 1779	La Bravoure des femmes	Simonet		1780
15 5 1779	Les Paysans volés			
14 12 1779	Il Desertore			
22 1 1780	La Bergère coquette			
22 4 1780	The Rural Sports	Favre-Guiardel; Simonet (1781)		1781
22 4 1780	La Fête pastorale	Favre-Guiardel		
9 5 1780	Il Filosofo	Zucchelli		
25 11 1780	The Fortunate Escape	Simonet		
25 11 1780	The Country Gallant	Simonet		
2 12 1780	The Squire Outwitted	Zucchelli		
16 12 1780	Les Amants surpris	Simonet		1786
13 1 1781	The Pert Country-maid	Simonet		
22 2 1781	The Country Diversions	Simonet		
22 2 1781	Ninette à la cour	G. Vestris, after M. Gardel; Rossi (1806)	Martini (1806)	1786, 89, 91, 1806
29 3 1781	Les Caprices de Galathée	G. Vestris, after Noverre; Noverre (1789)		1789

Date	Title of Ballet	Choreo-grapher	Composer	Revivals
29 3 1781	Médée et Jason	G. Vestris, after Noverre; Noverre (1782)	Noseri, Gluck	1782
17 11 1781	Les Amants réunis	Noverre		
11 12 1781	Les Petits Riens	Noverre	Barthélemon	
10 1 1782	Le Triomphe de l'amour conjugal	Noverre		
23 2 1782	Rinaldo and Armida	Noverre	Le Brun	
19 3 1782	La Rosière de Salency	Noverre		
11 4 1782	Adela of Ponthieu	Noverre	Le Brun	1788
2 5 1782	Apollon et les Muses	Noverre	Noverre, Le Brun	
9 5 1782	Mirsa	M. & P. Gardel		
6 6 1782	Apelles et Campaspe	Noverre		1783
2 11 1782	La Bergère constante	Simonet		
12 12 1782	Il Ratto delle Sabine	Le Picq	Vincentio	
11 1 1783	Le Tuteur trompé	Le Picq	Martini	1784, 85, 89
15 2 1783	Les Épouses persanes	Le Picq		
13 3 1783	Il Riposo del campo	Le Picq		
13 3 1783	La Bégueule	Le Picq	Borghi	
10 4 1783	The Amours of Alexander and Roxane	Le Picq	Barthélemon	
1 5 1783	Le Déjeuner espagnol	Simonet		
1 5 1783	Les Ruses de l'amour	after Noverre		
8 5 1783	La Dame bienfaisante	Le Picq	Floquet	
6 12 1783	The Pastimes of Terpsichore	Dauberval	Barthélemon	
9 12 1783	Friendship leads to Love	Dauberval		
3 2 1784	Le Réveil du bonheur	Dauberval	Barthélemon	
26 2 1784	Le Coq du village	Dauberval		
6 3 1784	Orpheo	Dauberval	Barthélemon	
11 3 1784	Le Magnifique	Dauberval		
25 3 1784	Pygmalion	Dauberval	J. J. Rousseau	
13 5 1784	Le Déserteur	Dauberval		1785, 88, 98, 99, 1813
20 5 1784	Sémiramis	Le Picq		
18 12 1784	La Partie de chasse d'Henri IV	Le Picq		
12 2 1785	Il Convito degli dei	Le Picq	Barthélemon	
12 2 1785	Le Jugement de Pâris	Le Picq	Barthélemon	
3 3 1785	À la plus sage	after M. Gardel		
12 3 1785	Il Convitato di Pietra	Le Picq	Gluck	
17 3 1785	Macbeth	Le Picq	Locke, arr. Barthélemon	

Date	Title of Ballet	Choreographer	Composer	Revivals
7 4 1785	L'Amour soldat			
7 4 1785	Don Juan			
14 4 1785	Les Amours d'été	Le Picq		
14 4 1785	Robin Gray		Barthélemon	
18 2 1786	Acis and Galatea	Giroux		
23 3 1786	Le Premier Navigateur	Aug. Vestris, after M. Gardel		
1 4 1786	L'Amour jardinier	P. d'Egville		
27 4 1786	La Fête marine	P. d'Egville		
18 5 1786	Les Deux Solitaires	Giroux		
23 12 1786	La Chercheuse d'esprit			
6 1 1787	Le Berger inconstant			
20 1 1787	L'Heureux Événement	Hus		
17 2 1787	Zemira and Azor	Hus	Mazzinghi	
10 3 1787	La Fête provençale	Hus		
22 3 1787	La Jardinière			
22 3 1787	Sylvie	Hus		
17 5 1787	Le Cossac jaloux	Hus		
3 1 1788	Les Offrandes à l'Amour	Noverre		
12 1 1788	The Military Dance	Chevalier		
29 1 1788	L'Amour et Psiche	Noverre	Mazzinghi	1797
28 2 1788	Les Fêtes du Tempe	Noverre		
13 3 1788	Euthyme et Eucharis	Noverre		
22 5 1788	La Bonté du seigneur	Didelot		
22 5 1788	Richard Cœur-de-lion	Didelot		
10 1 1789	L'Embarquement pour Cythère			
31 1 1789	Les Fêtes provençales	Noverre		
3 3 1789	La Nymphe et le chasseur	Coinde		
17 3 1789	Les Jalousies du sérail	Noverre		
2 4 1791	Orpheus and Eurydice			
11 4 1791	La Mort d'Hercule	G. Vestris	Von Esch	
14 4 1791	La Fête des matelots et des provençaux			
5 5 1791	L'Amadriade	G. Vestris		
26 5 1791	Les Folies d'Espagne	Aug. Vestris		
2 6 1791	La Capricieuse	G. Vestris		
25 6 1791	La Fête du seigneur	G. Vestris		
26 1 1793	Les Époux du Tempe	Noverre		
26 2 1793	Venus and Adonis	Noverre		
6 4 1793	Le Faune infidèle	Noverre		
23 4 1793	Iphiginia in Aulide	Noverre	Miller	
1 6 1793	Le Jaloux puni			
11 1 1794	Adélaïde	Noverre	Miller	
1 3 1794	L'Union des bergers	Noverre	Miller	
1 4 1794	Les Ruses de l'Amour	Noverre	Miller	
31 5 1794	Le Bon Prince	J. d'Egville	Tomich	
6 12 1794	Giustino I	Onorati		
20 12 1794	L'Éspiègle Soubrette	Onorati		

Date			Title of Ballet	Choreo-grapher	Composer	Revivals
20	1	1795	L'Amant retrouvé	Onorati		
26	3	1795	Paul et Virginie	Onorati	Mazzinghi	1796, 1802, 05
20	2	1796	Les Trois Sultanes	Onorati	Mazzinghi	
1	3	1796	Le Bouquet	Onorati	Mazzinghi	
2	4	1796	Alonso e Cora	Onorati		
21	4	1796	Little Peggy's Love	Didelot	Bossi	1797, 98, 99, 1802, 12
21	4	1796	L'Amant statue	Onorati		
12	5	1796	La Villageoise enlevée			
2	6	1796	The Caravan at Rest	Didelot		
2	6	1796	L'Amour vengé	Didelot		
7	7	1796	Flore et Zéphire	Didelot	Bossi	1797
7	7	1796	L'Heureux Naufrage	Didelot	Bossi	
27	12	1796	Apollon berger	Gallet		1803
17	1	1797	Les Délassements militaires	Gallet	Mazzinghi	
7	2	1797	Pizarre	Gallet	Mazzinghi	
28	3	1797	L'Heureux Retour	Gallet	Bossi	
6	4	1797	Sappho et Phaon	Didelot	Mazzinghi	
25	4	1797	Le Trompeur trompé	Gallet	Bossi	
11	5	1797	Le Rendez-vous	Gallet		
25	5	1797	Le Triomphe de Cupidon	Barré		
15	6	1797	Acis et Galathée	Didelot	Bossi	
28	11	1797	L'Offrande à Terpsichore	Gallet	Bossi	
28	11	1797	Ariadne et Bacchus	Gallet	Bossi	1799, 1803
20	12	1797	Le Triomphe de Thémis	Gallet	Bossi	
2	1	1798	Le Chasse d'amour	Gallet		
6	2	1798	Constance et Alcidonis	Gallet	Bossi	
6	3	1798	Les Rivaux généreux	Gallet		
15	3	1798	Les Scythas	Gallet		
22	3	1798	La Vengeance de l'Amour	Gallet		
19	4	1798	Énée et Didon	Gallet		
10	5	1798	Élisa	Gallet	Mazzinghi	1799
15	12	1798	Le Marchand de Smyrne	Barré	Bossi	
29	1	1799	Les Deux Jumelles	Barré	Bossi	
19	2	1799	Diane et Endymion			
26	3	1799	Télémaque [1]	J. d'Egville, after Dauberval	Haydn, &c., arr. Bossi; Miller (1819)	1800, 01
18	4	1799	Hylas et Témire	J. d'Egville	Bossi	1800
18	4	1799	La Fille mal gardée [2]	J. d'Egville, after Dauberval		1800, 02, 15
2	5	1799	Tarare et Irza	J. d'Egville		
17	6	1799	La Double Épreuve	J. d'Egville		
11	1	1800	Les Jeux d'Eglé	J. d'Egville, after Dauberval	Bossi	
25	2	1800	Le Mariage méxicain	J. d'Egville	J. d'Egville	

Date	Title of Ballet	Choreo-grapher	Composer	Revivals
4 3 1800	Hyppomène et Atalante	J. d'Egville		1801
8 5 1800	Laura et Lenza	Didelot	Bossi	1801
29 5 1800	Renaldo e Leonora	J. d'Egville	Bossi	
5 6 1800	Jamie's Return	J. d'Egville		
3 1 1801	Pigmalion	J. d'Egville	Bossi	
17 2 1801	Barbara and Allen	J. d'Egville	J. d'Egville	1802
26 3 1801	Alonzo the Brave and the Fair Imogen	Didelot	Bossi, Federici	
25 4 1801	Des Quatre Nations	J. d'Egville		
14 5 1801	Le Pied de bœuf [3]	after Aug. Vestris		
14 5 1801	Ken-si and Tao	Didelot	Bossi	
27 5 1801	Heliska	J. d'Egville	Bossi	1802
29 12 1801	Amintas et Sylvie	J. d'Egville		
2 2 1802	Irza	J. d'Egville	Bossi	1804
20 2 1802	Le Jugement de Midas	J. d'Egville		
20 3 1802	La Coquette villageoise	J. d'Egville		
19 6 1802	Paphos assiégé pas les Scythes	J. d'Egville, after Dauberval	Bossi	
4 12 1802	La Fête de Vénus	Gallet		
4 12 1802	La Forêt enchantée	Gallet		
8 1 1803	La Foire de Batavia	Gallet		
15 2 1803	Laurette	Gallet	Smart	
26 4 1803	Vologese, King of the Parthenes	Gallet	Winter	
21 6 1803	Le Débarquement			
14 1 1804	Le Vœu téméraire	J. d'Egville		
31 1 1804	Achille et Déidamie	J. d'Egville	Winter	1805
24 5 1804	Le Jugement du berger Pâris	J. d'Egville, after P. Gardel		1805, 11
26 1 1805	**La Belle Laitière**	J. d'Egville	Steibelt	1808
2 3 1805	L'Offrande à l'Amour			
4 4 1805	Crazy Jane	J. d'Egville	J. d'Egville	
16 5 1805	Ossian	J. d'Egville	Fiorillo	
30 5 1805	Édouard III	J. d'Egville		
6 6 1805	La Fille sauvage	J. d'Egville	Mortellari	1806, 08
7 12 1805	Naval Victory and Triumph of Lord Nelson	Rossi	Woelfl	
21 12 1805	La Surprise de Diane	Rossi	Woelfl	
11 2 1806	Tamerlane et Bajazet	Rossi	Bishop	1807, 18
29 4 1806	Les Jardiniers	Rossi		
15 5 1806	La Dansomanie	Deshayes, after P. Gardel		1807, 16, 17, 18
15 5 1806	Armide et Renaud	Rossi		
24 6 1806	Narcisse et les Grâces	Rossi	Bishop	1807, 10
13 12 1806	L'Agréable Réunion	Rossi	Venua	
27 1 1807	Alzire	Rossi	Woelfl	

Date	Title of Ballet	Choreographer	Composer	Revivals
21 3 1807	Mirtil et Amarillis	Rossi		
14 4 1807	Le Siège de Troye	Rossi	Fiorillo	
7 5 1807	L'Enlèvement d'Adonis	Deshayes	Venua	
11 6 1807	Le Sérail	Rossi		
23 7 1807	Énée et Lavinie	Rossi		
2 1 1808	L'Offrande à Bacchus	J. d'Egville		
9 2 1808	L'Enlèvement de Déjanire	J. d'Egville	Venua	
20 2 1808	La Fête chinoise	J. d'Egville		1809
26 3 1808	Le Mariage secret	J. d'Egville	Fiorillo	1809, 11, 26
19 5 1808	Constance and Almazor	J. d'Egville	Venua	
9 6 1808	Émilie	J. d'Egville	**Venua**	
6 1 1809	Les Amours de Glauque et Circe	J. d'Egville	Venua	
14 2 1809	Don Qichotte	J. d'Egville	Venua	
14 3 1809	Les Jeux floraux	J. d'Egville	Venua	
27 4 1809	La Naissance de Flore	J. d'Egville	Puccita	
11 5 1809	Le Calife de Bagdad	Armand Vestris	Lanza	1815
15 6 1809	Mora's Harp	J. d'Egville	Bishop	
14 12 1809	Borea e Zeffiro	Rossi	Ferrari	
14 12 1809	Pietro il Grande	Rossi	Venua	
13 1 1810	Li Contadini Tirolesi		Venua	
13 2 1810	La Dama di spirito in Napoli	Rossi	Ferrari	
12 4 1810	Psiche	Deshayes, after P. Gardel	Venua	1817
17 5 1810	Anacréon	Arm. Vestris (?)		
31 5 1810	L'Épouse persane	Rossi		1811
22 12 1810	La Fête provençale		Venua	
12 2 1811	Le Point du jour	Rossi		
9 3 1811	Les Amants généreux	Rossi		
30 4 1811	Les Amours de Mars et Vénus	Favier		
16 5 1811	Figaro	Deshayes, after Duport	Venua	1816, 17
30 5 1811	Ildamor et Zuléma	Arm. Vestris	Gianella	
14 1 1812	Le Marchand d'esclaves		Venua	
14 1 1812	Zélis	Didelot	Venua	1813
8 2 1812	L'Épreuve	Didelot	Venua	1814
7 4 1812	Zéphyr inconstant, puni et fixé (Flore et Zéphire)	Didelot	Venua	1814, 15, 21, 30, 31, 33
30 4 1812	La Rosière	Arm. Vestris (?)	Venua	
4 6 1812	Le Bal champêtre		Venua	
4 6 1812	La Reine de Golconde	Didelot	Venua	
9 2 1813	Le Pâtre et l'Hamadriade	Didelot	Venua	

Date	Title of Ballet	Choreographer	Composer	Revivals
23 2 1813	Une Soirée d'été			
20 4 1813	La Chaumière hongroise	Didelot	Venua	
13 5 1813	Les Amants péruviens	Didelot		
27 5 1813	Katchell (Russian *divertissement*)	Didelot	Fiorillo	
27 5 1813	Rosalie et Dozinval	Didelot	Mortellari	
10 6 1813	Le Troubadour	Didelot	Venua	
12 4 1814	Thamaida et Alonzo	Didelot	Jouve	
12 4 1814	Aminte et Sylvie	Favier		
18 5 1814	Karl et Lisbeth	Didelot	Horn	
2 6 1814	Le Calife voleur	Arm. Vestris	arr. Jouve	
28 1 1815	Les Petits Braconniers	Arm. Vestris	Venua	1816, 17
21 2 1815	Le Prince troubadour	Arm. Vestris	Venua	1816, 17 18
29 4 1815	Mars et l'Amour	Arm. Vestris		1816
8 6 1815	L'Enfant prodigue	after P. Gardel		
13 6 1815	Endymion			1816
6 7 1815	Caesar's Triumph over the Gauls (ballet-cantata)	Arm. Vestris	Liverati	
20 7 1815	Le Grand Bazar de Caire			1816
27 2 1816	La Partie de chasse d'Henri IV	Léon	Méhul	1817
6 4 1816	Gonzalve de Cordoue	Arm. Vestris	Venua	
20 4 1816	L'Amour et le poison	Arm. Vestris	Liverati	
21 5 1816	Le Bal			
20 6 1816	Emmeline	Arm. Vestris		
11 1 1817	L'Amour vengé	Léon		
18 2 1817	L'Amour et la folie	Léon		
8 5 1817	Les Fêtes espagnoles			
17 5 1817	Zulica			
7 6 1817	Les Deux Âges			
1 7 1817	Les Déguisements amoureux	Léon	Klose	
10 1 1818	Aetius et Fulvie	Favier		
10 1 1818	Le Départ de Sancho Panza	Favier	Favier	
31 1 1818	Acis et Galathée	Favier		
17 2 1818	La Fête villageoise			
21 2 1818	Zéphir	Guillet, after Duport	Klose	1819
11 4 1818	La Fée Urgèle	Favier		
18 5 1818	La Fête campestre			
27 6 1818	La Veille villageoise			
2 7 1818	Apelles et Campaspe	Favier, after Noverre	Jouve	
26 1 1819	La Réunion villageoise			
6 2 1819	Paul et Virginie	Guillet, after P. Gardel	Kreutzer	1835
2 3 1819	Télémaque	Guillet after P. Gardel	Miller	1820

Date	Title of Ballet	Choreo-grapher	Composer	Revivals
20 3 1819	Le Marchand d'esclaves	Guillet, Baptiste	Cooke	1820
1 5 1819	Adolphe et Matilde	Guillet, after Duport		1820
18 5 1819	La Rose	Duport		1820
8 7 1819	Le Séducteur		Venua	
17 7 1819	Les Ingénus	Duport		
18 12 1819	Le Sultan généreux	Hullin		
19 2 1820	Panurge			
9 5 1820	La Noce chinoise			
6 6 1820	Céphale et Procris	Hullin		
8 7 1820	Le Plumet rouge	Hullin		
10 3 1821	Le Prix	Deshayes		
27 3 1821	Oenone et Pâris	Albert		1822, 31
10 4 1821	La Paysanne supposée	Deshayes	Venua	
4 5 1821	Nina	after Milon	Persuis	1822, 35
31 5 1821	Le Carnaval de Venise	after Milon		1822, 23, 30
31 5 1821	Finette et l'éveillé	Albert		
3 7 1821	La Foire de Smyrne	J. d'Egville	Sor	
21 7 1821	Alcide	Albert, Deshayes		
26 7 1821	Le Seigneur généreux	Deshayes	Sor	
12 1 1822	Pandore	Anatole	Schneitz-hoeffer	
16 2 1822	Les Pages du duc de Ven-dôme	Anatole, after Aumer	Gyrowetz	1823, 28, 40
26 3 1822	Cendrillon	Albert	Sor	
13 6 1822	Le Triomphe de l'Amour			
13 6 1822	Le Petit Chaperon rouge	Anatole	Venua	1823
14 1 1823	L'Offrande aux Grâces	Aumer		1824, 25
15 2 1823	La Noce du village	Aumer		1824, 25
8 3 1823	Alfred le Grand	Aumer	Gallenberg, Dugazon	1825
16 5 1823	Aline, reine de Golconde	Aumer	Blum	
5 6 1823	Justin et Lisette			
19 6 1823	Alphonse et Léonore			
24 1 1824	Honneur aux dames	Aumer		
24 1 1824	L'Adoration au soleil	Aumer		
9 3 1824	Le Songe d'Ossian	Aumer		
6 4 1824	La Fête hongroise	Aumer	Gyrowetz	
10 6 1824	Le Page inconstant	Aumer, after Dauberval	Mozart, Beethoven, Gyrowetz	1825, 27
1 7 1824	Jadis et aujourd'hui	Aumer	Gyrowetz	
12 3 1825	La Coquette soumise [4]	Aumer	Lacy	
16 4 1825	Cléopâtre, reine d'Égypte	Aumer	Kreutzer & others	
9 6 1825	Clari	Aumer, after Milon	Kreutzer	

Date	Title of Ballet	Choreographer	Composer	Revivals
7 1 1826	Justine	J. d'Egville	Bochsa	
21 1 1826	Le Temple de la concorde	J. d'Egville	Bochsa	
18 2 1826	Le Bal champêtre	J. d'Egville	Bochsa	
8 4 1826	La Naissance de Vénus	J. d'Egville	Bochsa	
30 12 1826	Les Noces de Tamar et de Rose Blanche	J. d'Egville		
6 3 1827	Le Siège de Cythère	J. d'Egville	Bochsa	
26 5 1827	Le Rose et le bouton	J. d'Egville	Steibelt, Musard	
12 1 1828	Hassan et le Calife	Anatole	Sor	
5 2 1828	Phyllis et Mélibée	Anatole	overture by Vogt	
26 2 1828	Le Sicilien	Anatole	Sor, Schneitzhoeffer	
15 7 1828	Diane et Endymion	Anatole	Wade	
31 1 1829	La Somnambule	Deshayes, after Aumer	Hérold	1830, 31, 32, 33, 35, 58
24 3 1829	Masaniello	Deshayes	Auber	1830, 31, 32, 33, 34, 38
16 6 1829	Les Déguisements imprévus	Deshayes	Bochsa	
6 3 1830	Guillaume Tell	Léon	Rossini, arr. Costa, Nadaud	1831
3 3 1831	Kenilworth	Deshayes	Costa	
3 5 1831	La Naïade			
26 5 1831	La Bayadère	Deshayes	Auber, arr. Musard	1833, 34, 35, 38, 39
4 2 1832	Une Heure à Naples	Albert	Costa	
31 3 1832	L'Anneau magique	Albert	Gallenberg	
24 4 1832	Daphnis et Céphise			
30 6 1832	Amynthe et l'Amour	Albert		
16 2 1833	Faust	Deshayes	Adam	
9 5 1833	Nathalie (*also given in a shorter version as* La Ressemblance) [5]	F. Taglioni	Gyrowetz, Carafa	1834, 38
1 6 1833	Ines de Castro	Cortesi	Rossini & others	
13 6 1833	La Sylphide [6]	F. Taglioni	Schneitzhoeffer	1834, 35, 36, 37, 38, 41, 45, 46, 47, 51, 52
11 7 1833	La Fée et le Chevalier	T. Elssler		
20 3 1834	Sire Huon	F. Taglioni	Costa	
10 5 1834	Armide	T. Elssler		
21 6 1834	La Chasse des nymphes	F. Taglioni		1835
3 7 1834	Le Pouvoir de la danse	F. Taglioni		
30 4 1835	Zéphir berger	Deshayes		1836

Date	Title of Ballet	Choreo-grapher	Composer	Revivals
29 6 1835	Mazila	F. Taglioni	Nadaud	
5 3 1836	Le Rossignol	Deshayes	Nadaud	
5 5 1836	Beniowsky	Deshayes	Bochsa	1837, 38
16 6 1836	L'Amour et la folie			
25 2 1837	Le Brigand de Terracina	Deshayes	Auber, Pilati	1838, 40
29 6 1837	Le Corsaire	Albert	Bochsa	
19 4 1838	Le Chalet	Deshayes	Adam, Pilati	
14 6 1838	Miranda	F. Taglioni		
12 7 1838	L'Amour vengé	Guerra		
9 8 1838	Le Diable boiteux [7]	after J. Coralli	Gide	
9 3 1839	Robert le Diable	Guerra	Meyerbeer, arr. Nadaud	
18 4 1839	Une Nuit de bal	Guerra	Auber	1840
6 6 1839	La Gitana	Guerra, after F. Taglioni		1840, 41, 42, 46
25 7 1839	La Gipsy	after Mazilier	Benoist, Thomas, Marliani	1840, 43
21 3 1840	La Tarentule	Barrez, after J. Coralli	Gide	1843
14 5 1840	Le Lac des fées	Guerra	Auber, Nadaud	1841, 42, 44
18 6 1840	L'Ombre	F. Taglioni	Maurer	
6 8 1840	Le Toréador	Guerra	Nadaud	
11 3 1841	Le Diable amoureux		Nadaud	
4 5 1841	La Fille de l'exilé	Guerra	Nadaud	
8 7 1841	Aglaé	F. Taglioni		
15 7 1841	Matilde	F. Taglioni	Mussi	
12 3 1842	Giselle	Deshayes, Perrot	Adam	1843, 44, 45, 47, 49, 50
28 4 1842	Le Pêcheur napolitain	Perrot		1845
30 4 1842	La Fête des nymphes	Deshayes		
30 4 1842	La Fiancée		Auber, Nadaud	
14 5 1842	L'Élève d'Amour	Cerrito		
23 6 1842	Alma	Deshayes, Perrot, Cerrito	Costa	1843, 44, 45, 46, 47, 48
14 7 1842	Une Soirée de carnaval			1843, 47
11 3 1843	L'Aurore	Perrot	Pugni	1846, 52, 57
6 4 1843	Un Bal sous Louis XIV	Perrot	Nadaud	1844, 45, 46
27 4 1843	Les Houris	Perrot		
22 6 1843	Ondine	Perrot, Cerrito	Pugni	1844, 45 46, 47, 48, 51
3 8 1843	Le Délire d'un peintre	Perrot		1844, 46

Date	Title of Ballet	Choreographer	Composer	Revivals
9 3 1844	La Esmeralda	Perrot	Pugni	1845, 47, 48, 49, 50, 51, 57
23 5 1844	La Vivandière	Cerrito, Saint-Léon	Pugni	1845, 46, 48
25 6 1844	Zélia	Perrot	Pugni	
25 7 1844	La Paysanne Grande Dame	Perrot		
8 3 1845	Éoline	Perrot	Pugni	1846
17 4 1845	Kaya	Perrot, Weiss	Pugni	
1 5 1845	La Bacchante	Perrot	Pugni	1846, 47
29 5 1845	Rosida	Saint-Léon	Pugni	
12 7 1845	Pas de Quatre	Perrot	Pugni	1847
24 7 1845	Diane	Perrot	Pugni	
3 3 1846	Catarina	Perrot	Pugni	
11 6 1846	Lalla Rookh	Perrot	Pugni, David	1847
23 7 1846	Le Jugement de Pâris	Perrot	Pugni	1847, 48
16 2 1847	Coralia	P. Taglioni	Pugni	1848
18 3 1847	Théa	P. Taglioni	Pugni	1848, 49, 50
15 4 1847	Orithia	P. Taglioni	Pugni	
26 6 1847	Les Éléments	Perrot	Bajetti	1848
19 2 1848	Fiorita et la reine des Elfrides	P. Taglioni	Pugni	1849
13 6 1848	Les Quatre Saisons	Perrot	Pugni	
15 3 1849	Le Diable à quatre [8]	after Mazilier	Adam	1851
17 4 1849	Electra	P. Taglioni	Pugni	
14 6 1849	La Prima Ballerina	P. Taglioni	Pugni	1850
5 7 1849	Les Plaisirs de l'hiver	P. Taglioni	Pugni	1850
12 3 1850	Les Métamorphoses	P. Taglioni	Pugni	1851
2 5 1850	Les Grâces	P. Taglioni	Pugni	1851
15 7 1850	Les Délices du sérail	Gosselin	Pugni	
22 3 1851	L'Île des amours	P. Taglioni	Nadaud	
15 5 1851	Les Cosmopolites			
1 4 1852	Un Baile de Candil			
24 4 1852	La Fête des rosières	Gosselin	Nadaud	
24 6 1852	Zélie	Gosselin	Nadaud	
24 7 1852	La Bouquetière			
10 5 1856	Les Quatre Saisons	after L. Petipa	Verdi	
22 5 1856	La Manola			
26 6 1856	La Bouquetière	P. Taglioni		
8 7 1856	Le Corsaire	Ronzani	Adam	
16 5 1857	Acalista	Massot	Nadaud	
20 6 1857	Les Roses	Massot		
7 7 1857	Marco Spada	Ronzani	Auber	
18 7 1857	Alphea	P. Taglioni		
23 1 1858	L'Hyménée	Massot	Balfe	
15 4 1858	Calisto	Massot		

Date	Title of Ballet	Choreo-grapher	Composer	Revivals
1 5 1858	Fleur des champs	Massot		1860
29 5 1858	La Reine des songes	Massot		
17 7 1858	Lucilla			
15 5 1860	Scintilla	Borri		
7 6 1860	Adelina	Borri		
6 5 1862	Diavoletta			
2 7 1862	La Réveil de Flore	Petit		
16 4 1863	La Farfaletta	Diani	Giorza	
26 5 1863	Bianchi e Negri	Rota	Giorza	
7 7 1863	L'Enfant de l'armée	Borri		
19 4 1864	Bacco ed Arianna	Magri		
20 6 1864	La Festa di Ballo			
9 5 1865	Le Bouquet	Diani		
8 6 1865	Le Harem			
10 7 1877	Les Nymphes de la forêt	K. Lanner		1879
24 7 1877	Une Fête de pêcheurs à Pausilippe	K. Lanner		1878
17 5 1878	Les Papillons	K. Lanner	Hansen	

NOTES TO APPENDIX B

[1] As *Telemachus in the Island of Calypso,* previously produced by Dauberval himself at the Pantheon in 1791.   (See Appendix D.)

[2] Previously performed by Dauberval himself at the Pantheon in 1791. (See Appendix D.)

[3] Announced as a revival 'not danced these eight years'.

[4] The first performance, on this date, took place at the Theatre Royal, Haymarket, the company having temporarily migrated there while the King's Theatre was undergoing repairs.

[5] As *La Ressemblance,* previously performed at Covent Garden in 1832. (See Appendix D.)

[6] Previously performed at Covent Garden in 1832. (See Appendix D.)

[7] As *The Devil on Two Sticks,* previously performed at Covent Garden in 1837. (See Appendix D.) A *divertissement* from this ballet was given at the King's Theatre in 1837.

[8] As *The Devil to Pay,* previously performed at Drury Lane in 1845. (See Appendix D.)

Appendix C

PRINCIPAL DANCERS AND CHOREOGRAPHERS AT THE KING'S (LATER HER MAJESTY'S) THEATRE,

1750–1881

NOTE: The dates given refer to seasons. The following seasons commenced in the latter part of the previous year: all seasons to 1785, 1787, 1795 to 1799, 1802, 1803, 1805 to 1807, 1810, 1811, 1827.

DANSEUSES

Aimée, 1791
Aimée [Petit], 1823
Albert, Élisa, 1828
Albertine [Coquillard], 1840
Anatole, Constance, 1822, 1823, 1828
Angiolini, Fortunata, 1809–12, 1814
Arányváry, Emilia, 1864
Asselin, 1760–2
Athalie, 1830
Aumer, Julie, 1824–6
Aurélie [Vente], 1823
Auretti, 1764, 1765
Aussandon, Esther, 1848–51

Baccelli, Giovanna, 1775–83, 1786
Banti, 1756
Banti, Felicita, 1778, 1779
Baptiste-Duport, Mme, 1816–18
Bartoletti, Malvina, 1878
Barville, Jenny, 1844
Beaucourt, Caroline, 1847
Beaupré, Zoé, 1831
Bellon, Eliza [Albert-], 1838–40, 1856
Bénard, Adèle, 1842, 1843
Beretta, Caterina, 1863, 1864
Bias, Fanny, 1821
Boschetti, Amina, 1856–8
Brocard, Caroline, 1826–8, 1830, 1831
Brugnoli, Amalia, 1832

Cámara, Petra, 1851
Camille, 1842, 1843
Capdeville, 1765
Cavalazzi, Malvina, 1878–81
Cerale, Luigia, 1878
Cerrito, Fanny, 1840–8, 1851
Chavigny, Geneviève, 1833–6
Clavelle, Hortense, 1858

Copère, Mme, 1826–31, 1833, 1835–47
Coralli, Teresa, 1803
Coulon, Anne-Jacqueline, 1788
Court, Louisa, 1819, 1821–3, 1825, 1826, 1828
Cranfield, 1802, 1804–8
Cucchi, Claudina, 1860

Danseuses Viennoises, 1845
Del Caro, 1794–6, 1803
Del Caro, 1815
Deshayes, Mme, 1804–10
De Varennes, Julia, 1821–3, 1830
Didelot, Rose (née Paul), 1796–1801
Didelot, Rose (née Colinette), 1812–14
Dorival, Anne-Marguerite, 1785, 1791
Dorsé, Aline, 1836, 1837
Dumilâtre, Adèle, 1843
Dupont, Mme Alexis, 1834
Duport, Mme, 1819
Dupuis, Mimi, 1828
Duval, Mélanie, 1826
Duvernay, Pauline, 1834, 1837

Elssler, Fanny, 1833, 1834, 1838–40, 1843, 1844
Elssler, Hermine, 1837, 1839
Elssler, Therese, 1833, 1834, 1838, 1839
Emarot, Célestine, 1841
Esper, Mathilde, 1851, 1852

Favier, Mimi, 1774
Favier, Nina, 1774
Favre-Guiardel, 1794, 1800–2
Ferdinand, Thérèse, 1844, 1845
Ferraris, Amalia, 1850, 1851, 1860, 1863
Fitzjames, Nathalie, 1838
Fleury, Louise, 1842, 1852
Forli, Regina, 1852
Forster, Caroline, 1838

Frassi, Adelaide, 1844
Friedberg, Katrine, 1856, 1857, 1862

Ginetti, Teresa, 1818
Gosselin, 1822, 1823
Grahn, Lucile, 1845–7
Grisi, Carlotta, 1836, 1842, 1844, 1845, 1847–51
Guichard, Pauline, 1832
Guimard, Madeleine, 1789
Guy-Stéphan, Marie, 1841–3, 1852

Heberle, Teresa, 1832
Heinel, Anne, 1772–4, 1776
Hilligsberg, 1788, 1791, 1793–1803
Hullin, Félicité, 1819
Hullin, Joséphine, 1830, 1832
Hullin, Virginie, 1818, 1820–2

Karliski, Isabella, 1857
Kohlenberg, Josephine, 1851

Lanner, Katti, 1877–81
Lanza, Lauretta, 1867
Lecomte, Mme, 1828, 1832
Léon, Virginie, 1814–17
Lequine, Rosalie, 1860
Leroux, Pauline, 1824, 1826, 1829, 1833
Lisereux, Julie, 1856
Lupino, 1809, 1813, 1814
Lydia [Thompson], 1852

Marinette, 1815, 1818, 1826
Mélanie, 1815–21
Mercandotti, Maria, 1814, 1822, 1823
Mersie, Julie, 1829–31
Michelet, Zilia, 1857
Miller, 1793
Millet, Marie, 1865
Montessu, Pauline, 1831, 1833, 1837
Montez, Lola, 1843
Monti, Adelaide, 1878–80
Monti, Carolina, 1878–80
Monti, Paolina, 1851
Mori, 1810, 1811, 1813–16, 1818, 1819
Morlacchi, Giuseppina, 1857, 1858, 1860, 1862, 1866

Mozon, 1786, 1787, 1791
Müller, Marie, 1877–9

Noblet, Lise, 1821, 1822, 1824, 1834

Oliva, Pepita de, 1852
Orsini, Annetta, 1858

Palladino, Emma, 1879, 1880
Pallerini, Antonia, 1833
Parisot, 1796, 1797, 1800–7
Perea, Manuela (La Nena), 1845, 1857
Petit-Stéphan, Joséphine, 1845–51
Pierron, Louise, 1856
Pitrot-Angiolini, Carolina, 1785, 1786
Plunkett, Adeline, 1843, 1844
Pochini, Carolina, 1857, 1858, 1860, 1863
Proche-Giubilei, Augustine, 1831–4, 1838, 1839, 1842

Radicati, 1762, 1767–9, 1771, 1772
Roland, 1822
Rolla, Teresa, 1857
Ronzi-Vestris, Carolina, 1822–5
Rosati, Carolina, 1847–9, 1851, 1852, 1856–1858
Rossi, Mme, 1783–5

Saint-Romain, Angelica, 1836
Salvioni, Elvira, 1857
Simonet, Mme, 1777–84
Sophie [Louillé], 1775, 1776

Taglioni, Louise, 1846
Taglioni, Marie, 1830, 1831, 1833–5, 1838–1841, 1845–7
Taglioni, Marie, the younger, 1847–50, 1856–8
Théodore (Mme Dauberval), 1782–4
Troisvallets, Élisa, 1865

Vallouy, Mme Noel, 1775–7
Vaque-Moulin, Élise, 1820, 1829
Varin, Élise, 1832, 1835, 1836

Weiss, Louise, 1845

Zucchelli, 1777–81

Appendix C

163

Nivelon, Louis, 1782, 1785, 1789, 1793

Noble, 1809, 1812–14

Noverre, Jean-Georges, 1782, 1788, 1789, 1793, 1794

Onorati, 1795, 1796

Paul, Alessandro, 1863

Paul, Antoine, 1822, 1831

Paul, Cesare, 1866

Perrot, Jules, 1830, 1833–6, 1842–8

Petit, Émile, 1848–52, 1856–8, 1862, 1863, 1866

Pitrot, 1774, 1784, 1785

Ragaine, 1821

Ronzani, Domenico, 1833, 1856, 1857

Rossi, F., 1806, 1807, 1810, 1811

Rota, Giuseppe, 1863

Rozier, 1814

Ruiz, Antonio, 1851

Saint-Léon, Arthur, 1843–8

Samengo, Paolo, 1832

Silvain, James (formerly Sullivan), 1824 and 1826 as Sullivan, 1843 and 1851 as Silvain

Simonet, 1777–9, 1781–3

Slingsby, 1767–70, 1772–4, 1779–85

Taglioni, Filippo, 1834, 1835, 1838, 1840, 1841

Taglioni, Paul, 1847–51, 1856, 1857

Vallouy, Simonin, 1770, 1775–7

Vandris, 1856

Venafra, 1824, 1825, 1828, 1834–52, 1856

Vestris, Armand, 1809–16

Vestris, Auguste, 1781, 1784, 1786, 1791, 1815

Vestris, Charles, 1814, 1816, 1817, 1819, 1822–5

Vestris, Gaëtan, 1781, 1788, 1791

Vitalba, 1775

Zucchelli, 1777–81, 1783–5, 1789

Appendix D

SELECTED LIST OF BALLETS PERFORMED AT OTHER LONDON THEATRES (EXCEPT THE ALHAMBRA)

ABBREVIATIONS: CG—Covent Garden; DL—Drury Lane; H—Theatre Royal, Haymarket; Pn—Pantheon; Ps—Princess's; R-CG—Royal Italian Opera, Covent Garden; R-L—Royal Italian Opera, Lyceum.

Date	Ballet	Choreographer	Composer	Theatre
19 2 1791	Amphion et Thalie	Dauberval		Pn
19 3 1791	Telemachus in the Island of Calypso	Dauberval		Pn
30 4 1791	La Fille mal gardée	Dauberval		Pn
3 5 1791	Le Triomphe de la folie	Dauberval		Pn
9 5 1791	Le Siège de Cythère	Dauberval		Pn
17 12 1791	La Fontaine d'amour	Dauberval		Pn
17 12 1791	L'Amant déguisé	Dauberval		Pn
31 12 1791	La Fête villageoise	Dauberval		Pn
10 3 1792	Le Volage fixé	Dauberval		H
14 4 1792	La Foire de Smirne	Dauberval		H
10 2 1795	Alexander the Great	J. d'Egville	Krazinsky Miller	DL
14 5 1800	Telasco and Amgahi	J. d'Egville		DL
6 6 1803	The Black Knight	J. Byrne	Bossi	DL
4 2 1807	Emily	J. d'Egville	Venua	DL
22 4 1808	Caractacus	J. d'Egville	Bishop, etc.	DL
12 6 1815	Drive Love out of the Door	J. d'Egville		DL
14 7 1832	La Ressemblance	F. Taglioni		CG
26 7 1832	La Sylphide	F. Taglioni	Schneitzhoeffer, Adam	CG
13 2 1833	The Sleeping Beauty [1]	Anatole, after Aumer	Hérold	DL
5 2 1834	The Revolt of the Harem [2]	after F. Taglioni	Labarre	CG
23 6 1834	The Fair Sicilian	Albert	Sor	CG
25 4 1836	Zulema	J. d'Egville		H
30 5 1836	Swiss Nuptials	J. d'Egville	Reid	H
1 12 1836	The Devil on Two Sticks [3]	Mazilier (?), after J. Coralli	Gide	DL
21 11 1837	The Daughter of the Danube [4]	Gilbert, after F. Taglioni	Adam	DL

Date	Ballet	Choreo-grapher	Composer	Theatre
30 9 1843	The Peri [5]	E. Coralli, after J. Coralli	Burgmüller	DL
17 2 1844	The Beauty of Ghent [6]	Albert	Adam	DL
9 3 1844	Leola	Gilbert, Védy	Corri	Ps
28 3 1844	The Fête of Terpsichore	Albert		DL
15 4 1844	Lady Henrietta [7]	Varin, after Mazilier	Flotow, Burgmüller, Deldevez	DL
9 11 1844	The Enchanted Bell	Rousset	Hérold, etc.	Ps
4 2 1845	Les Danaïdes	Hoguet	Schmidt	DL
24 3 1845	Robert et Bertrand	Hoguet	Schmidt	DL
27 9 1845	The Marble Maiden	Albert	Adam	DL
24 11 1845	The Devil to Pay [8]	Barrez, after Mazilier	Adam	DL
12 2 1846	The Island Nymph	Barrez	Schira	DL
20 4 1846	Imelda	Barrez	Hughes	DL
3 6 1846	Paquita	Silvain, after Mazilier	Deldevez	DL
3 10 1846	The Offspring of Flowers	Bretin	Scaramelli	DL
16 11 1846	The Wags of Wapping [9]	after Mazilier	Thomas	DL
2 12 1846	Le Verven	Barrez	Hughes	DL
4 2 1847	The Pretty Sicilian	Blasis	F. A. Blasis, Senna, Bajetti	DL
4 3 1847	Spanish Gallantries	Blasis	F. A. Blasis	DL
15 3 1847	La Pléiade de Terpsichore	Blasis		DL
6 4 1847	L'Odalisque	Albert	Curmi	R-CG
20 4 1847	La Reine des fées	Albert	Curmi	R-CG
1 5 1847	La Bouquetière de Venise	Albert	Curmi	R-CG
18 5 1847	La Salamandrine	Blasis	Curmi	R-CG
12 6 1847	Manon Lescaut	Casati	P. Bellini	R-CG
3 7 1847	L'Amour et la danse [10]	Casati		R-CG
22 7 1847	La Rosiera	Casati	Curmi	R-CG
14 8 1847	La Naïade	Casati	P. Bellini	R-CG
9 3 1848	La Reine des feux-follets	Appiani	Biletta	R-CG
16 5 1848	Nirène	Appiani	Biletta	R-CG
11 7 1848	Corilla	Casati, Appiani	P. Bellini	R-CG
9 10 1848	The Amazons [11]	Barrez, after A. Mabille	Benoit	CG
5 12 1848	Le Bal masqué	Barrez		CG
6 2 1852	Vert-Vert	Barrez, after Mazilier	Deldevez, Tolbecque	DL

Date	Ballet	Choreographer	Composer	Theatre
24 2 1852	The Star of the Rhine	Barrez	Boisselot	DL
6 5 1853	The Spirit of the Valley [12]	Saint-Léon	E. Gautier	DL
18 6 1853	Fleurette	Desplaces	Panizza	R-CG
3 6 1854	Une Étoile	Desplaces	Panizza	R-CG
19 4 1855	Eva	Desplaces	Panizza	R-CG
14 4 1857	Les Abeilles	Desplaces		R-L
2 5 1857	La Brésilienne	Desplaces	Panizza	R-L
23 6 1857	Terpsichore	Desplaces		R-L
24 7 1858	L'Amour d'une rose	Desplaces	Mellon	R-CG
19 7 1859	Azelia	Desplaces		R-CG
8 11 1859	La Fiancée	Petit		CG
24 5 1860	Les Amours de Diane	Desplaces	arr. Nadaud	R-CG
5 5 1862	Les Sylphides	Desplaces		R-CG
14 5 1864	L'Île enchantée	Desplaces	Sullivan	R-CG
25 10 1865	Gitta la Ballerina	Desplaces	Bosselet	R-CG

NOTES TO APPENDIX D

[1] In Paris Opéra version, entitled *La Belle au bois dormant*.

[2] In Paris Opéra version, entitled *La Révolte au sérail*.

[3] In Paris Opéra version, entitled *Le Diable boiteux*.

[4] In Paris Opéra version, entitled *La Fille du Danube*.

[5] In Paris Opéra version, entitled *La Péri*.

[6] In Paris Opéra version, entitled *La Jolie fille de Gand*.

[7] In Paris Opéra version, entitled *Lady Henriette*.

[8] In Paris Opéra version, entitled *Le Diable à quatre*.

[9] In Paris Opéra version, entitled *Betty*.

[10] Included a *pas* arranged for Marietta Baderna by Carlo Blasis—*La Bayonnaise*—to music from Donizetti's *La Figlia del Reggimento* ('Rataplan, rataplan').

[11] In Paris Opéra version, entitled *Nisida*.

[12] In Théâtre Lyrique (Paris) version, entitled *Le Lutin de la vallée*.

Appendix E

SELECTED LIST OF PRINCIPAL DANCERS
APPEARING AT OTHER LONDON THEATRES
(EXCEPT THE ALHAMBRA)

ABBREVIATIONS: A—Adelphi; CG—Covent Garden; DL—Drury Lane; H—Theatre Royal, Haymarket; L—Lyceum; Pn—Pantheon; SJ—St James's.

NOTE: The 1792 season at the Pantheon began in December 1791.

DANSEUSES

Andreanova, Elena, CG 1852
Baderna, Marietta, CG and DL 1847
Battaglini, CG 1854, 1855, 1858, 1862
Cámara, Petra, SJ 1859
Cerrito, Fanny, CG 1855; L 1856, 1857
Danseuses Viennoises, DL 1846
Del Caro (Mme Bossi), DL 1796–1801
Dor, Henriette, CG 1868, 1869, 1872
Dumilâtre, Adèle, DL 1844, 1845; CG 1847
Duvernay, Pauline, DL 1833, 1836, 1837
Elssler, Fanny, CG 1847
Elssler, Hermine, DL 1838
Fabbri, Flora, DL 1845, 1846; CG 1848
Fleury, Louise, DL 1844; CG 1847
Fuoco, Sofia, DL 1846, 1848; CG 1847
Grahn, Lucile, DL 1844, 1848; CG 1848
Grisi, Carlotta, DL 1843, 1846
Hilligsberg, Pn 1792
Legrain, Victorine, DL 1851
Leroux, Pauline, CG 1832–4, 1849; DL 1843
Maria [Jacob], DL 1845, 1846
Mariquita, A 1855; CG 1860
Morlacchi, Giuseppina, CG 1859; DL 1859, 1860
Noblet, Lise, CG 1834
Parisot, DL 1799, 1807
Perea, Manuela (La Nena), H 1854–6, 1858
Pertoldi, Erminia, CG 1874
Plunkett, Adeline, DL 1844, 1845, 1852, 1853; CG 1847, 1848, 1853
Richard, Zina, CG 1858–60
Robert, Élisabeth, CG 1848, 1852
Salvioni, Guglielmina, CG 1861–5
Taglioni, Amalia, CG 1832; DL 1837
Taglioni, Louise, CG 1849–51
Taglioni, Marie, CG 1832; DL 1837
Théodore (Mme Dauberval), Pn 1791, 1792
Webster, Clara, H 1838, 1839; DL 1841–4
Wuthier, Margherita, CG 1848, 1849
Yella, Gabriella, CG 1853
Zucchi, Amalia, CG 1867
Zucchi, Virginia, CG 1878, 1879

DANSEURS

Albert, Auguste, CG 1834
Albert, François, CG 1834, 1847; DL 1844, 1845
Alexandre [Fuchs], CG 1849–52
Anatole [Petit], DL 1833
Barrez, DL 1845, 1846
Boisgirard, Louis, Pn 1791, 1812
Bretin, Louis, DL 1845, 1846; CG 1848
Carey, Édouard, DL 1843
Coralli, Eugène, DL 1843
Coulon, Antoine, CG 1832–4
Dauberval, Pn 1791, 1792
Didelot, Charles, Pn 1791
Hoguet-Vestris, DL 1844, 1845
Laborie, Pn 1792
Mabille, Auguste, CG 1847
Massot, Pierre, H 1836
Mazilier, Joseph, CG 1836, 1837
Montessu, François, DL 1844
Paul, Antoine, DL 1833
Petipa, Lucien, DL 1843, 1845; CG 1847, 1848
Saint-Léon, Arthur, DL 1853
Silvain, James, DL 1833, 1844–6; CG 1834, 1848; SJ 1839
Taglioni, Paul, CG 1832; DL 1837
Viganò, Salvatore, Pn 1791

Index

Index

Note: the Appendices are not indexed

171

Index